RESTORING the SOUL
of the WORLD

"David Fideler is a scholar and thinker of the first rank, and this marvelous book presents his profound historical, scientific, and philosophical expertise in a brilliant synthesis that is accessible to everyone. It is a beautifully written and wide-ranging guide to the history of the soul of the world. Drawing together threads from every field of human endeavor, from theology to poetry and astrophysics to biology, it is the most exciting, uplifting, and optimistic exhortation to engage with and restore the magical world around us that I have read in a long time."

TOM CHEETHAM, PH.D., AUTHOR OF *ALL THE WORLD AN ICON*

"*Restoring the Soul of the World* goes beyond the goal of 'sustainability' to a new vision of our role here on Earth as renewing and regenerating a world that we feel emotionally committed to and want to care for and understand from a long-term view. This book is optimistic in the best way—based not just on hope or determination but on science, on an exciting array of successful solutions, and a daring kind of spiritual freedom rooted in the cosmos. This outlook could transform the world."

NANCY ELLEN ABRAMS AND JOEL R. PRIMACK, AUTHORS OF
THE NEW UNIVERSE AND THE HUMAN FUTURE

"*Restoring the Soul of the World* is the most far-reaching book available on more profound ways of understanding how we are connected to the cosmos. David Fideler reveals previously hidden traditions and ways of understanding ourselves and nature, exploring our relationships to nature's intelligence as no one has before. A classic: you need to read this book."

ARTHUR VERSLUIS, PROFESSOR OF AMERICAN STUDIES AT
MICHIGAN STATE UNIVERSITY AND AUTHOR OF
PERENNIAL PHILOSOPHY AND SACRED EARTH

"In *Restoring the Soul of the World,* David Fideler highlights the paradigmatic foundations of seemingly intransigent religious, scientific, and economic beliefs. But he then takes the crucial—and all too rare—step of interpreting and integrating these histories to illuminate a path forward. He pragmatically demonstrates how models of regenerative strategies can be found all around, and that restoring the soul of the world begins with becoming attuned to the cycles and patterns of a living universe."

DAVID MCCONVILLE, CHAIRMAN OF THE BOARD OF THE
BUCKMINSTER FULLER INSTITUTE

"In this timely and absorbing book, David Fideler traces our long relationship with the world soul, chronicling how our experience of the spiritual power of nature was lost in a mechanized world. Yet Fideler brings real hope. Drawing on recent scientific discoveries and solutions, he envisions a way for humanity to collaborate in a 'living but damaged paradise.' This book will help many people take heart."

TRACY COCHRAN, EDITOR FOR *PARABOLA* MAGAZINE

"*Restoring the Soul of the World* is a wonderful book. I challenge anyone to read it intently and not feel the presence of *the anima mundi* or hear the hum of the music of the spheres. David Fideler is an inspiring guide on an enlivening excursion through the intelligence of nature. He brings together heart and mind in an alchemical fusion uniquely his own."

GARY LACHMAN, AUTHOR OF *THE CARETAKERS OF THE COSMOS*

"*Restoring the Soul of the World* is a timely rallying call to reimagine our relationship with our world, our culture, and our cosmos. Through a masterful overview of the history of forgotten knowledge, Fideler reveals the unsuspected connections between ancient thought and the cutting edge of contemporary natural science."

LEON MARVELL, DEAKIN UNIVERSITY FACULTY MEMBER
AND AUTHOR OF *TRANSFIGURED LIGHT*

RESTORING *the* SOUL *of the* WORLD

OUR LIVING BOND
WITH NATURE'S INTELLIGENCE

DAVID FIDELER

Inner Traditions
Rochester, Vermont • Toronto, Canada

Inner Traditions
One Park Street
Rochester, Vermont 05767
www.InnerTraditions.com

Text stock is SFI certified

Library of Congress Cataloging-in-Publication Data
Fideler, David R., 1961– author.
  Restoring the soul of the world : our living bond with nature's intelligence /
David Fideler.
     pages cm
  Includes bibliographical references and index.
  ISBN 978-1-62055-359-6 (pbk.) — ISBN 978-1-62055-360-2 (e-book)
  1. Human ecology—Philosophy. 2. Philosophy of nature. I. Title.
  GF21.F53 2014
  304.201—dc23
                                                                    2014018193

Printed and bound in the United States by Lake Book Manufacturing, Inc.
The text stock is SFI certified. The Sustainable Forestry Initiative® program
promotes sustainable forest management.

10 9 8 7 6 5 4 3 2 1

Text design by Debbie Glogover and layout by Priscilla Baker
This book was typeset in Garamond Premier Pro with Helvetica Neue, Gill Sans,
and Legacy Sans used as display typefaces

To send correspondence to the author of this book, mail a first-class letter to the
author c/o Inner Traditions • Bear & Company, One Park Street, Rochester, VT
05767, and we will forward the communication, or contact the author directly at
www.cosmopolisproject.org.

For Almira and Benjamin,
my two nearest bonds
with the living universe.

Contents

PART II

THE DEATH OF NATURE
AND THE RISE OF ALIENATION

PART III

ANIMA MUNDI
Rediscovering the Living Universe

PART IV

A WORLD WITH A FUTURE
Cultivating Life in a Global Community

Introduction

In Search of the Living Universe

The most beautiful experience we can have is the mysterious. It is the fundamental emotion which stands at the cradle of true art and true science. He to whom this emotion is a stranger, who can no longer wonder and stand rapt in awe, is as good as dead.

ALBERT EINSTEIN

We have the greatest technological knowledge of any civilization, but we have forgotten what it means to be alive in the world, to be alive in a living universe. Yet without this living connection to the world, our lives become trivial, routine, and mechanical. Being cut off, we start to wonder about the meaning of life and raise other abstract questions, while meaning itself is an experience of being bonded to the world and others at the very deepest level.

It's strange how the history of Western civilization has in some ways mirrored the unfolding life stages of individuals. We start life enraptured and ecstatic, intoxicated by the beauty and wonder from which we have emerged, the brilliant epiphanies that surround us on every side. The world is sensed, tasted, and felt spontaneously in deeply intimate ways. As children, the world fits us like a glove. To color, sound, or a glimmer of light, we respond with sympathy and curiosity. To the face of a loved one, we respond with instantaneous joy. Childhood is a time of belonging, and we sense the world as deeply mysterious, luminous, and awe-inspiring. The world is not something distant or remote, but a part of our own being that is bubbling with life, full of excitement and infinite mystery.

As we grow older, that begins to change. At an early age, the educational system starts, bit by bit, to erode our native enthusiasm, preparing us for the adult world of duty and responsibility. Things are not studied to be loved but to be mastered. We learn discipline, hard work, and self-control, all of which are necessary for our personal development. But despite the need for these skills, something is lost in the process. The very best teachers seek to inspire enthusiasm, but even with their good efforts our view of the world begins to subtly change. By the time we are young adults, the world is becoming less of an epiphany and more of a distant object—something to be approached with control to ensure our success in life. We become highly concerned with our role in society, and life becomes a maze, something that needs to be navigated with foresight in order to attain our goals. In essence, we become calculating and manipulative, and—though born out of luminous depths—the living, vibrant world begins to recede in the background. As we prepare for the hard work of adult life, we are simultaneously strengthened and diminished.

A similar thing has happened historically. In many ways the ancient and traditional peoples had a far more intimate relationship to the world than we do today. While they lacked the rational autonomy of the modern analytical self, the world for them was alive, numinous, and sacred—animated by a living spirit. And they were part of that world. Every part of creation spoke to them—brooks, trees, and mountains—and they responded appropriately with myth, story, and song, in a vital spirit of participation. They could directly experience the kinship and living sympathy that connects all things, perhaps more so than we modern, urbanized individuals who are considerably more insulated from the vitality of nature by our gadgets and technological conveniences. For traditional peoples, their bond with the living planet was an *experience;* for us, Gaia is a theory introduced by scientists.

As T. S. Eliot once asked, "Where is the Life we have lost in living? / Where is the wisdom we have lost in knowledge? / Where is the knowledge we have lost in information?"[1]

The primordial response to the vitality and mystery of creation is the beginning of all science, art, philosophy, and religion. As Socrates said, "Wonder is the beginning of all philosophy." This living response to the world is still something within our grasp. But in the same way that the individual ego begins to crystallize, take hold, and crowd out other parts of the personality during our individual development, a growing disconnect with the natural world has crowded out our sense of wonder historically and collectively.

The ancient Greeks saw life and divinity in all things. Deeply moved by the order and beauty of nature, the ancient thinkers set out on a quest to understand the cosmic pattern and our own relation to it. Until very recent times, the greatest philosophers and thinkers had tended to see the cosmos as a living organism with which we are bound in vital participation. In the words of Plato, the universe is a "single Living Creature that contains all living creatures within it."

For many centuries, from ancient Greece through the Renaissance, the idea of living nature helped to maintain a healthy bond between humanity and the larger-than-human world in which we are embedded. These ideas about living nature are examined in part I of this book.

In the sixteenth and seventeenth centuries, a new analytical spirit emerged that was highly mathematical. Associated with the great geniuses of the Scientific Revolution, this new way of looking at the world portrayed the cosmos not as alive, but as a dead clockwork mechanism, perpetually ticking along according to eternal laws. At this time, when Western humanity was crystallizing a scientific ego, a new, charismatic image of divinity emerged, which was highly compelling to the scientific thinkers of the Enlightenment. God came to be pictured as a remote, rational, divine engineer, who laid down the laws of the universe. After the laws were set up, the universe was set in motion, and allowed to run on its own like a giant clock, after which God stepped back, only to view the universe as a spectator.

At this key turning point in the development of scientific awareness, all of reality came to be increasingly pictured in terms of two main categories or principles: dead, inanimate matter, and motion, the external cause that powered it. In the process, nature came to be seen as radically other and different from humanity. Animals, for example, came to be seen as unconscious machines. If you hit a dog and it yelped, it was only an automatic response, just like the sound given off by a mechanical doorbell. The cosmos could now be modeled mathematically, and mathematics gave us control over the external world, which was coming to be pictured more and more as an exploitable resource rather than as a living community of which we are a part. This historical process, through which the world came to be modeled as a machine, is described in part II of this book.

While the machine-model of the universe proved to be very useful in many ways, it wasn't an accurate picture of the world, and over the last century or so every single premise on which it was based has been proven false. Matter, for example, doesn't even remotely resemble hard billiard balls being passively knocked around by external forces. At its deepest level, matter is creative, energetic, and community building. Rather than being unintelligent, it "knows" how to act in different circumstances, how to ward off outside disturbances, and how to maintain natural structures. Similarly, living organisms don't resemble machines at all; like human beings, they are embodiments of life's evolutionary intelligence, which is an outgrowth of the greater natural intelligence of the world in which we are all rooted. In part III of this book, I explore the most important scientific breakthroughs or "cosmological revolutions" of recent times, in physics, astronomy, and biology, demonstrating how these new discoveries undermine the assumptions of the mechanistic worldview and how they once again point toward the metaphor of a living, intelligent universe, in which we are not distant spectators but expressions of, and participants in, nature's creative process.

Every worldview sanctions specific ways of picturing the world and specific ways of knowing; these, in turn, sanction different ways of relating to the world and to other people. In the mechanistic worldview, for example, when the world was seen as a nonliving machine, the world became pictured as a collection of objects, meant for human consumption; and nature itself was seen as an object of scientific control. Writing toward the end of the sixteenth century—and using language that is shocking to many contemporary readers—Francis Bacon wrote that the emerging scientific method would render nature "the slave of mankind," enable humanity "to storm and occupy" the natural world, and establish the "Dominion of Man over the Universe" (see chapter 8). And while he may have been one of the first to use this kind of language, this way of thinking quickly became a widely accepted guiding ethos, at least on an unconscious level.

Fortunately, scientific knowledge—and the mythic visions that inspire it—continues to unfold over time. And at our current point in time, the biologist Edward O. Wilson has economically summed things up. He writes, "The question of the century is: How best can we shift to a culture of permanence, both for ourselves and for the biosphere that sustains us?"[2]

Because of overpopulation and the related ecological crisis, we now live at a pivotal time in both human and planetary history. Since the year 1800, human population has soared 700 percent, increasing from 1 billion to over 7 billion today. In the last century alone, human population has quadrupled, and we now live in a period of "ecological overshoot": it now takes the planet more than one year to absorb and regenerate what humans take from it in a single year.

In a symbolic sense, one crucial turning point for us came when humans were finally able to look back and see the fragile beauty of our home planet from space. This vision, as I explore in chapter 12, transformed our way of thinking about the world and our place in it. After those stunning images, which continue to pour in, no one could be a disembodied spectator any longer when thinking about the Earth. When we experience the deeply moving beauty of the Earth seen from space and intuitively realize that all life is bound together, facing a common fate, we automatically sense ourselves as *participants* in life's tapestry, not as disembodied spectators.

The idea that nature possesses a living intelligence is not something of just historical or academic interest; I wrote this book out of my strongly held belief that a deeper and more accurate worldview is needed if future generations will be able to inhabit a beautiful and flourishing world in which life is truly worth living. In this sense, *Restoring the Soul of the World* is not about the past, but about our own time and the future. In part IV of this book, I discuss how we are beginning to see hints of a new, emerging worldview, based not on exploitation, but on the idea of learning from nature—and collaborating with nature's intelligence—to create a better, more healthy, and more fulfilling world for all. If both human beings and the living planet are going to have a flourishing future, gone are the days in which we can think of ourselves as the masters and controllers of nature. The alternative to control is a spirit of partnership, in which we work in collaboration with nature's living systems, a topic explored in this book's final chapter.

At its deepest level, the new science of ecological design shows how we can solve our most pressing human problems by drawing upon, and working with, the genius of nature's design intelligence, developed and tested over the course of 3.8 billion years. In one stunning example, ecological designer John Todd has shown how it is possible to collaborate with communities of living organisms to turn wastewater into pure water and how to restore some of the most toxic waste sites known to humanity.

In purifying highly toxic bodies of water with the help of living organisms, John Todd has shown how it is possible to help regenerate degraded ecosystems in very short periods of time—weeks or months—that would normally take decades or even centuries to restore without human help. While species loss is not reversible, the Earth's living systems are resilient (until they reach a certain point), and regeneration is possible. We already know how to make this happen. Should we also possess the love, desire, and will needed to accomplish it, through the use of ecological design, we humans—working in true collaboration with nature—could restore health to the world's living systems, and radically reduce our own ecological footprint.

PART I

AWAKENING TO THE BEAUTY OF NATURE

Humanity and the Cosmological Impulse

The astronomical universe is sensuous infinity.

CECIL COLLINS

1

Starlight and Cosmovision

Awakening to the Universe

Everything begins with starlight.

Our intellects divide and categorize. During the day we have tasks to do and roles to play. But at nighttime under the fire of starlight, another way of knowing comes into being. Boundaries dissolve and we recognize a kinship with the radiant stars above. The fire that burns in them is the same fire that burns in us.

Ever since I was a child I have had a love for the stars. Growing up away from city lights, I knew what it meant to be enveloped in the darkness of night. On a pitch black summer night, my home was an island of light and repose, embedded in the greater life of the world. Through open windows the loud chant of insects would lead me outside into the velvet backdrop of night. Their hypnotic voices spoke of a mystery and reflected the living depths of the world, the primordial vibration of rhythm and instinct from which the fabric of life emerges. We humans may pride ourselves on being more clever than crickets, but insects have been chanting to the stars for eternity, relatively speaking. Should some catastrophe befall the human race—should our cities and shopping malls and all our technical achievements someday be overgrown and reclaimed by the natural world from which they have emerged—then still, hundreds of years later, the crickets will remain, chanting to the stars. By entering their chorus, we touch upon an ancient mystery, and tangibly sense the eternal music and rhythms from which we arose.

After stepping outside on a warm summer night, my own voice would join the chorus of the greater world. Approaching the darkness, I would move through the boundary of light surrounding our home, accompanied by a friend or my father. What was hidden during the day was now manifest in the darkest hour. Nature's soul revealed an exuberance of hidden life in a velvety carpet of moths and tiny insects that blanketed the window screens and danced prolifically around the patio spotlights. Somehow, somewhere, these delicate creatures hibernated during the day, only to emerge and vibrate under the cover of darkness. The Sun can block out that which is subtle and delicate. Night is a period of rejuvenation and for contacting everything that is blotted out by the harsh glare of noon.

Moving away from the house and walking down our long driveway, the lights would fall away and the night sky would open up. Darkness can be frightening and disorienting as you enter into the insect chorus and the shadowy depths of the world. Our egos seek control and certainty, afraid of unseen obstacles or creatures that might be wandering in the forest stand. But as the sounds of night beckoned me onward, hesitation began to fall away. Suddenly, as the brilliant stars came into focus, blazing like diamonds and colored gems, a feeling of wonder and amazement began to overpower the ego's frail timidity. Under the sparkling cover of starlight, our souls open to the depths of the universe. Overpowered by a sense of astonishment and belonging, our fears begin to fall away.

WONDERING ABOUT THE STARS: PHILOSOPHY, SCIENCE, AND CONTEMPLATION

Had we never seen the stars, and the sun, and the heaven,
none of the words which we have spoken about the universe
would ever have been uttered. But now the sight of day
and night, and the months and the revolutions of the years,
have created number, and have given us a conception of

*time, and the power of enquiring about the nature of the
universe; and from this source we have derived philosophy,
than which no greater good ever was or will be given by the
gods to mortal man.*

PLATO

Wondering about our place in the cosmic pattern is the beginning of
all philosophy, science, and religion. And it is the stars, above all, that
inspire awe, wonder, and contemplation.

Plato summed it up perfectly: Through their regular cyclical movements, the stars and planets beat out patterns and rhythms. These
rhythms teach us number, which then develops into mathematics.
Mathematics allows us to inquire into the order of nature, giving birth
to philosophy and science in the process. Thus the stars teach us philosophy, and awaken us to the underlying regularities of the cosmic pattern in which we find ourselves embroidered.[1]

In the beginning, philosophy and science were the same—and both
were connected with religion, because the desire to understand the cosmos has always been a spiritual quest. As Einstein wrote, "I maintain
that the cosmic religious feeling is the strongest and noblest motive for
scientific research."[2] The order and beauty of nature awakens wonder,
awe, and amazement. Thus, the sense of wonder is the cosmological
impulse, the common seed from which religion, philosophy, and science
emerge. Over time, religion, science, and philosophy may go their different ways, but at their root they emerge from the same fundamental
experience that defines an essential aspect of human nature. By understanding their common origin in the cosmological impulse, we can see
directly their intimate relation.

The first philosopher-scientists in ancient Greece, the Presocratics,
were awestruck by their vision of the stars and the quest for mental insight that vision inspired. This is a theme that comes up time
and again in the stories associated with them. The stars and celestial
phenomena overpowered them with a desire to understand, and they
withdrew from the daily activities of society in order to study and contemplate the order of nature. The deep perception of the world's fair

order inspires *contemplation,* which means "to observe." The words *idea, wisdom,* and *vision* all originate from a common Indo-European root, *weid-,* which means "to see," and the language of vision is also the language of contemplation. We experience "insight," "illumination," and "reflect on" the nature of things. The word for imaginary reflection, speculation, comes from the Latin *speculum,* a mirror. People have "bright ideas" and, in understanding, I can "see" another person's point. A person with great ideas is a "man of vision." Through contemplation and speculation, we reflect deeply on things, tracing them back to their source or inner meaning.

In early Greek philosophy, the contemplative faculty that experiences beauty, wonder, and awe was identified as the flower, the highest part of human nature. And for the first philosophers, it was the vision of the stars and the regularity of the celestial movements that inspired contemplation and the search for scientific understanding. For the early Greek philosopher Anaxagoras (ca. 500–ca. 428 B.C.), contemplation was the true end of human nature. When he was asked why anyone should wish to have been born rather than not, he answered, "In order to contemplate the heaven[s] and the structure of the world-order as a whole."[3] In another account, when Anaxagoras was accused of ignoring the affairs of his native land, he said "I am greatly concerned with my fatherland," and pointed toward the heavens.[4] A similar story was told about the Greek philosopher Empedocles (ca. 493–ca. 433 B.C.). When asked why he was alive, Empedocles replied, "That I may behold the stars; take away the firmament, and I will be nothing."[5] The human desire to understand our relationship to the universe is charged with passion, and such ardent devotion has inspired the greatest philosophers and scientists throughout history.

Accounts like this could be extended. A particularly entertaining one is told about Thales, the sixth century B.C. philosopher, astronomer, and mathematician. One evening Thales was contemplating the stars when, distracted by the pursuit, he tumbled down a well. A very attractive woman who was standing nearby then chastised him for ignoring the things at his feet—such as her beauty—and for having his head up in the clouds. Such are the dangers of the contemplative life, and as

Socrates warned, "Anyone who gives his life to philosophy is open to such mockery."[6]

Plato took the perfect, rational regularity of the celestial bodies to be reflective of a divine order. But that divine order, he said, is present in us too, especially in the contemplative faculty of the soul. Our innermost nature is rooted in the immortal heavens, but when the soul descends to Earth and becomes engrossed in endless appetites and ambitions, we forget about the soul's true nature and nourish our mortality. But by contemplating the cosmic order through the love of learning and wisdom, we remember our connection to the divine order, and philosophy allows us to "possess immortality in the fullest measure that human nature admits."[7] In Plato's view, contemplation is ultimately transformative, for by contemplating what is beautiful and timeless, we partake of beauty, participate consciously in the deep structure of the world, and bring about the fulfillment of our essential nature.

MODELING THE UNIVERSE: SCIENCE, CREATIVITY, AND HUMAN EXPERIENCE

The Greeks started writing philosophy only around 500 B.C., but philosophy and the cosmological impulse are as old as human nature. As philosopher Stephen Clark points out, "It is too often assumed that 'ancient Greeks' were the first to speculate, and reason, about the world, the first to exchange and criticize each other's thoughts." On the contrary, he continues, "The philosophical temperament, on the available evidence, is found throughout the world and may be assumed to have been present throughout the hundred thousand years of human being."[8] Similarly, lunar tallies and artwork from Paleolithic times suggest that humans were actively observing and recording celestial phenomena thirty thousand years ago (see figure 1.1).[9]

For the Greeks, writing was a relatively late invention. Long before the appearance of the written word, highly skilled and "literate" bards memorized and recited the Homeric epics at athletic contests and religious festivals. When the phonetic alphabet was adopted, those epics were finally written down. It was only in 415 B.C., during the lifetime of

Figure 1.1. Paleolithic artwork from Spain showing the Moon God (?) and the days of the lunar month. Circa 28,000 B.C.

Plato, that the vowels were officially incorporated into the Greek alphabet in Athens. But even Plato, great artist that he was, was distrustful of the written word. For him philosophy was a process of ongoing *dialogue* in which ideas were developed and tested among living people. To write philosophy down in a book seemed to falsify its very nature, because books are frozen and, unlike living people, cannot respond to questions. Plato wrote his dialogues to give an idea of the philosophical process, but he believed that the highest form of knowledge was not expressible in written words. Consequently, he refused to write down his ultimate thoughts about the universe, fearing they would be misunderstood or mocked by those who had not attained a similar level of insight.[10]

As David Abram argues in his book *Spell of the Sensuous,* another problem with writing is that it leads us to live in an overly abstract, conceptualized world. The living world is a realm of dynamic processes. A flower is not a thing, but an *event,* like a butterfly emerging from a chrysalis. But with the word, we take a living event and freeze it forever into a useful but stable category. As Goethe wrote, "How difficult it is, though, to refrain from replacing the thing with its sign, to keep the object alive before us instead of killing it with a word."[11]

Certainly, we all need words to get by. But if spoken words take us away from the world, written words and technical models take us much farther still into a disembodied, conceptual sphere. Spoken language goes back tens of thousands of years, but written language is only about twenty-five hundred years old. Widespread literacy is perhaps only a couple of *hundred* years old. In the five-billion-year history of our planet, written literacy is less than an eye blink. But concurrent with that eye blink is an accelerating development of human ingenuity and technology that has progressively taken us into an artificial world of our own creation, away from the living streams, trees, and mountains that once spoke to our ancestors. So as the written word has continued to increasingly proliferate, we have found ourselves increasingly distant from nature—increasingly encased by appliances, technological comforts, conceptualized strategies, and handy categories—buried in emails and distracted by text messages. The ability to write and conceptualize is one of our greatest achievements, but at the same time it isolates us. For in the wake of increasing conceptualization, we have lost a sense of our natural bondedness with the world and the primordial energies that shape existence.

Greek science and philosophy began with wonder—a sense of wonder that led directly to conceptualization and the development of the first important scientific models in the history of Western thought. Yet while models, concepts, and words are useful tools, contemporary philosophers have become increasingly aware that even our very best scientific models do not correspond to reality in an absolutely precise one-to-one way, which seems to rule out the possibility of an "ultimate theory of everything."[12] Like Plato who believed that philosophy is a perpetual, ongoing dialogue, we can now see that science is not a fixed doctrine but an open and ongoing conversation with the world—an ongoing investigation in which new questions will always be raised, and in which no model is absolutely final. As philosopher and scientist Alfred Korzybski so aptly put it, "the map is not the territory," and this especially applies to evolving scientific models. Ideally, the models we develop and the primordial wonder they arise from can fruitfully coexist.

In the best of all worlds our models can provide new ways of seeing, inspire curiosity, and challenge us to raise further questions. But if we fail to use caution, it is easy to slip into idolatry. Then models become false gods. They ask us to worship at the altar of conceptualization, and thus deaden our perception of the living universe by insulating us from the world of experience. By maintaining a fertile tension between wonder and conceptualization, we can stay open to the realities of inspiration and nonverbal experience while at the same time satisfying our needs for rationalization, prediction, and creative model building. By striking such a balance between living experience and theory, we can benefit from the many ways of knowing, experiencing, and relating to the world. In this way, the conversation will continue. When we realize that science is partly rooted in logic but that it is even more deeply a creative, human pursuit, then science, art, and creative inspiration can work in harmony to illuminate the many facets of life and the world fabric.[13]

UNDERSTANDING COSMOVISION

In the last analysis it is the ultimate picture which an age forms of the nature of its world that is its most fundamental possession. It is the final controlling factor in all thinking whatever.

E. A. Burtt, *The Metaphysical Foundations of Modern Physical Science*

A worldview is a culture's most valuable inheritance because it fashions the way in which we envision and relate to the world and other people. A worldview or cosmovision provides the means through which a culture weaves all the threads of human experience into a meaningful pattern. Moreover, every worldview reflects cultural ideas and has social consequences. The history of culture and ideas is nothing other than the story of changing worldviews and the myths, stories, and concepts behind them. We edit reality selectively, often in useful ways, and those ways that we collectively agree upon shape the way in which society functions.

Worldviews change. Sometimes they collide painfully. And then there are the dissenters who refuse to play the game, try to change the rules, or try to see a little further than they are encouraged to by society. In earlier times, visionary individuals like Socrates, Jesus, or Giordano Bruno were put to death for trying to expand the vision of their time and place.

In every society, artists, visionaries, healers, priests, and musicians provide the tribe with access to the spiritual realm, with new forms of inspiration. In traditional cultures, these roles were combined in the person of the tribal shaman, a visionary healer who possessed the power to enter into trance, traverse the celestial and hidden regions, enter into dialogue with spirits, and return to normal consciousness with useful knowledge for the tribe. Human culture is based on imagination, rooted within the greater imagination of the unfolding universe. Despite the oftentimes conservative nature of worldviews and social cosmologies, the myths on which our lives are based must be constantly renewed. If the gateway to inspiration remains too closed, our lives dry up and the world becomes a wasteland; as in the well-known biblical line, "where there is no vision the people perish." A living bond with creativity and the spirit world must be maintained even today in our secular and technological age if human life is to remain meaningful.

In addition to the necessity of renewal, worldviews change and expand. Sometimes a long period of stability passes, like the Middle Ages, in which a worldview reigns supreme for hundreds of years. The cosmology works, and it works very well. In the Middle Ages, for example, the universe and society were neatly compartmentalized. It was a comfortable vision in which everyone knew their place, their social role, and what was expected of them. Individuals were born into a certain station in life and, beyond that, no real advancement was possible. The very thought of questioning the social structure or the religious ideas on which it rested rarely occurred to anyone. But change can only be avoided for so long. In the twelfth century, the troubadours arose, celebrating in song the idea of romantic love for a specific individual, an idea that went against the standard medieval notion of socially arranged marriage as a utilitarian, economic convention. In the theological sphere, the writings of Aristotle became available and stimulated a hunger for reason as well as for faith—a hunger that would eventually lead to the Scientific Revolution following the Renaissance. And when

Copernicus's heliocentric hypothesis was finally validated by Kepler and Newton, it destroyed the cosmological scaffolding on which the entire medieval worldview had been based.

Like shamans or witch doctors, philosophers and scientists have often lived at the fringes of society, dedicating their lives to expanding the boundaries of knowledge and the ways in which we see, imagine, and investigate the world. True philosophy is characterized by visionary courage and a willingness to look at the world in new and unfamiliar ways. In this way, the greatest philosophers and scientists have assumed a heroic risk. Certainly, some have risked their very lives by asking unsettling questions or by holding unconventional views. Like a shaman's journey to the Otherworld, the heroic quest is often lonely and fraught with danger. But if successful, the true hero is able to attain a new level of insight or way of being, which upon return to society, he or she can share with everyone who is capable of receiving it. In this way, through the work and sacrifice of creative individuals, our worldview—our cosmovision—is constantly being expanded, rewoven, and enriched.

MYTH, THE GREAT ATTRACTOR

A myth is an attractor in the world of ideas.

DAVID SHIRE

Science and philosophy always develop from two different sources: 1) Empiricism and rational thought; 2) Unconscious presuppositions which may even be more influential than the tools of rational analysis. . . . The danger is when we think that we have left all mythic thought behind.

W. K. C. GUTHRIE

Our lives are shaped by myth or story. At its deepest level, myth has the power to shape and inspire human action on both an individual and collective level.

When the medieval, theological myth of the geocentric universe fell apart, it was replaced by a new secular myth of scientific progress. Yet even the secular idea of scientific progress was highly colored and animated by underlying religious and mythological ideas. For example, the ideas of "salvation" and "utopia" are heavily charged symbolic and mythic images that are highly compelling to the human spirit. While the medieval Church offered its own vision of redemption, the new idea of technological progress popularized after the Renaissance catalyzed human action by offering a new, mythic vision of salvation in which scientific knowledge could establish a utopian heaven on Earth. In this way, the myth of scientific progress actively sanctified the formation of a community of "the faithful"—a community in which individuals could transcend their isolation and participate in the gradual establishment of a utopian paradise. To continue the analogy, some scientists held an almost unshakable religious belief that their particular way of understanding the world was supremely authoritative and "theologically correct" above all others—a belief that allowed those individuals to make a total life commitment to the scientific worldview. The point I am raising here is not whether the medieval or scientific myths of salvation were true or false, but the fact that they possessed parallel structures and fulfilled similar human needs.

Observations such as this have led some scholars to conclude that the greatest force shaping any culture's worldview is myth. As mythologist Joseph Campbell pointed out, myth has four primary functions:

- The mystical dimension opens us up to the awesome, numinous energies of existence in which human life is situated.
- The cosmological dimension paints a picture of the universe that is congruent with society's current understanding of the world-structure.
- The sociological dimension validates, supports, and imprints the norms of the social order in which an individual needs to live.
- The educational dimension shows us how to live a useful life under any circumstances.[14]

Myth and worldview are inseparable. They feed off of one another. One of the most helpful insights of contemporary times is the realization that all human activity is mythological and imaginal to some degree. Behind every desire, activity, or mode of behavior is a story, a narrative, a mythos. Whether we decide to climb the corporate ladder, withdraw to monastic life in the woods, dedicate our lives to a political cause, or believe literally in a scientific theory or spiritual teaching, each pathway is the embodiment of a certain myth, magnetized and given energy by archetypal or symbolic ideas. But because everything is mythological in some sense, and since myth has a powerful life of its own, we need to be selective and reflect consciously on the myths we are living or drawn to. By choosing to cultivate those myths that embody deeper levels of beauty, value, and awareness, human life is nourished and enriched. Myth liberates human energy and allows us to experience life in the deepest and most vital way; but without conscious reflection, individuals are swept away to become devotees of passing fads or totalitarian ideologies.

Without myth, the energy never would have been catalyzed to build the Egyptian pyramids or gothic cathedrals. Without myth, Plato and Socrates never would have achieved their intellectual brilliance. Without myth, Jesus never would have challenged the Pharisees and found the courage to give up his life for a cause greater than himself. Without the myth of the contemplative life, the great monasteries of medieval civilization never would have emerged. Without the myth of the creative genius, Michelangelo and Beethoven never would have discovered the inspiration necessary to bring forth their masterpieces. Without the myth of progress, experimental science and technology never would have emerged in their startling way. Without the myth of national socialism, Hitler never would have risen to messianic power. Without the myth of imperialism and dominion, slavery and the industrial exploitation of the Earth would not have been possible. Without the myth of democracy, the Berlin wall might not have fallen; without the myth of communism, it would not have risen. Without the myth of unlimited growth, our unquestioning adherence to modern economic theories would be severely shaken. Without the myth of ecological sustainability and a tangible perception of our fragile living planet, our children's children may inhabit a despoiled, paved-over wasteland, in which the quality of life will be severely impoverished. Understanding myth shows how there can be no split between the worlds of fact and value, because the values we adopt are instantaneously translated into the world of action.

Myth structures behavior and influences everyone on the collective level, but myth, and the reframing of myth, is something that emerges from the creative encounter with reality. Mathematician and cultural historian Ralph Abraham notes that myths, like worldviews, are not static, but change and evolve: "The evolution of myth is the evolution of the self-representation, or self-image, of society, which guides our behavior today, and tomorrow. If we reflect on our myth . . . we can participate consciously in the creation of our future."[15] Like truth, myth is not something handed to us ready made on a platter, but something that we actively participate in discovering and shaping. As he notes, "In mythogenesis, we can apply our creative hand, our will, our understanding. We can change the myth, and history may follow."[16]

COSMOVISION REVISITED: HUMANITY IN HARMONY WITH THE UNIVERSE

One of the best ways to understand the all-encompassing totality of a worldview or cosmovision is to look at the monuments of prehistoric and traditional peoples that are aligned to the stars and other celestial phenomena. In these sacred sites we can see a synthesis of scientific knowledge, spiritual yearnings, and cultural realities. The wonder aroused by the heavens is as old as human nature. The early Greek philosophers were just the first to write about it, but before them the people who built Newgrange and Stonehenge *acted on it.*

As astronomy writer E. C. Krupp notes, places like Stonehenge

had power because they matched and reflected the structure of the cosmos itself. In them, the entire universe was miniaturized through symbol. The universe and the shrine shared what those who study the nature of the structure would call a homologous relationship. Each element of the shrine mimics—through placement, function, and meaning—a corresponding aspect of the universe itself. Invested, then, with cosmic symbolism, such shrines were sacred venues, places where it was believed the magical power of the universe could be encountered and tapped.

Cosmovision, or world view, is the link between the architecture of the universe, the pattern of nature, the fabric of society, and the personal environment. It integrates these notions and forges a system of relationships between the cosmic and the divine with human society and individual destiny. Ideas about the structure of the world, about the rhythms of time, and about the origin of the cosmos are all combined into a ceremonial landscape.[17]

No matter where you go on the Earth, since the dawn of time people have sought to align themselves with the cosmos. In the primordial experience of humanity, the heavens were alive, pulsating with living, moving beings. And the life of these heavenly bodies sustains us too. Without the Sun, all life would expire. Without the Moon, it would be impossible to count off the month. Without the stars, we would lose track of the seasons. Poised under the living sky, traditional people had a far more intimate relationship with the heavens than we modern city dwellers could ever imagine.

To be fully alive is to be engaged with the rhythms and patterns of the natural world, but to be fully human is to reflect upon and celebrate this relationship. And this is precisely what we find in the monuments of the ancient peoples. Even though they have left us no manuscripts or elaborate instruction manuals, their careful writings in stone convey a message of awareness, self-reflection, and celebration. The message itself couldn't be clearer.

At a deep level of human experience the world reveals itself as a circle: the circle of the horizon; the circle of the seasons; the cycle of the Moon; the circle of birth, development, maturity, death, and regeneration; the circle of learning, testing, and revisioning. *Circle* and *cycle* come from the same root. And in the same way the circle encompasses the greatest area using the least possible perimeter, the cycle as circle joins the beginning to end in the most efficient way. No wonder that the circle has often been celebrated as the most perfect form and that the ancient peoples of the British Isles often built stone circles as meeting places and ritual structures to link their societies with the cosmos.

Speaking historically, we know that the first astronomers were priests, and the first observatories were temples. The Latin word *templum* literally means "a place set aside for observing the heavens," and the act of observing the heavens from the temple gave rise to the word *contemplation*. The word *temple* comes from the prehistoric Indo-European root *tem-,* which means "to cut."[18] A temple is a sacred space, a place of retreat that is literally cut out from the busy demands of everyday existence. Sometimes only by separating and purifying ourselves from external distractions—whether through ritual, contemplation, or intensive study—is it possible to experience renewal and discover a deeper relationship with the world.

The Latin word *religio* means to "relink" or "rebind," and the ritual performed in a temple is a religious act, designed to relink us to the universe and ensure that the proper balance is maintained between humanity and the cosmos. From this perspective, gazing into the night sky is a primordial "religious" activity, for it is a contemplative act that relinks us with the universe and the mysterious depths of our own being. As Henry Corbin writes in his book *Temple and Contemplation:*

> It is significant that the Latin word *templum* originally meant a vast space, open on all sides, from which one could survey the whole surrounding landscape as far as the horizon. This is what it means to *contemplate:* to "set one's sights on" Heaven from the *temple* that defines the field of vision. . . . The term was actually used above all to designate the field of Heaven, the expanse of the open Heaven where the flight of birds could be observed and interpreted. . . . The *temple* is the place, the organ, of vision.[19]

Since the first temples were open places for observing the heavens, it is not surprising, as sacred architecture developed, that many temples were oriented toward celestial bodies. *Orientation* means "to face the east" or the orient—to face the rising Sun or some other heavenly object. Sir Norman Lockyer, one of the first individuals to research the astronomical features of sacred sites, discovered that some Egyptian temples were oriented toward the rising or setting Sun on a special day of the year. On the feast day of the temple god, and only on that day, the Sun would send a flash of light down a long, narrow corridor, where it would finally enter the holy of holies, illuminating the cult statue of the divinity.[20] Similarly, the five-thousand-year-old mound at Newgrange in Ireland is oriented toward the rising Sun on the winter solstice (December 21), the shortest day of the year. On that morning a shaft of light penetrates a long tunnel and illuminates the back wall of the innermost chamber. Thus, at the turning point of the year, the Sun plants its fertilizing seed deep within womb of the Earth, initiating the return of life in the spring.

If space permitted, dozens of other aligned sites could be listed from all around the world, ranging from Stonehenge to Greek temples to Native American medicine wheels to Central American pyramids. In all such cases, scientific knowledge has been united with the practical, magical act of maintaining harmony between human life and the larger life of the cosmos. As modern human beings, we still have the need to channel the fertilizing energies of the cosmos into our everyday lives through science, art, and the imagination.

There are barriers in trying to understand sacred sites like Newgrange or Stonehenge and the cosmovision of the people that built them. The greatest obstacle is the lack of written records. Drawing upon the structure and symbolism of these sites, their alignments, what we know about human nature, and our historical imagination, we have to reconstruct what occurred there.

In the British Isles there are literally hundreds of megalithic stone circles. They come in a variety of sizes. But Stonehenge stands apart from them all in terms of its structure, scale, and the amount of human effort involved (see figure 1.2 on page 24). In its scope and grandeur, Stonehenge resembles a national sanctuary. Its construction began around 2800 B.C., before the construction of the Great Pyramid in Egypt, and went on for several hundred years as it progressed through a number of stages.

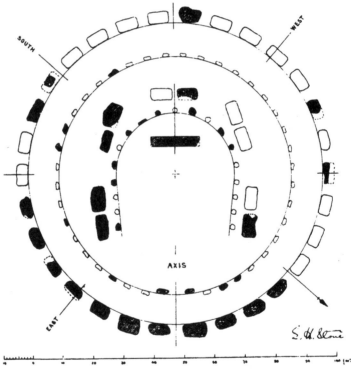

Figure 1.2. Above: Engraving of "Stonehenge Restored." Below: Ground plan and alignment of the monument. The central axis of Stonehenge is aligned with the rising of the Sun on the summer solstice (June 21), the longest day of the year.

The bluestones out of which it was constructed were transported by raft and over land from Wales—over a 230-mile route. Stonehenge does not stand in isolation, but rises from the Salisbury plain in an area richly saturated with mounds, banks, rings, long barrows, and other earthworks.

As some scholars have argued, most recently science historian John North, Stonehenge may well have functioned as a sophisticated astronomical observatory.[21] The flat plain surrounding the structure would have provided ample opportunity to measure and track the movement of the celestial bodies in relation to the standing stones of the monument. Certainly there can be no doubt that the axis of the structure is aligned with the sunrise point of the summer solstice, the longest day of the year. On that day, the Sun rises over an outlying marker called the Heel Stone, to shine its rays into the horseshoe-shaped structure in the heart of the monument designed to capture and cradle the vital energy.

To further highlight the alignment, in the past there was an earth-banked causeway leading out from the great circle toward the Heel Stone. On the summer solstice, a beam of light would travel down the causeway toward the center. On that day before dawn, we can also imagine a group of privileged individuals, dressed in colorful robes and accompanied by song, making a ritual procession across the Salisbury plain, down the causeway and into the structure. There they would wait and greet the rising Sun, the source of life and light. What words were spoken there we can only guess, but it is likely that the ceremonial energy generated by the meeting of Sun, Earth, and humanity then radiated out into the greater culture as a stimulus for festive thanksgiving and celebration. In ancient times, under the spell of the cosmological impulse, storytellers, artists, priests, and their societies were expert at weaving human life into the cosmic pattern by celebrating the natural bonds that unite us with the world.

Stonehenge may have been an observatory and place for scientific research, but first and foremost it was a temple, "the place, the organ, of vision." Certainly Stonehenge was far more than a solstice marker. On one hand, it was a structure designed to channel the life-giving energies of the cosmos into human society. On the other hand, it was a ceremonial instrument used to reinforce humanity's bond with the living

Figure 1.3. While based on scientific knowledge, Stonehenge was a ceremonial instrument used to reinforce humanity's bond with the patterns and energies of the greater cosmos.

universe. In the megalithic worldview, science, art, mathematics, and priestcraft were integrated for magical purposes in the service of the larger society (see figure 1.3). As John North notes, the astronomical activities of these early peoples were truly scientific, in the sense that they reduced what was observed to a series of rules that could also be used for purposes of prediction.[22] But the motivation behind the science was mystical, religious, and social, in the same way that modern technology is science applied for a practical end.

The magical dimension of ancient astronomical knowledge is even more evident at Newgrange, the oldest surviving structure in Europe that is aligned with the cosmic pattern (see figure 1.4).[23] Located in the Boyne Valley in Ireland some twenty-five miles north of Dublin, Newgrange is a vast artificial mound. Measuring 280 feet in diameter and 36 feet high at the center, it could easily enclose the bluestone ring of Stonehenge. But more amazing than its size, or the 800,000 hours that it took to build, is the fact that Newgrange was constructed in 3500 B.C.

Newgrange before restoration

Newgrange after archaeological restoration, as it appears today

Interior ground plan showing the path of light on the winter solstice

Entrance stone, doorway, and roof box

Sunbeam entering the roof box and penetrating the inner chamber on the winter solstice

Figure 1.4. Dating from 3500 B.C., Newgrange is the oldest astronomically aligned structure surviving in Europe. On the winter solstice, a beam of light from the rising Sun enters the roof box to penetrate the innermost chamber.

Earlier in this century, residents around Newgrange thought of it as a fairy mound, an entrance to the Otherworld. That was before the archeologists got involved. Then in 1969 Michael J. O'Kelly discovered that the rising Sun on the winter solstice cast a beam of light down the long passageway to illuminate the innermost depths of the Earth. The artistry and elaborate precision of construction are astonishing. Once overgrown and covered by fifty centuries of debris, Newgrange has been excavated and restored to its original state. Placed like a gleaming white button on the plain, we can now view the mound as it was originally built: surrounded by a stone ring at its base, flanked with radiant quartz, and covered in turf. Situated in front of the passage doorway is an entrance stone with beautifully carved spirals, while above the doorway is a window now known as the "roof box."

The placement of the roof box is just one element that reveals the intricate design of the structure. According to local tradition, a triple spiral on a stone in the deepest part of the structure was illuminated by the Sun on a certain day of the year. But because of the upward slant of the passageway, no sunlight entering the doorway could enter the inner chamber. During his excavation, however, O'Kelly discovered the roof box that had been sealed by two blocks of quartz. One was still in place and the other nearby. Together, they exactly fit the opening. Once the roof box was open, the rays of the Sun were allowed to *precisely* enter the innermost chamber.

Following an intuition, O'Kelly entered the chamber on the winter solstice, December 21, 1969, before sunrise. As day began to break, a brilliant beam of sunlight passed through the roof box to dance across the spiral carvings of the stones in the innermost chamber. Taking into account the shift of the Earth's axis, in prehistoric times the solstice Sun would have been reflected off the upright stones to illuminate the mysterious triple spiral located deep within the structure (see figure 1.5).

The spiral is a central theme of Newgrange. Symbolically, the spiral represents the unfurling of life. As plants and trees unfold, they whirl out, engaging in a spiral dance. The spiral is one of nature's most dynamic patterns and embodies the fertile energies of cosmic regeneration. As such, it throws light on the inner meaning of Newgrange.

Figure 1.5. The triple spiral located within the interior of Newgrange.

The winter solstice, when the light enters the chamber, is the shortest day of the year. It marks the death of the old year, but also the birth of the new year, for the winter solstice is the turning point at which the days begin to grow longer. Similarly, Newgrange is a place of death and rebirth. It is not an astronomical observatory, but a passage grave—a tomb, not a temple. While not a community cemetery, it contained the cremated bones of a few individuals, probably chieftains, priests, or other individuals of a special social status. More than a tomb, it may have been a sanctuary for ritual activities. The mound with its inner chamber is the womb of the Earth Mother. Entering the passageway, the shaft of heavenly light embodies the fertilizing energy of the Sky Father. When Earth and sky are conjoined in their alchemical union, the spiral dance of life is set in motion. Together, Sun and Earth bring forth a vibrant tapestry of vegetation, the spiraling source of vitality on which all creatures ultimately depend.

Similarly, our lives embody a spiral, circular structure. At our birth we emerge from the root mystery of the cosmos, a deep and silent mystery into which we will one day be reabsorbed. Our own lives are a spiral pattern of creative unfolding, death, and regeneration. Fashioned out of the creative power of starlight and the fecund body of the Earth, we are the children of Earth and the starry heavens caught up in the timeless rhythms of the celestial dance.

While we cannot reconstruct the rituals that took place at Stonehenge or Newgrange with certainty, it seems evident that an important function of these structures was to maintain society's harmony with the cosmos and the natural world. And in this enterprise, mathematics, astronomy, religion, and art were all conjoined. The word *harmony* means "to fit together" and conjures up the most primordial images of cosmic order. The Greek word *harmonia* comes from a prehistoric Indo-European root *ar-*, which also means "to fit together." More revealing, however, are all of the other familiar words that grew out of this ancient root. These include *order, arithmos* (number), *ritual, ratio* (proportion), *ornament,* and *art.*[24] Through the arithmetic divisions of space and the temporal rhythms of ritual, the ancient peoples sought to emphasize their proportional relationship to—their being woven into— the greater cosmic order.

In this way, they underscored the sacred quality of life. Abstract theological ideas about God and divinity vary from culture to culture and from person to person. But common to all spiritual yearning is a desire to be bonded with the cosmos or to a reality larger than oneself. In this way, "the sacred" is not a theoretical idea, but an experience of being deeply connected with everything in the visible universe and all the forces that lie behind it. When we experience this vital sense of con- nectedness, life becomes engaging and meaningful. In a living cosmo- vision, humanity is bonded with the heavens and the living Earth—an embodiment of the starlight from which all things flow.

2

Beauty, Desire, and the Soul of the World

THE UNDIVIDED UNIVERSE

The things of the universe are not sliced off from one another with a hatchet, neither the hot from the cold nor the cold from the hot.

ANAXAGORAS

Science is the search for unity, the search for understanding the fundamental patterns of nature. The very earliest philosophers, captivated by the beauty of nature, believed that nature was orderly and that there was one fundamental principle that the entire universe originated from. This principle was thought to be self-moving and the author of its own transformations. In this way, the earliest philosophers, who were known as the *physikoi*—the "physicists" or "naturalists"—believed that nature has the ability to create and sustain itself. — doesn't it?

The Greek word for nature, *physis,* is the source of our word "physics." But like the Latin word *natura,* it also means "birth." *Phuō,* the root of physis, means to sprout like a plant. The forms of nature are always germinating, growing, and coming into being. Because of this, the universe is alive, a continual birthing—a living event of creative unfolding.

The earliest Greek philosophers—Thales, Anaxagoras, and Anaximenes—postulated a radical unity that some later thinkers found difficult to understand. There is no difference between spirit and matter, but matter is itself a dynamic, living activity. The word *psychē* means "life," and the characteristic energy of life is movement. Because the world is ever-moving and ever-changing, it is ensouled and alive. And since the primordial root of the physical world is eternal, self-moving, and the cause of all ordered phenomena, it was also described as being divine.[1]

There are numerous ideas of God and divinity, but Western people have been influenced by the Judeo-Christian idea of a creator God who stands outside of the universe, and also by the mechanistic worldview in which matter is dead and passive, acted upon by external forces. To understand the vision of the Presocratics, however, we must leave all these ideas behind. In the Judeo-Christian image, divinity has been pictured in very anthropocentric terms, much like an engineer who draws up a plan for the universe and then sets it in motion. But for the Presocratics there was nothing *outside* of nature itself. For them the two characteristics of the divine were movement and eternal activity. Because of this, the universe itself was believed to be permeated by divinity, but not a type of divinity that stands outside of the world. The Presocratics felt no necessity to divide up the universe into a type of passive matter and an external force that acts upon it. In this way the basic idea of the earliest scientists was remarkably modern, for contemporary physics demonstrates that matter is not a dead substance, but rather a dancing pattern of activity.

Thales, the very first philosopher, saw the entire universe as a living organism. For him the *archē*—the originating principle of the universe—was water, which then changed itself into all things through a process of self-transformation. This *archē* was alive and everlasting, capable of self-organization. Ultimately, everything is alive and animate. Thales pointed out that even the magnet possesses a soul because it is

Truth

capable of attracting iron. When Thales said that "all things are full of gods," he meant that soul, or the divine power of movement and transformation, is inherent in all things.[2]

Not only is the world alive but it is also intelligent. We see that the universe is alive because all of reality is a ceaseless flow of activity, and motion is a sign of life. Secondly, the ever-shifting universe exhibits recurring patterns of order and form—and order and form are expressions of intelligence.[3] Put another way, the deployment of order and form are strategies of organization, and anything that possesses a strategy also possesses some type of intelligence. The order of the universe is not imposed upon it by some outside source, but is a natural expression of its own inner life, intelligence, and being. In this way the vision of the Presocratics very strongly resembles the modern cosmological theories of the evolutionary, self-organizing universe.

THE DISCOVERY OF THE COSMOS: THE ORDER AND BEAUTY OF NATURE

The universe is a kosmos, *because it is perfect and "adorned" with infinite beauty and living beings.*

PYTHAGORAS

If nature were not beautiful, it would not be worth knowing.

HENRI POINCARÉ

One of the most captivating aspects of the universe is its beauty. On one hand, the beauty of the world arrests us, causing us to halt in our tracks. On the other hand, it entices us, leads us onward, and calls out to us. According to one ancient writer, the very word *beauty* (*kalon*) originates from the verb *to call* (*kalein*).[4] Beauty can influence us powerfully because in some deep, subliminal, and nonverbal way, it reminds us of our own inner nature.

In a living cosmovision, the world is luminous and transparent. It radiates a divine beauty in which we are embedded. In the modern world, however, a great confusion has arisen about beauty. Because some people confuse beauty with personal taste, they see it as subjective, "in the eye of the beholder," or as culture-specific, rather than seeing it as an objective quality of nature. Under the spell of materialism and the quest for efficiency, the world grows increasingly heavy and opaque. We are surrounded by the beauty of nature on every side; but when we become anesthetized to the beauty of the world, the world itself becomes exploitable—just "a natural resource" for human consumption. If we could consistently see the world with unclouded vision and appreciation, we would treat it with reverence and realize that beauty reveals a deep and essential aspect of the cosmic pattern. While our human *tastes* are certainly individual and culture-specific in many ways, beauty itself is rooted in the deep structure of the world.

As often happens, by destroying or despoiling the beauty of nature in the name of economic growth, we are destroying one of our most vital links with the depths of the cosmic pattern. In terms of our evolutionary heritage, we emerged from the beautiful, organic harmonies of the world fabric, but when we no longer have direct access to the living patterns and forms of nature something of our own nature is lost or forgotten too.[5] As the biologist Gregory Bateson pointed out, the aesthetic unity of nature reveals an ultimate unifying pattern far deeper and more complete than the findings of quantitative science can describe. He also wrote that the lost sense of this aesthetic unity—the common possession of all traditional peoples—is one of the most serious failings of the modern world.[6] By entering into a deep experience of nature's beauty, we are able to experience directly the vital patterns that connect flowers, starfish, galaxies, and our own human lives with the greater tapestry of the living universe. As Goethe wrote, "The beautiful is a manifestation of secret laws of nature, which, without its presence, would have never been revealed."[7] Ultimately, the beauty that we can perceive directly at all levels of existence and scale reveals the whole of nature to be an organically interconnected and comprehensive unity.

The Greek word *kosmos* cannot be translated into a single English word, but refers to an equal presence of order and beauty. When the Greek philosopher Pythagoras first called the universe a *kosmos,* he did so because it is a living embodiment of nature's order, beauty, and harmony.

The fact that the physical world embodies beauty and harmony can be demonstrated in many ways, but rational proof is only required when we have forgotten our own connection with the underlying web of life. When we can view the exquisite grandeur of a forest, mountain range, or the form of a distant galaxy with a clear and untroubled heart, the beauty and harmony of the universe becomes immediately obvious— not through argument, but through direct perception. As William Blake wrote, "If the doors of perception were cleansed everything would appear to man as it is, infinite."[8]

In this sense, the perception of the world's deep, intrinsic beauty and harmony was the starting point of ancient science and philosophy. In the vision of the ancient philosophers, the universe itself was seen as an embodiment of beauty, which is itself a manifestation of value. Hence, Pythagoras (570–496 B.C.) called the universe a *cosmos*—a "beautiful order"—and explained that the world-structure arises from *harmony* or the "fitting together" of different elements through proportional relationships.[9] We can see the patterns of harmony reflected in the structure of galaxies, trees, snowflakes, in the deeply elegant forms of living creatures, and in the proportions of the human body. In the harmonic structure of the living universe, all the individual parts fit together to make up the greater whole.

For Pythagoras there could be no separation between the realms of science and religion or fact and value. The cosmos reflects a universal order, which is a fact, but is also an embodiment of beauty, which is a manifestation of value. From this perspective, fact and value are not opposed, but two interrelated aspects of the same pattern. The cosmos is a living unity in which all things are related through kinship, harmony, proportion, and sympathy. Referring to the teachings of the Pythagoreans, Plato wrote that "the wise men say that one community embraces heaven and earth and gods and men and friendship and order and temperance and righteousness, and for this reason they call this whole a cosmos, my friend, for it is not without order nor yet is there excess."[10] Or, in the words of another ancient writer, "There is a certain community uniting us not only with each other and with the gods but even with the brute creation. There is in fact one breath pervading the whole cosmos like soul, and uniting us with them."[11]

While the earlier Greek naturalists speculated about the structure of the universe, for Pythagoras philosophy was a broader enterprise of liberation and self-transformation. Cosmology is a search to understand the common order that embraces humanity and the larger universe. But if the order of the universe embodies a divine intelligence, that intelligence is reflected in us, too. For the Pythagoreans, philosophy and science was a process through which our essential vision of reality would become more purified and increasingly luminous. Put in religious language, by studying the divine structure of the cosmos, the philosopher would cultivate and come to know more clearly the divine element in himself.[12] By understanding our innate bond with the cosmic pattern, we also discover our essential nature.

Behind the divine harmony of the cosmos, Pythagoras discerned a mathematical order. His studies of musical harmony on the monochord, a one-stringed musical instrument, showed that the perfect intervals of music—the octave, the perfect fifth, and the perfect fourth—corresponded to simple whole number proportions. He created a symbol of this mathematical arrangement called the Tetraktys, a pyramid of ten dots (see figure 2.1). In addition to other relationships, this symbol represented the perfect harmonies in music: the octave (1:2), the perfect fifth (2:3), and the perfect fourth (3:4). As a symbol of cosmic attunement, the Pythagoreans referred to it as "Nature's fount and root." Where the earlier philosophers said that the essential root of nature was water, air, or fire, Pythagoras claimed that the root of nature's order lies in its mathematical harmony. In this perception, he discovered the mathematical order of nature and laid the foundation of the Western scientific tradition.

Mathematics is defined today as the study of patterns in time and space. According to Pythagoras, number and proportion is a primordial, archetypal reality that structures the patterns of space and time. Through proportion, parts are related to larger wholes in the most perfect and integrated way possible. In the dynamic patterns of nature, from the unfolding of a flower to the orbital dance of a planet, there is

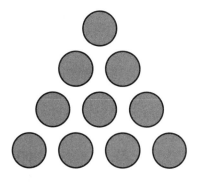

Figure 2.1. Right: The Tetraktys, a Pythagorean symbol of the perfect harmonies of music: octave (1:2), perfect fifth (2:3), and perfect fourth (3:4). Below: The polychord—a monochord with more than one string—used in antiquity to study the mathematical intervals of harmony and tuning theory.

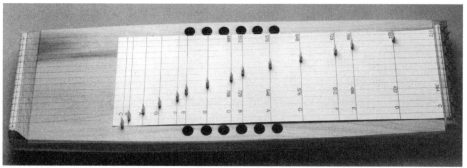

a harmonious efficiency at work that reflects the mathematical order at the heart of creation. But for Pythagoras mathematics was not primarily a quantitative study in terms of weight, volume, or mass, but a study of the qualitative relationships and patterns that bind things together. As Einstein once said, "The most incomprehensible thing about the universe is that it is comprehensible."[13] Many physicists have wondered how we can account for "the unreasonable effectiveness of mathematics," which is one of the central mysteries of Western science. How and why does the universe have such perfect interconnected balance? And how, through science and mathematics, can we discover and understand this order in our own minds? Pythagoras claimed that like can know like. The very fact that we encapsulate the cosmic order gives us access to its innermost nature. Or as the French poet Paul Valéry put it, "The Universe is built upon a plan the profound symmetry of which is somehow present in the inner structure of our intellect."[14] In some mysterious way, the human mind embodies the deepest reaches of the cosmic pattern and can peer into its order.

THE RHAPSODIC INTELLECT AND
THE WAYS OF KNOWING

While intelligence treats everything mechanically, instinct proceeds, so to speak, organically. If the consciousness that slumbers in it should awake, if it were wound up into knowledge instead of being wound off into action, if we could ask and it could reply, it would give up to us the most intimate secrets of life.

HENRI BERGSON

To know is not all, it is only half. To love is the other half.

JOHN BURROUGHS

Philosophy is often thought of as a dry, abstract, intellectual pursuit. Certainly, as it developed, philosophy came to be more and more limited to the discursive, reasoning intellect. But in the beginning, when philosophy stood closer to the cosmological impulse, things were different. Philosophy began with wonder and a deep perception of the aesthetic fitness of the universe. Feeling, wonder, awe, beauty, and desire are all tied up with the innermost heart of the philosophical quest. As Emerson wrote, "The true philosopher and the true poet are one, and a beauty, which is a truth, and a truth, which is a beauty, is the aim of both."[15]

Plato was a great believer in the power of the rational intellect, but he also recognized its limitations. We need to carefully analyze problems, note inconsistencies, and draw conclusions. We need to make judgments and test the waters. But the intellect remains removed from life. It is, in some sense, artificial. As French philosopher Henri Bergson wrote, it "treats everything mechanically."[16] As Plato noted, the analytical intellect polarizes reality into subject and object, overlooking the essential unity that exists between the self and the world.[17] From Plato's point of view, we must develop the intellect, but we must also know how to move beyond it into a more intimate connection with the world. The intellect needs to point beyond itself to a deeper way of knowing in which there is a merging with the essential nature of reality. In this way we can enter a nonverbal mode of perception in which the sense of intellectual alienation is overcome.

In this way the intellect is limited. Like a finely crafted car, it can take us far, but at the end of the drive we need to get out, enter the living world, and travel on foot with a valued companion along the most beautiful part of our journey. As philosopher Stephen Rowe writes, "The intellect must serve a way of being and relating that is ultimately beyond its grasp."[18] In order to enter the depths of the world, we need to move beyond conceptualization and embrace the vital energies that animate the universe and have brought us into being. As poet Bruce Nelson notes, the ego "loves the hermetic, the complex and the distant—it is always stepping back, avoiding directness."[19] Because the ego is always looking from the outside and lacks a deep connection with the inner nature of things, ego consciousness, which has strengthened since the Scientific Revolution, has assumed that the world is dead and Other. But the world itself remains alive. As Nelson writes, "It is not a problem of a dead world, for the world has always possessed soul, but of a dead vision, one which numbs and deadens us until we extricate ourselves from it."[20]

The word *science* means "to know," but it comes from an Indo-European root that literally means "to cut" or "to split." The same root gave birth to the word *schism*. The scientific method literally cuts reality up into little parts for the purpose of controlled experimentation. But if science and the discursive intellect is analytical, or tends to break things down, other ways of knowing are synthetic. They situate human life in a larger context. Through the knowledge conveyed by music, art, poetry, and symbolic imagery, it is possible to move beyond the path of mere analysis to experience a deeper connection with the vital energies of the world. Other human capabilities like intimacy, the unfolding rhythm of conversation, and the experience of creativity all offer valid pathways that reconnect us with the fundamental structures from which we have emerged.

The beauty of the cosmos inspires ecstasy, and *ekstasis* means to go outside of oneself. Inspiration is a mysterious quality but a fundamental aspect of human experience. The greatest works of art and scientific discovery result from a collaboration between critical self-awareness and the mysterious, nonverbal depths of our inner nature. How we are able to creatively contact the intelligence of the universe remains unknown, but intuition and inspiration are as important in serious scientific work as any other factor. In antiquity, inspiration was attributed to the Muses, minor goddesses who presided over culture and the branches of learning. According to Plato, there were four types of divine madness or *mania*—not to be confused with insanity—that took the soul outside of itself to experience a larger reality.[21] Poetic madness was sent by the Muses. Mystic madness was sent by Dionysus, the god of ecstasy and liberation. Prophetic madness was sent by far-seeing Apollo. And erotic madness was sent by Aphrodite, the goddess of love. Under the spell of such rhapsodic inspiration, we are touched by an enthusiasm that carries us beyond our normal, limited boundaries.

The Presocratics, Pythagoras, Plato, and Aristotle, all spoke of the virtues of contemplation and the fact that philosophy is inspired by wonder. But with Aristotle the sense of wonder that we can tangibly *feel* in the work of the greatest early philosophers was replaced with the quest for certitude and "verificationism."[22] For Socrates, philosophy was not the construction of an intellectual system but a total engagement with life. He envisioned knowledge as an *event* worked out through rigorous conversation and engagement with others. For Socrates, philosophy was a way of life, a way of being, and a way of relating to the world that leads to transformation. But with Aristotle this earlier vision of philosophy came to be overshadowed by intellectualism.

For Aristotle, the intellect, rather than pointing *toward* ultimate reality in a Zen sense, became mistaken as the goal in itself. As philosopher Robert Cushman points out, Aristotle "was subtly lured by definitive answers of supposedly enforceable demonstrations."[23] Consequently, he "was impatient with dialogue and preferred the declarative treatise."[24] Writing of Aristotle's attraction to "verificationism," philosopher Jon Moline notes that "verificationism's paradigm of inquiry is the quest for certainty. Its methods are restricted to what are conceived to be ways of showing that a given proposition is certainly true."[25] While such an approach is sometimes useful, its reductionism results in a greatly diminished vision of the world's richness. As the artist Cecil Collins put it, "Logic is a superficial form of the imagination for the organization of certain local fields of activity in time and space for the needs of the creatures of humanity."[26]

Compared with the vitality of Socrates and Plato, in Aristotle's approach contemplation lost its emotional and aesthetic engagement with the living universe and pulled back into the abstractions of the intellect—a shift in orientation that powerfully influenced philosophy and theology for many hundreds of years. While we must respect Aristotle's accomplishments, as Stephen Rowe suggests, Aristotle's demand for intellectual certainty

> has led to the elevation of intellectual/cognitive knowledge over all others, and to the fragmentation and specialization of knowledge, to an "intellectualist bias." As a result, the greatness of our tradition, philosophy as "the love of wisdom" (*philo-sophia*), is hardly visible as an option today.[27]

While the verifiable, deductive logic that Aristotle championed provides an excellent way to clarify an argument, the problem with all logic is that it never produces anything that is new. The conclusion is already contained in the initial premises. *By contrast, philosophy and science—as vibrant human activities—ask us to assume a greater risk by creatively and courageously questioning the initial premises of thought. They ask us to question our assumptions and look at the world in a new way.* Only then is it possible to arrive at new insights.

While all of the Greek thinkers stressed the rationality of the cosmos, the universe possesses its own rationality that cannot ultimately be reduced once and for all to simple, either/or formulas of symbolic logic. And since the universe has many faces, we may speak of it as holding a great, if not infinite, depth. From this perspective, the more sensitivities and ways of knowing we possess, the more comprehensive our knowledge of the universe will be. Philosophy today has become a dead way of looking at the world because the world itself is complex, engaging, and multivalent; it calls out to be known in multiple ways.[28]

Yet with Aristotle's influence, philosophy began to close itself off from the numinosity of the universe and the deep experience of being by sealing itself off in the bubble of the analytical intellect. In order to revitalize our lives and our tradition, we must once again make room for art, beauty, the rhapsodic intellect, and the multiple ways of knowing. In addition to employing rigorous logic when called for, in the words of William James we need to move beyond "vicious intellectualism" and realize that "the immediate experience of life solves the problems which so baffle our conceptual intelligence."[29] Ultimately, we need to go beyond our conceptual categories in order to directly experience the deep structure of the world in the most profound way possible.

THE EROTIC PHILOSOPHER

The world thus exists to the soul to satisfy the desire of beauty. This element I call an ultimate end. No reason can be asked or given why the soul seeks beauty. Beauty, in its largest and profoundest sense, is one expression for the universe.

RALPH WALDO EMERSON

By inspiring wonder, the stars and the beauty of nature excite a love for learning and exploration. Yet love is more than merely a human emotion. In the Greek tradition, the power of Eros was seen as the underlying force that moves the heavenly spheres and animates all of existence. Love is the magnetic pull that binds all of creation together into a seamless unity. When we speak of Eros today, ideas of sexual desire immediately come to mind. But our modern conception excludes the ancient understanding that sexual love is just one aspect of a much larger cosmic force. Viewed as a universal power, it is the magnetic pull of Eros that inspires the electron to desire the proton, lovers to desire conjugal union, and the soul of the mystic to desire union with the ineffable source of creation. When Dante spoke of "the Love which moves the sun and the other stars" in the final line of *The Divine Comedy,* he was referring to the ancient idea that cosmic desire energizes the motion of the entire universe.

For Plato, true philosophy was inspired by love. When we are touched by the divine power of Eros, it sets us down a path that leads to the soul's awakening. Using a myth, Plato explained the experience of love in the following way:[30] Before birth, each human soul possesses wings and follows in the train of the gods. There, in the winged, cosmic procession, each soul glimpses beauty and true knowledge to varying degrees, feeding upon the vision like ambrosia and nectar. Due to forgetfulness, however, the soul grows heavy; it loses its wings and sinks down toward Earth in a state of amnesia. We are all thus born in varying states of forgetfulness. When we fall in love, the vision of the beloved held in the imagination incites a form of divine madness. Eros is the desire to possess the beauty of the beloved, and in this condition "the whole soul throbs and palpitates."[31] The effluence of beauty moistens the hard, atrophied roots of the soul's feathers, which again begin to swell and sprout. This causes an itching and feverish sensation like the cutting of teeth. When the beloved is near, the sensation of beauty moistens the follicles of the feathers; this soothes the discomfort and fills the soul with joy. But when separated from the beloved, the follicles start to harden and close up; they prick the soul, and throb painfully like pulsating arteries.

Socrates explains that the beauty of the beloved reminds the soul of its true, winged nature. The soul is reminded of the beauty that it gazed upon in the heavenly realms before being dragged down into a state of forgetfulness. Love is a reawakening to recover our essential nature, but, in the experience of love, we often do not see what is really happening. There is a well-known tendency to fall down and worship the beloved as the ultimate source of the lover's experience, rather than seeing the beloved as a catalyst of transformation; and in the misplaced literalism of this perception, there exists the danger of not viewing the soul's awakening within a larger context. The suggestion is that an individual love, while beautiful in itself, can also awaken us to greater realities. Love is a noble end in itself, but also the means to greater ends.

Eros leads beyond itself, but it also leads to a potentially deeper understanding of our own inner nature. For Plato, the experience of love was the beginning of the soul's awakening and education; it reminds us of what we truly are, and of our intimate connection with the beauty of the cosmos. Ultimately, there is no distinction between the beauty pursued externally and the beauty that resides within the soul. Eros demands that we go beyond our limited views of self and reality so that we can arrive at a deeper experience of our innate connection with the greater soul of the world.

In the *Symposium,* Socrates describes his initiation into the mysteries of love by Diotima, a wise and prophetic priestess. In the famous "ladder of love" speech, Socrates relates her teachings. In the philosopher's erotic awakening, he first falls in love with a particular person. Next, he realizes that beauty is not limited to one particular form, but belongs to many. From the beauty of bodies he advances to gaze upon the beauty of the soul and the fair order of human conduct. The philosopher is next led to contemplate the beauty of knowledge and scientific understanding, and from this he is led to the ultimate vision and "final secret," the vision of pure Beauty-in-itself. This Beauty is "the final object of all those previous toils" and is "ever-existent and neither comes to be nor perishes." In coming to know the very essence of beauty (reflected in all levels of existence), "a man finds it truly worthwhile to live."[32] Thus the path of Eros leads from the outer vision of physical beauty toward the inner vision of expanded, contemplative insight.

In the *Symposium,* Eros himself is described as a great *daimōn,* a mediating spirit between the mortal and immortal levels of being. Love is described as the offspring of Fullness (*Poros*) and Poverty (*Peneia*), and consequently partakes of both. Love possesses a fullness and richness of being, but is simultaneously a desire for that which it lacks. The lover, painfully aware of his emptiness, desires to possess the beauty of the beloved; the philosopher, keenly aware of his lack of wisdom, desires the wisdom that eludes him. Love and philosophy are seen as an *identical* movement toward knowledge, wisdom, and the deepening of human experience. In this sense, says Diotima, even Eros is a philosopher, "a lover of wisdom," because he too exists between wisdom and ignorance. Love and philosophy are revealed not as the idealized destinations of one's quest, but as the arduous journey itself. Philosophy is revealed as the practice of eros: the desire for the Good, or that which is best.

Psychologist James Hillman writes that "an inflated vision of supreme beauty is a necessary idea for the soul-making opus we call our lifetime,"[33] and without beauty the soul wouldn't be able to situate itself in relationship to the deeper levels of being. The world stands before us at every moment, but in order for us to really see it and grasp its nature, something in us needs to be activated. Through the power of beauty, the universe conspires to ignite our vision and passion, to awaken our essential nature. At their root, both human love and the unquenchable wonder aroused by the beauty of the cosmic pattern are part of a common erotic movement to grasp and participate in the deepest levels of reality.

THE WORLD SOUL AND THE SOUL OF THE WORLD

The kosmos was harmonized by proportion and brought into existence.

PLATO

God has not made some beautiful things, but Beauty is the creator of the universe.

RALPH WALDO EMERSON

According to Thomas Aquinas three things are needed for beauty—wholeness, harmony, and radiance. In the radiant forms of nature, beauty arises from the delicate relatedness that unifies the tiniest part with the greater whole, and in the natural world this type of relatedness is achieved through harmony, symmetry, and proportion. Commenting on the beauty of the physical universe, Plato called the cosmos "a perceptible god, image of the intelligible, greatest and best, most beautiful and most perfect."[34] He said that the universe is "one Whole of wholes"[35] and "a single Living Creature which encompasses all of the living creatures that are within it."[36]

The cosmos is a living reality woven together through dynamic patterns of relatedness, and in his famous and influential dialogue the *Timaeus,* Plato offers a Pythagorean account of how the beauty and order of the cosmos came into existence. When speaking about ultimate matters Plato would never give a literalistic description, but he offered a myth or story to point his readers in the right direction. This is especially true in the creation myth of the *Timaeus,* where he describes the underlying structure and creation of the universe. Plato did not pretend to offer us "the final truth," but only a story, which he characterized as the "most likely account." And in this account he described the nature of the World Soul, the vital pattern of relatedness in which the life, beauty, and order of the cosmos are rooted.

The overall theme of the dialogue is simple enough. Plato invented a mythical figure, the demiurge, who brought the universe into being. *Demiourgos* simply means "craftsperson," "artist," or "fabricator." In the creation myth, the demiurge looks toward the eternal Good as its guiding light, and using this as a model, brings the physical universe into being in the extended realm of time and space. While the physical universe is not absolutely perfect because of disturbances caused by eddies in the sea of change, it is a living manifestation of divine beauty and "the best possible image" of the Good in space and time. For this reason, the cosmos is "greatest and best," "most beautiful and most perfect," the physical image of the spiritual realm, "a perceptible god."

In overall outline the account is absolutely straightforward. The mysterious part that has puzzled commentators is Plato's description of the World Soul—the Soul of the Cosmos—that lies at the heart of the cosmic pattern. With his eyes fixed on the Good, the demiurge weaves together the cosmic soul that animates the universe. But when Plato starts describing this operation, he begins to speak of mathematics and the exact musical ratios the demiurge used to create the cosmic soul. Tuning theory, or the study of musical proportions, was closely studied by the Pythagoreans and members of Plato's Academy. As in his other dialogues, Plato included here a musical and mathematical puzzle for the contemplation of his more advanced readers.

Fortunately for the general reader, the mathematical details are not important as long as the overall idea is understood. For the Pythagoreans the musical scale was seen as the purest expression of mathematical and cosmic harmony. Through the use of simple mathematical proportions that are present in the actual universe, the musical scale is created. And through the use of these proportions, the two extremes of the musical scale or octave—low C and high C—are reconciled and brought together. *Harmonia* means "fitting together" and *scala* means ladder. Through the perfect proportions of harmony, a continuous bridge is constructed between the two extremes of the octave. They are bound together in harmony and—like the cosmos itself—all of the parts are perfectly and beautifully interrelated in the overall pattern.

In the creation of the World Soul, the demiurge takes the principles of Sameness and Difference and weaves them together through the ratios of the musical scale (see figure 2.2 on page 48). Existence has two faces, Sameness and Difference, in which everything participates. In order for something to exist, it first needs to be itself through the principle of Sameness or self-identity; but it also needs to be Different from everything else. Sameness is unity, Difference is diversity. The universe is both one and many, woven out of these primordial strands. For Plato, "The *kosmos* was harmonized by proportion and brought into existence."[37] The World Soul is the living bond between extremes and "partakes in harmony and reason."[38] In Plato's description, *the World Soul is the intelligent and harmonious principle of proportion or relatedness that exists at the heart of the cosmic pattern and allows all things to unfold in the best possible way.*

In addition to allowing the goodness of the universe to flower forth, the World Soul accounts for the divine beauty that we can see reflected at all levels of the physical cosmos. In Plato's story, the central Pythagorean ideas of harmony, proportion, and kinship are transformed into the World Soul, the central organizing principle of the cosmic pattern. And because of the World Soul, the entire cosmos is one life, in which every part is related to the whole through proportion, harmony, and resonance.

Sameness, Difference, and Proportion are not just abstractions—they

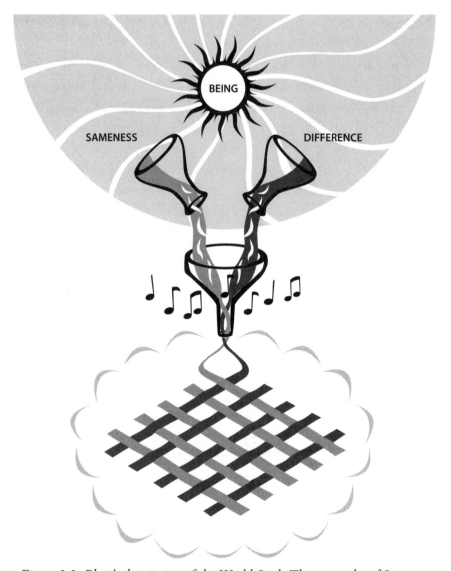

Figure 2.2. Plato's description of the World Soul: The principles of Sameness and Difference woven together through the mathematical ratios of the musical scale. Through harmony and proportional relationships, the cosmos and living organisms unfold in the best and most beautiful way.

are living ideas or principles manifest in the natural world. A nautilus shell, for example, integrates Sameness and Difference through Proportion (see figure 2.3a). The sea creature needs to grow and change,

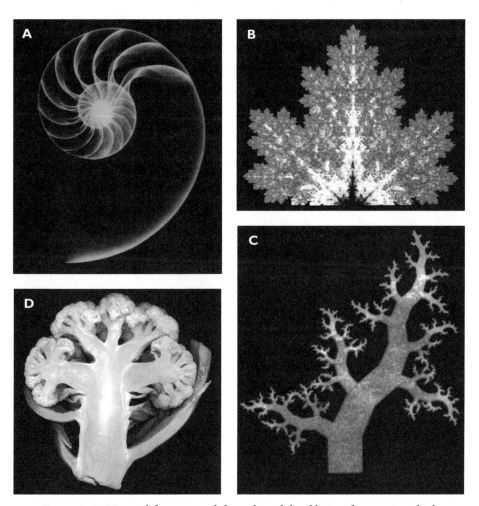

Figure 2.3. Natural forms—and fractal models of living forms—in which Sameness and Difference are united by Proportion.

which is a form of "difference." But by employing continuous geometrical proportion or "sameness," the nautilus can accommodate change in a regular way. Through the use of proportion, the nautilus can integrate the polarities of stability and change in an ordered and beautiful way.

Many of nature's forms integrate Sameness and Difference through the use of proportional relationships. In the fractal model of a maple leaf shown in figure 2.3b, we can see how the part is a model of the entire leaf, and how the pattern of the whole is reflected in the parts.

Fractal geometry embodies self-similarity at different levels of scale, and harmonizes Sameness with Difference through Proportion. The pattern is the same, but it appears at different levels of magnification, as we can see in the computer-generated model of a coral shown in figure 2.3c. Each tendril is a model of the branch, and each branch is a model of the entire coral. Another example can be seen in the cross-section of a cauliflower shown in figure 2.3d. Each little floret is a model of the branch in which it resides, and each branch is a model of the entire plant.

It is the very elegance, integration, and harmony between opposing tensions that makes the cosmos an embodiment of beauty. Nature takes the shortest route and, while exhibiting exuberant creativity, does little in vain. For as Ralph Waldo Emerson observed, "Elegance of form in bird or beast, or in the human figure, marks some excellence of structure . . . in the construction of any fabric or organism, any real increase of fitness to its end, is an increase in beauty."[39] As he wrote:

> Beauty rests on necessities. The line of beauty is the result of perfect economy. The cell of the bee is built at that angle which gives the most strength with the least wax; the bone or the quill of the bird give the most alar strength with the least weight. . . . There is not a particle to spare in natural structures. There is a compelling reason in the uses of the plant, for every novelty of color or form.[40]

The study of harmony demonstrates why the forms of nature are so beautiful. Nature is economical and embodies its organic harmonies of sharing in the most fit, graceful, and elegant patterns. Drawing on the insights of the Pythagoreans, Plato explained that Proportion, Beauty, and Goodness are all related phenomena.[41] Good proportion—a fit relationship between the part and the whole—gives birth to beauty, and allows nature's forms to work in the most efficient way possible. This principle of relatedness is just what Plato meant by the World Soul, for the most vital principle of the cosmos harmonizes Sameness with Difference, stability with change, and unity with diversity, and allows the beauty and goodness of life to unfold in just the right way.

As Emerson said, beauty is not arbitrary but reflects necessity. Beauty is also necessary for a flourishing life, for without beauty and elegance we depart from the cosmic pattern. Our individual souls, rooted in the cosmic soul, feed on beauty. In order to feel fulfilled as humans we need to taste and deeply savor our relation with the greater whole from which we have emerged. Nature's elegant patterns of sharing radiate beauty and goodness, a beauty and goodness that we embody in the most profound ways. When we can sense the vitally exuberant power of the World Soul and perceive its radiance shining through the forms of nature, we become tangibly aware of our innermost bond with the living universe.

3

Life in the Cosmopolis

> *This entire cosmos, a great divinity, is a fullness of life . . .*
> *and through the whole of eternity there is nothing in the*
> *cosmos that does not live, neither in the whole nor in its*
> *parts.*
>
> ALEXANDRIAN HERMETIC WRITING

ON AN ALEXANDRIAN SHORE

As in antiquity, so today. The Sun still dominates life in Egypt.

It's morning, a few hours after daybreak, and the sun is mounting skyward as I move along the shoreline. Its clear rays suffuse earth and sky, breathe life into the world, and crisply articulate the white buildings, date palms, and tropical flowers that lie before me. Walking to the muffled sounds of buses and tugboats I move forward, the Sun behind me and the Mediterranean on my right. As I shuffle along the coastline seagulls cavort and cry above, unearthly white forms poised between the blue-green sea and the indigo depths of the brightening sky.

The place is Alexandria, once the greatest city of the ancient world. I'm walking along the coast of the harbor, still the central heart of the city. While no one knows the exact spot, the royal palaces once stood very near, and across the harbor towered the Pharos Lighthouse, one of the Seven Wonders of the ancient world. Rising four hundred feet above the sea, the Pharos dominated the skyline of Alexandria in the same way that the Eiffel Tower defines the skyline of Paris. Its bright beacon, fueled by wood and focused with mirrors, could be seen thirty miles out to sea. And even though it was eventually toppled by an earthquake, the lighthouse's legacy lived on. The tall, spindly structure inspired the design of the minaret, duplicated countless times at mosques around the world, from which the daily calls to prayer ring out.

Still the symbol of Alexandria, the great lighthouse is appropriate in another way, for the city became the foremost center of learning, a focal point of intellectual brilliance. Home of the famous Museum and Library, Alexandria was an international center of scholarship, the greatest center in the ancient world. The Library itself held some five hundred thousand papyrus rolls. The Museum and Library were financed by the wealthy Ptolemaic dynasty of Egypt, which went to any length to ensure that the Library was the most comprehensive in the world. According to one account, all ships entering the harbor of Alexandria were searched, and if any books were discovered they were confiscated until copies could be made.

How this all came to be is one of history's most intriguing stories. Alexandria was a planned city that grew out of Alexander the Great's imperial ambitions. Located on the Mediterranean Sea to the west of the Nile Delta, which was inaccessible to many ships, Alexandria featured a protected harbor, enabling it to become the world's richest sea port. Thanks to its centrally located position, it emerged as the pivot of Hellenistic civilization and the meeting point of East and West.

Alexander the Great's military conquests marked the beginning of the Hellenistic age and transformed the known world into a unified empire that included Greece, Egypt, Asia Minor, and Persia and stretched all the way to India in the East. Greek became the common language of this empire, and following the death of Alexander, his trusted friend Ptolemy transferred the capital of Egypt from Memphis to Alexandria. Ptolemy declared himself king in 304 B.C., and established the dynasty that would rule Egypt for many decades.

Under the Ptolemies, Alexandria flourished as the greatest commercial and cultural center in the world. Each day ships would enter the harbor from distant ports, carrying exotic cargo and people from all nations. Alexandria became a meeting point in which myriad cultures, religions, and philosophies intermingled with one another. The Stoic philosophers came to speak of the *cosmopolis* or "world city," and Alexandria seemed to physically embody this idea and the new cultural reality of the Hellenistic age. In many uncanny ways the environment of ancient Alexandria closely anticipated our current planetary civilization by two thousand years.

The presiding genius behind the activities of the Museum and Library was Aristotle, and members of Aristotle's school were called to Alexandria to help set up these institutions. Aristotle was the sharp-dressing son of a wealthy physician to the Macedonian court. At the early age of seventeen, he was sent to Athens to study with Plato at the Academy, where he stayed for twenty years. Later in life at the age of forty-two, he was called back to Macedonia where he was hired to teach Alexander, the son and heir apparent of ruler Philip II, and his youthful court companions. One of those friends who sat in on Aristotle's lectures was Ptolemy, who would many years later found the great Museum and Library.

What Aristotle taught Alexander, Ptolemy, and friends we have no idea. But after returning to Athens, Aristotle set up his own philosophical school in a public park, the Lyceum. While Plato's school, which met in the park Academus, was devoted to the practice of joint discussion and mathematical research, Aristotle's approach was far more structured. He gave daily lectures and set about collecting, organizing, and systematically classifying information. For example, he collected the constitutions of 158 Greek states, which he classified. In another instance, Aristotle and his nephew won an award from the city of Delphi for drawing up a list of the winners of the athletic games. The modus operandi of his school was to collect information, classify it, and add further material as research continued. When the Library and Museum were set up in Alexandria, they were established to continue the research methods of Aristotle's school.

CULTURE AND COSMOS
AT THE CROSSROADS OF ALEXANDRIA

With the beginning of the Hellenistic age, both philosophy and culture reflected a new spirit. In the age of classical Athens, the emphasis was on the local community of the *polis* or city-state. Living a meaningful life entails being an integral member of a community and the Greek city-state provided just what was needed in the time of Plato. But as the Hellenistic empire emerged, all that started to change. In the new cultural landscape, the world expanded to encompass the entire globe. The power of the city-state declined and individuals found themselves swimming in new waters—not as clearly defined members of a community, but as *individuals* adrift in a vastly larger and less comforting world.

In this new environment, the character of philosophy began to change. The grandeur of Plato and Aristotle gave way to more pressing, personal concerns. If philosophy for Plato had been a means of liberation, in Hellenistic times it became more a means of salvation—a way of coping with life in an uncertain and anxiety-provoking world. As in our own time, specialization began to set in. The idea of professional scholarship was born in Alexandria, and Strato of Lampsacus, the third head of Aristotle's school, was the first example of "the pure scientist." Before him, science, philosophy, ethics, and social concerns were always joined together. But Strato focused on the study of mechanical and pneumatic devices and believed that this type of pure research had little to do with ethics or social concerns.

With the emergence of the Hellenistic age and Alexandria, we enter a more complex, international, and multifaceted period of human history. In contrast to the straightforward life of the city-state in which everyone knew their place and proper role, the Hellenistic period was one of unprecedented options—and a greater share of confusion. In Alexandria especially, world cultures were coming together and sometimes colliding. Walking the streets of the cosmopolis you would encounter Egyptians, Greeks, Phoenicians, Greek-speaking Jews, and even Buddhists and Hindus from the Far East. Alexandria was the first great multicultural city, and it was also a seedbed where philosophical, spiritual, and scientific ideas intermingled to create vital new syntheses. Set against the background of the Museum and Library, it was the greatest university town of the ancient world, and an exotic port of call in which ideas and artifacts from every great culture were readily available.

In Alexandria the entire world was on tap. Not only was it a center of scientific research, but it was also the place where the first urbane and educated Christians drew upon older Greek ideas to frame the message of the new faith in philosophical terms. In this way, by giving Christianity a philosophical and theological foundation, these pioneers transformed it into something that the educated pagans could take seriously, and this helped to fashion it into an emerging world religion.

IN THE BEGINNING WAS THE LOGOS

Just as our one body is composed of many members which are held together by one soul, so I think that the universe ought to be thought of as an immense, complex organism held together by the power and reason (logos) of God as by a single soul.

Origen of Alexandria

The Logos is God's likeness, by whom the whole cosmos was fashioned.

Philo of Alexandria

The central idea of Alexandrian spiritual thought was the Logos, a notion that united religious, philosophical, and cosmological ideas. *Logos* has many meanings, including "reason," "ratio," "intelligent pattern," "order," and "an account" or "that which is spoken." Unfortunately, *Logos* is usually translated into English as "Word," which is highly misleading because it so greatly diminishes the full meaning of the Greek term. When the prologue to the gospel of John starts off with the lines, "In the beginning was the Word, and the Word was with God," the Greek term Logos appears in the original.

Used in this context Logos refers to the rational order of the cosmic pattern. We live in an ordered universe, a cosmos in which the parts are harmonized within the whole through ratio, pattern, and proportion. This organic pattern that lies at the heart of nature is the Logos. As Plato said, the cosmos itself is harmonized by logos or proportion, but *logos* also means "reason." Not only is there a cosmic pattern, but it is rational. The reason or ratio that is present in us, in our souls and our intellects, is part of the same Logos that underlies the cosmic pattern. In short, our own minds embody the reason and intelligence of the universe, and the Hellenistic idea of the Logos is just, essentially, another name for what Plato called the World Soul. According to the ancient philosophers, the Logos is the divine, rational power that orders and enlivens the resplendent universe.

Ever since the birth of humanity, and long before the beginnings of written history, thoughtful people have noticed an order of nature reflected in the changing seasons, the course of the Sun, the wheeling stars, the growth patterns of plants and animals, the ratios of music—the list goes on. For the Greeks, all of these things reflected the nature of Logos, the living pattern behind the cosmic order. It was only natural, in a poetic sense, that this cosmic order would be personified as divinities or divine powers. For example, the ancient Egyptian god Thoth, the lord of celestial mathematics who spoke the primordial words that ordained the course of the planets, was a personification of the Logos. So too was his Greek counterpart Hermes, the messenger of Zeus, who was said to be the inventor of the alphabet and writing. Apollo, the Greek god of music, harmony, and the mediation between extremes, also symbolized the Logos. And in the Hymn to Zeus by the Stoic philosopher Cleanthes, Zeus himself is identified as the Logos, the World Soul, and intelligence behind the universe. Thus, when the early Christian writers identified Jesus as the Logos, they were following in an ancient tradition that was culturally and philosophically sanctioned.[1]

Christ as Logos was seen not as merely a human person, but as the cosmic power that shapes the universe and is revealed in its rationality. "In the beginning was the Word." Human consciousness, "the light of life," is a manifestation of this same living power that animates the Sun and shining stars. Clement of Alexandria was just one early writer who personified Christ in cosmic terms as the Spiritual Sun, noting that when the Logos, "the Sun of the soul," rises in "the depth of the mind, the soul's eye is illuminated."[2]

THE ATOMISTIC UNIVERSE VS. THE INTELLIGENT COSMOS

Nothing which is devoid of life and intelligence can give birth to any living creature which has intelligence. But the universe does give birth to living creatures which partake of intelligence in their degree. The universe is therefore itself a living intelligence.

ZENO OF CITTIUM

When the early Christians referred to the Logos, it was an idea they had assimilated from the Greeks. Plato had spoken of the rationality of the cosmos and even referred to the mind and soul of the universe, but it was the Stoics who developed these ideas in an even grander way.[3]

After Plato's Academy and Aristotle's Lyceum, the Epicureans and the Stoics were the two great philosophical schools to emerge in Athens. With the Epicureans and Stoics we have already entered the threshold of the Hellenistic age. For them "philosophy most clearly became what, in ordinary language, it still is: a way of coping with a world at war."[4] Yet despite their emphasis on philosophy as a means for achieving peace of mind in an unpredictable world, both the Epicureans and Stoics appealed to scientific ideas in support of their opposing viewpoints.

Epicurus established a philosophical school in Athens around 307 B.C. at his private home and garden, which he bestowed to his students after his death. Known as the Garden, the Epicurean community was a circle of friends who shared their lives and meals in common. Epicurus was a materialist insofar as he adopted the atomism of the earlier philosopher Democritus. According to Democritus, the world is made out of tiny, solid particles of matter that adhere together. The smallest discrete bits of matter are *atomē* or "indivisible," the source of our word *atom*. Only atoms and the void in which they move are real, but since the ever-moving atoms are infinite, what can possibly come into being actually does, however rare it might be. Everything that happens in the universe does so for a cause, but for the atomists there is no purpose or design to the universe.

The materialism of the Epicureans was used as a means of refuting popular superstitions regarding the afterlife. If someone coined a motto to sum up the thought of the Epicureans, it might read "science removes the fear of the gods." One of the greatest fears of humankind is everlasting punishment in an afterlife, but Epicurus pointed out that the soul, like everything else, is ultimately material, merely formed out of an especially fine substance. At death, the atoms of the soul are released back into the universe, and the soul as such ceases to exist. There is no reason to fear the pain of death because when the soul dissolves there is nothing left to experience the pain, let alone anything to suffer eternal torment. In essence, when we die, we won't even know that we are dead.

For Epicurus, the pathway to happiness involved cultivating a life of simple pleasure among friends. Pleasure involves a freedom from physical pain and mental agitation. The philosopher should live simply, free of empty fears and vain ambitions. In order to attain a quiet mind, it is necessary to withdraw from the active responsibilities of the world and to "live unnoticed." Ironically, despite his rejection of religious ideas regarding the afterlife, Epicurus did accept the existence of the gods. He reasoned that because the universe is infinite, there is room for infinite possibilities to become real; what can physically come into being actually does. He believed that the bodies of the gods are composed of the finest matter and they live forever in a state of perfect tranquility because they alone possess the power and knowledge to guard themselves against all disturbances. In this sense, the gods are models of what the philosopher's life should become.

While the Epicureans developed a wide following, most Greek philosophers viewed the ideas of atomism as woefully incomplete. For if everything is made out of tiny particles of matter, what is it that *causes* the atoms to fit together to form complex organisms? In a universe of randomly colliding billiard balls, what is the glue that holds everything together in such a stunningly coherent and beautiful way? What causes the order of nature to arise? For most philosophers, the answer was soul, which bestows form on living things. Over a period of several weeks, every single molecule of our physical body is replaced by other molecules. Every several weeks we are made of different stuff, but the actual *form* of the organism remains largely unchanged. From this perspective the most important aspect of anything is the form that makes an organism cohere, and it was this aspect that the atomistic theories fell short of addressing. As philosopher Stephen Toulmin writes, "Wherever men looked they saw bodies preserving a structure and form more organized and permanent than Greek atomism could easily explain."[5]

Contrary to the Epicureans and the atomists stood the Stoics. Founded by Zeno of Cittium in 301 B.C., the school held its discussions near the painted Porch, or Stoa, in Athens, a local landmark that gave the school its name. Like the Epicureans, the Stoics sought to discover a pathway to an untroubled life of self-sufficiency—but beyond that similar desire, no two perspectives could be further apart.

Zeno believed that Plato and Aristotle had been dualistic in outlook, pitting spirit against matter. For Zeno, the world was made out of only one thing, and there is no difference ultimately between mind and matter. They are only different aspects of the same phenomenon. We can speak of mind and matter as a figure of speech, but since the universe is one, mind and matter are ultimately the same. For Zeno, God was mind, matter, and the entire universe simultaneously. God is not something outside of nature, but a vital force and intelligence that permeates the living universe.

For the Stoics, the entire universe was a living organism, synonymous with God, and permeated by a vital, animating spirit. This spirit or *pneuma*, like everything else, is "material," but at the same time intelligent and dynamic. While the Epicureans said that everything was composed of tiny, discrete atoms, for the Stoics the emphasis was on continuity. The world is not an empty void in which atoms collide mindlessly, but a plenum, a living ocean saturated by spirit and intelligence.

Zeno rejected atomism because the universe is finely ordered.

Atomism left too much to chance. For Zeno the world is divinely ordered, but like every other Greek philosopher he did not suggest the existence of an external creator God that brought the universe into being, like an engineer who draws up a plan. Instead, Zeno's universe arose from a divine ordering principle that was synonymous with the universe itself and existed at the heart of creation. This principle he called the Logos, which might best be translated as "intelligence."

SELF, COSMOS, AND SOCIETY

Without an understanding of the nature of the universe, a man cannot know where he is; without an understanding of its purpose, he cannot know what he is, nor what the universe itself is. Let either of these discoveries be hid from him, and he will not be able so much as to give a reason for his own existence.

MARCUS AURELIUS

For the Stoics cosmology and ethics were tightly interwoven. As the Roman emperor and Stoic philosopher Marcus Aurelius pointed out, without knowledge of the nature and purpose of the universe, we cannot know ourselves. Yet without knowledge of our own true nature, we cannot understand the universe. Philosophy, like science, is an unfolding spiral of discovery in which the part comes to more deeply understand its relationship with the living whole.

While the Epicureans based their ethics on pleasure and the avoidance of pain, the Stoics based their ethics on reason. Logos, the luminous rationality of the world structure, is also present in humanity. Human rationality embodies the intelligence of the cosmos, and the Stoics taught that this faculty must be actualized and cultivated in order for one to become fully human. To achieve happiness, we must "follow nature" and live in harmony with the world. But to follow nature, each being must realize its own true nature and fulfill its inner potential. In the case of humans, this means cultivating the rational spark within, which binds us with the deepest heart of the cosmic pattern.

For Plato and the Pythagoreans, all things are connected through the proportional relationships of the World Soul. The entire cosmos is a coherent pattern in which humanity is profoundly interwoven. For Plato, the harmonies of nature provided a standard on which to base the good order of society. Through proportion, humanity is linked with every part of creation, for "one community embraces heaven and earth."[6] Disease and disorder appear when nature's equilibrium is disrupted, both in the individual soul and in the larger society. Plato said that it is the philosopher's job to first study the harmonious patterns of the cosmos as a guide, and to then therapeutically cultivate such relationships in human society or the *polis*.[7]

The Stoics took this idea further and spoke of the *cosmopolis* or "world community"—literally the community of the cosmos or the entire universe. Because of the spark of cosmic reason that dwells in human beings, all persons are equal and united in a universal brotherhood of humanity—men, women, and the people of every race. As Seneca wrote, "Life must proceed on the conviction that 'I am not born for any one corner of the universe; this whole world is my country.'"[8] For the Stoics at the dawn of the Hellenistic age, humans were no longer seen as being restricted to the boundaries of their local village or tribe. As in our own time, individuals became not only global citizens, but citizens of the larger universe.

In the cosmopolis, there is a moral community of rational beings, implying collaboration with others and society. Our own inner nature demands that we fulfill our potential and become vitally involved in the world community of which we are part. In this way, individual fulfillment, fulfillment of the human race, and the fulfillment of the entire cosmic process are all intertwined.[9] As Seneca wrote in another passage, "Philosophy's first promise is a sense of participation, of belonging to mankind, being a member of society."[10] But this entire matrix of human community is more than just a human invention. It is rooted in the deep order, harmony, and relatedness of the cosmic pattern. Thus, while the Epicureans claimed that happiness could be obtained only by a selfish withdrawal from public life, the Stoics maintained that true human flourishing depends on an involvement in the world community.

THE COMPLEXITY OF THE WEB

*Always think of the universe as one living organism, with
a single substance and a single soul; and observe how all
things are submitted to the single perceptivity of this one
whole, all are moved by its single impulse, and all play
their part in the causation of every event that happens.
Remark the intricacy of skein, the complexity of the web.*

MARCUS AURELIUS

For Plato the World Soul was the pattern of relatedness that allows
the cosmos to unfold, but for the Stoics it was an even more tangible
reality—the fiery, rational breath that permeates the stars, Sun, and all
living things. The universe is one event manifesting itself in a variety
of ways. It is permeated by an active intelligence that has many names:
Logos, Mind, Nature, God, Providence, Zeus, Destiny, the World Soul.
Mind is not something exclusive to humans, but our individual minds
emerge from the larger rationality and intelligence of the greater whole
to which we belong.[11] As Marcus Aurelius wrote in a passage reminiscent of modern ecological thought, "All things are interwoven with one
another; a sacred bond unites them; there is scarcely one thing that is
isolated from one another. Everything is coordinated, everything works
together in giving form to the one universe."[12]

Because we are woven into the warp and woof of the cosmic tapestry,
each person is implicated in ever-widening circles and ever-larger wholes.
An individual is rooted in human community, human community is
rooted in the greater community of the biosphere, the biosphere is rooted
in the living dynamics of the solar system, and the solar system is rooted
in the great community of the Milky Way Galaxy. For the Stoics "the
Mind of the universe is social"[13] and the world is "that supreme City in
which all other cities are as households."[14] "The chief good of a rational
being is fellowship with his neighbors,"[15] and as a part of the world order
we help to create the social whole; therefore, our actions should support
the social life.[16] But as Marcus Aurelius pointed out, we are not merely
"parts" of the whole, but "limbs" of the universe. If we think of ourselves

only as parts, we act only out of "bare duty" and not out of "love from the heart of mankind."[17] Because of its emphasis on the universal fellowship of humanity, Stoicism not only inspired Roman statesmen like Marcus Aurelius but provided the foundation for the early Christian idea of "the brotherhood of man."

PLOTINUS ON THE ENSOULED UNIVERSE

By the power of the Soul the manifold and diverse heavenly system is a unit: through soul this universe is a God because it is ensouled; so too the stars: and whatsoever we ourselves may be, it is all in virtue of soul.

PLOTINUS

Alexandria, the earthly cosmopolis, was a center of trade, scientific research, higher education, and religious speculation. Ancient Egyptian spiritual teachings mingled with the ideas of Greek philosophy to produce influential new syntheses, like the Hermetic writings. These writings, written in Greek, were produced by spiritual communities in the neighborhood of Alexandria, and were attributed to Thrice-Great Hermes, a mythical Egyptian sage and revealer of hidden knowledge. Like other Alexandrian writings, they tended to focus on the Logos, the structure of the cosmos, and humanity's relationship to the cosmic pattern. Humanity was pictured as the microcosm, the world-order in miniature, with an intimate bond to the larger universe. Life and mind were revealed as universal principles—not limited to one individual or even locked away in human nature, but inherent aspects of existence itself. The universe was described as the very image of divine beauty and harmony, a hierarchical pattern in which all levels of creation were united in one Great Chain of Being. In the words of one Hermetic writing, "This great body of the world is a soul, full of intellect and of God, who fills it within and without and vivifies the All."[18] Another exhorted the reader to contemplate "the beautiful arrangement of the world and see that it is alive, and that all matter is full of life."[19]

It was against this remarkable cultural and intellectual backdrop of

Alexandria that Plotinus (A.D. 205–270) emerged, the last truly great philosopher of the ancient world. Often portrayed as "the founder of Neoplatonism," Plotinus drew on his own personal insight and experience, in addition to the teachings of Plato, Aristotle, and the Stoics. Yet while his ideas certainly resemble those of the Hermetic writings, they were presented as philosophical arguments, sometimes deeply poetic, but not as revelation discourses.

Plotinus was an Egyptian by birth and studied for some years with Ammonious Saccas, a mysterious figure in Alexandria about whom little is known. After joining an ill-fated army expedition to the East on which he had hoped to learn the wisdom of the Persians, Plotinus ended up in Rome where he lectured and on the side acted as a guardian for orphaned children. His school consisted of a small circle of individuals who would come to hear him speak and respond to questions. Most of his writings were composed in response to issues and questions that came up in the school discussions.

Plotinus is important in our story because he offers the most detailed account of the World Soul and its place in the cosmic structure to be found in any ancient philosopher. He was one of the greatest writers in the Platonic tradition on beauty and contemplation, and he was also very careful to point out the inadequacy of human language when it came to discussing the deepest nature of reality. So while forced to use poetic images and metaphors taken from the world of time and space, Plotinus frequently warned that the metaphors are not exact, but only meant to point the mind in a certain direction.

For Plotinus all reality was essentially spiritual in nature. The source of the universe was unlimited, ineffable, and of infinite power. He gave the Source a variety of names, even though they were all inadequate. The purpose of giving it a name was not to define the source of creation but only to point toward its nature. His most common name for the unlimited source was "the One," which suggests its simple, unified nature. Everything that exists is something definite and particular, but this cannot be said of the One, which is unlimited. In this sense, the One lies even "beyond being" or existence itself. It is literally "no thing," yet the infinite source from which all reality emerges.

Because it is perfect, unlimited, and a source of infinite power, the One overflows like a fountain. Since its own perfection cannot be contained, it spontaneously gives forth from itself in a movement of generosity in the same way that the Sun spontaneously gives forth rays of light. As it overflows, it gives birth to *Nous* or Mind, which is the first and most essential level of reality. In thinking of Nous, we must not envision it in human terms. Rather, Nous is the universal principle of Mind or Intelligence out of which our own minds and the entire cosmic pattern emerges.

The Nous is a perfect harmony in which every part is related to every other part. It is the Logos, the cosmic blueprint of all reality, but unlike the Stoic Logos, the Nous is entirely nonmaterial. Because it exists beyond time and space, the Nous is not limited but present everywhere.[20] As Plotinus pointed out, Mind is not something in us, but we are in Mind. The very fact that you can understand these words is due to the common matrix of intelligence in which we all are rooted. Everywhere in nature we see the same sorts of repeating patterns, from galaxies to flowers, and these patterns of order and intelligence are rooted in the Nous. If modern scientists speak of "the laws of nature" which shape the fabric of everything, Plotinus would see those laws as a form of intelligence, and situate that intelligence in the Nous.

Like the One, the Nous is perfect. It continues to overflow and emanate outward, giving birth to the Word Soul, the soul of the cosmos. The Nous is a harmonically differentiated image of the One and the World Soul is a further differentiated image of the Nous. Like Mind, the Cosmic Soul is entirely immaterial. There is a continuity between Mind and Soul and no firm dividing line can be drawn between them. Soul is life, and life is always informed by intelligence.

Finally, in the same way that Intelligence gives birth to Soul or Life, Soul gives birth to Nature. It is the World Soul that brings the space-time cosmos into being and animates the world.[21] In this way, the entire universe is a living organism and all levels of being are related as links in one unbroken chain. Nature is an image of Soul, Soul is an image of Mind, and Mind is an image of the One. Plotinus described things in another way based on the idea of increasing differentiation. The One is a perfect unity; the Nous is a One–Many; the World Soul is a One-

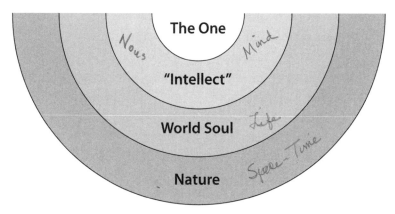

Figure 3.1. The place of the World Soul, according to Plotinus. As the levels of reality "move away" from the One, they become more differentiated. "Intellect" is a One–Many, the World Soul is a One-and-Many, and Nature appears to be made of many things. But behind the diversity of the natural world there is an underlying, intelligent, and harmonious unity, revealed by the universe's order and beauty.

and-Many; and Nature appears to be made up of many things but is, in reality, a coherent organism (see figure 3.1).

As Emerson wrote in the spirit of Plotinus:

> The problem of restoring to the world original and eternal beauty, is solved by the redemption of the soul. The ruin or the blank, that we see when we look at nature, is in our own eye. The axis of vision is not coincident with the axis of things, and so they appear not transparent but opaque. The reason why the world lacks unity, and lies broken and in heaps, is because man is disunited with himself.[22]

For Plotinus the central task of philosophy was remembering our essential nature and awakening to "another way of seeing, which everyone has but few use."[23] Should our vision be purified, we would see the world as it is: not as a collection of things, lying broken and in heaps, but as a radiant image of divine beauty and intelligence in which every part is related to every other part. We would see the universe itself as the living "image" of intelligence and soul, as "one closely knit organism"[24] in which we are joined in "the cosmic fellowship."[25] But, as Plotinus pointed out, such a seeing involves a transformation of vision:

> No eye ever saw the sun without becoming sun-like, nor can a soul see beauty without becoming beautiful. You must become first of all godlike and all beautiful if you intend to see God and beauty.[26]

For Plotinus the world was a thought, a pattern of intelligence, at its most essential level. The Nous is a thought that thinks itself: thinker, thought, and object of thought are one.[27] Or as some astronomers now like to say, when we think and wonder about the stars that have given us birth, the stars themselves are thinking through us.

Because the cosmos springs from the closely knit unity of the Nous, the universe is a "single living being which encompasses all the living beings that are within it."[28] It has a soul, "one soul, which extends to all its members in the degree of participant membership held by each."[29] Because of this, the cosmos is a "One–All," "a sympathetic total" which "stands as one living being."[30] As in a single animal with many organs, there is a harmonious coordination of all the parts because "a single reason-principle is at work."[31] Ultimately, the entire universe is holy and "there is nothing which is without a share of soul."[32]

As members of the cosmic fellowship, our individual souls are rooted in the World Soul in the same way that our individual minds are rooted in the Nous. But that does not make us the insignificant parts of a greater and more important whole, a whole that overshadows us. Since the whole is present in the part, there is nothing to prevent a part from also being the whole.[33] Plotinus described the World Soul not as our mother, but as our elder sister. Because the World Soul is older than us and shapes the divine beauty of the cosmic pattern, she deserves our respect and reverence. But if we clarify our vision and discover our true nature, we become her equal and collaborator. By realizing our true identity, we become one with the fundamental power that orders the universe and brings the world to creative fruition.

4

The Light of Nature and the Alchemical Imagination

SPRING FEVER AND BLACK EARTH

Twenty minutes from my old home in Michigan lies a park with ever-changing vistas. Tall leafy maples blanket the hilly landscape, shifting into pristine groves of towering pine. At some places, the tree-lined canopy opens to expansive, grassy meadows that reach off into the distance, skirted again by the green boundaries of hardwood forest. Trails stretch for miles like arteries, weaving together the multiple landscapes. It's amazing, for if you could be transported to different spots without journeying along the trails, you might think that you had visited several different parks rather than adjacent places. At one point the trail moves through lush, swampy lowlands; at another, it climbs skyward in a pine cathedral. At one point you descend through an old apple orchard, and at another you move along a gurgling, rock-lined stream.

At one eerie spot, the landscape changes into a couple of huge, sand-filled craters, encircled by large, creaky oaks. The change is so unexpected, and the craters so out of place, it feels like you have stepped onto another planet; even the wind brushing against the dry leaves sounds extraterrestrial. Open to the sky above and encircled by the oaks below, the shining dune craters always give me the feeling of being in a secret grove. I often wonder what it would be like to be there at night, with moonlight and starlight glistening off the pure white sands.

Whenever possible, I drive out to the park and often discover that I am the only one there. It's wonderful to be there at different times of the year, though in the wintertime cross-country skiers make the steeper trails icy and dangerous. And while it's not the most beautiful time of the year, I have had several noteworthy experiences there in the early spring, in that pregnant moment right before the emergence of the season's first growth.

A typical experience goes like this. It's that time of year when cabin fever turns into spring fever, and the first really hot day comes along. Having been cooped up over a long winter, everyone is feeling stale, confined, and ready to break free. Finally, it appears—that first memorable day in which the fertilizing heat of the Sun bears down on the landscape and everything responds to it. In the human sphere, there is an anxious rush to get outside and feel the warmth of the air, which releases a wild, carefree abandon. People become animated and are ready to cut loose. On the first hot day of spring, car windows roll down, the music is turned up to a blare, and automobiles careen by at speeds much higher than normal. I respond by hopping into my car and traveling to the country, also at speeds much higher than normal.

Pulling into the parking lot, I switch off the music as shards of gravel crunch beneath the tires. After coming to a stop and turning off the engine, the car door opens, engages with a hearty slam, and my journey down the trail begins.

The time and place is one of pregnant possibility. All of nature is in a state of unfolding gestation. As I head down the trail, the pathway curves and meanders along the bank of Honey Creek, which is now swiftly boiling from the winter melt off. There are a few birds, but the atmosphere is mostly quiet. It is as though everything is ready to break out, but is, as yet, on pause, in a state of suspended animation. The atmosphere is one of anticipation.

The sharp heat of the Sun beats down and is embraced by the moist, black earth. Every now and then I come across a patch of lingering ice that is being worked away relentlessly by the Sun's rays. I'm moving along at a good pace and feel the first sting of sweat on my back, arms, and shoulders. Perhaps I'm starting to melt, too.

Everywhere I look, I feel the presence of emergent life, but it is not yet realized. While there are no leaves on the trees, saplings display tiny points of new growth. Everything is black, brown, maize, silver, or the color of driftwood. Despite this neutrality, under the Sun and hot air the radiant presence of life is unseen yet tangible. It impinges on every sense and you can taste it in the air. In reality, everything is cooking in the primordial heat of gestation.

My attention is repeatedly drawn to the warmth of the air and what is happening in the rich, black soil along the stream. The air itself is like a moist, hot breath. As I breathe in, I take in the living breath of the Earth, and when I exhale I offer back my own life essence. As nature breathes and cooks, there is a continuity of the inner and the outer.

Pounding along the trail, I am struck by the immediate perception that the black earth is alive and twisting beneath the surface, ready to send forth shoots and carpets of green. And it is this on which I linger. Cooked by the heat of the Sun, the black earth is animated by a life power that is ready to burst forth. The importance of the perception lies in its tangible, experiential nature: *the body of the Earth, warmed by the alchemical heat of the Sun, is itself alive.* The force of the living Earth is sensed and present, a manifest perception that cuts to the deepest core of reality. It is an intoxicating sensation, and one that the calculating intellect could never hope to grasp or explain. When the spring fever of the hot Sun cooks the black body of the Earth, it is then when you can most tangibly feel the living spirit of nature. The alchemists called it Mercurius, quicksilver, the World Soul, *anima mundi, spiritus mundi,* the light hidden in nature, and a dozen other names. It is a vital force, a living presence, the Holy Spirit that penetrates all things. My breath and the breath of the living Earth are one. And when the hot sap of spring fever mounts upward in exfoliation and celebration, it mounts upward in us, too.

THE ALCHEMICAL VISION OF LIVING NATURE

Go to the streamings of the Nile, and there you will find a stone that has a spirit.

OSTANES

The direct experience of living nature has been felt in all times in places, but it is in the alchemical tradition where "soul" and "spirit" take on their most tangible, living form. In the alchemical vision, all matter is alive and animated with spirit. The Earth is a single living organism. It is fertilized and impregnated by the celestial spirit of the Sun, stars, and planets. All matter is evolutionary, striving toward higher forms, and deep within the bowels of the Earth all metals are ripening toward gold. Because of this, alchemy is not an attempt to manipulate matter, but the cultivation of a natural process.

Alchemy is rooted in the perception that nature is an unfolding, dynamic process, characterized by the power of transformation. Around 4000 B.C. smelting was applied to copper and bronze, and later, around 1200 B.C., to iron. The workings of the first metallurgists took place as a ritualized activity in an atmosphere of secrecy. Working with molten metals involved risk and directly exposed the practitioners to the elemental and numinous powers of nature. Smelting involved a purification by fire, and the ritual activities of the first metallurgists involved their own purification as well.[1]

The beginnings of alchemy are lost in prehistory, but European alchemy begins in Egypt. The ancient Egyptians had always seen their land as an image of the heavens. The Nile was pictured as a terrestrial reflection of the celestial stream on which the gods and planets sailed. The Sun is a source of fertility, but in Egypt life depends equally on the cool waters of the Nile. Each year like clockwork in late July, the Nile would flood, depositing rich black silt in the regions surrounding it. The Arabic word *al-kemi* means "the black land," an ancient name of Egypt. Dredged up from the depths, moistened by the stream of life, and fertilized by the Sun, the black earth of Egypt embodied the vital energies of the gods and cosmic powers. This rich effluence of the earth, when cooked by the Sun, gave birth to crops, animals, and the dazzling pageantry of life. From Earth and Sun arose the baking of bread, every art and science, and the sound of hymns that reverberated in the temples. From Earth and Sun arose the entire social structure, culminating in the image of the pharaoh, the divine, golden spark who encapsulated on Earth the cosmic powers of regeneration and eternal life. Through the transformation of black earth into the living tapestry of a high civilization, life in Egypt was itself an alchemical process.

The earliest alchemical texts that survive are Greek writings that appeared in Egypt. Some are merely collections of recipes; others endow the alchemical process with spiritual and mystical implications.

Alchemical theory as it has come down to us is heavily influenced by the ideas of Greek philosophy and rests on several assumptions. From the ideas of Democritus and Plato the alchemists assumed that matter is capable of transformation. From the writings of Aristotle the alchemists developed the idea that nature is teleological or developmental. Teleology is most readily seen in living organisms, which unfold in a goal-oriented, expanding way. Given an adequate opportunity, it is the nature of an acorn to mature into an oak tree, just as it is the nature of a child to grow into a mature, self-realized adult. The Stoics identified the creative power of nature, the Logos, as a "seed power" present in all things. It is the nature of the *spermatikos logos* or seminal essence to carry all things to the fruition of their essential nature.

Like the unfolding life of plants and animals, metals grow and develop within the womb of the Earth. Aristotle taught that the moist exhalations of the Earth give birth to metals, which then grow and mature. Veins of metal spread outward from a seed and, given enough time, will grow back if harvested. The active growth process is fueled by the vital power of the Sun in the same way that the Sun causes plants and other organisms to emerge from the dark soil of the Earth.[2]

Ancient Greek mystery religions celebrated the *hieros gamos,* the sacred marriage of heaven and Earth that brings forth the fruit of life.

Certainly for anyone who lives close to nature, the fertilizing influence of the masculine heavens on the receptive, feminine Earth is a fact of daily existence. When speaking of the virtues of the Sun, Copernicus duly noted that "the Earth conceives from the Sun and is made pregnant with annual offspring."[3] In the Renaissance, the philosopher Bernardino Telesio wrote that "we can see that the sky and the Earth are not merely large parts of the world universe, but are of primary—even principal rank. . . . They are like mother and father to all the others."[4] His contemporary, Giordano Bruno, similarly described himself as "a citizen and servant of the world, a child of Father Sun and Mother Earth."[5]

The early alchemists, who saw the entire cosmos as an organism, drew upon the ideas of Greek philosophy to offer a coherent explanation of the development of metals within the Earth. Behind everything is a type of prime matter, which is itself formless. The four elements of fire, air, water, and earth are qualitative forms of matter that exist in tension with one another. One element can be transformed into another, and the soul, spirit, or pneuma within anything is the determining formal element, the essential spark that bestows qualities on the prima materia.

The Stoics taught that all matter was alive and dynamic, permeated by spirit and intelligence. This intelligence, the Logos, was often associated with the fire of the heavenly bodies and the life-giving power of the Sun.[6] Aristotle, too, had spoken of *aether,* the fifth element, or *quinta essentia,* out of which the heavenly bodies were fashioned. Compared to the four elements, this was a pure and heavenly radiance, a glowing ethereal substance akin to spirit. It was practically inevitable that all of these principles would become identified with one another. For the ancient alchemists, aether, or the quinta essentia, came to be seen as the form-giving logos, the fiery life principle that ensouled plants, animals, and the gestating metals within the womb of the Earth. Within each living thing was a spark of star fire, a celestial, animating flame.

In the same way that the universe was composed of the terrestrial sphere and the starry heavens, so too was each thing composed of body and spirit. At night the dew of heaven would descend to the Earth, charged with the rays of the glowing celestial bodies. This dew, rich in heavenly and ethereal essences, would nourish plants, revitalize the soul of the Earth, and stimulate the generation of metals. As early as Babylonian times, the seven metals were identified with the seven planets. The Sun ruled over gold, the Moon over silver, Mercury over quicksilver, and so on. And the divine, ethereal rays of the planets seeded their kindred metals to grow in the Earth. As the fifth-century alchemist Proclus of Byzantium wrote,

> Gold and silver, as found in nature, as well as all other metals and substances, are engendered in the earth by the celestial divinities and the effluvia that come from them. The Sun produces gold; the Moon silver; Saturn lead; and Mars iron.[7]

Seeded by the heavens, matter takes form, yet all matter is evolutionary and aspires to return to a more spiritual state. As Meister Eckhart wrote, "copper is restless until it becomes gold."[8] Over the course of centuries, metals naturally develop and mature in the Earth. The alchemist merely acts as a midwife to accelerate and nurse along the natural process. As one alchemical writer clearly explained, "We help the metals to arrive at maturity, just as a gardener may assist fruit, which by accident is prevented from ripening."[9] The greatly sought after Philosophers' Stone was the miraculous catalyst that would speed up the natural process of transformation.

If the Earth is the matrix or womb of gestation, the alchemist's flask is an artificial womb in which the work takes place. Gazing into the flask, the alchemist discovers every process of nature reflected (see figure 4.1 on page 76). Gestation, fermentation, cooking, transformation, sublimation, creative decay, dismemberment, dissolution, coagulation, circulation, and regeneration are all keywords of the alchemical process. There is no absolute distinction between the alchemist and nature, between the inner and outer worlds. All are part of one creative, evolutionary process. Because of this, alchemy has always possessed a spiritual dimension, since it is not possible to participate in the Great Work of Nature without experiencing a self-transformation. In order for the work to be successful, total participation is required. Alchemy is a comprehensive

*Figure 4.1. Gazing into the flask, the alchemist discovers every process of
nature reflected. There is no absolute distinction between the alchemist
and nature, between the inner and outer worlds, because all are
part of one creative, evolutionary process.*

science of the cosmos in which both humanity and the larger universe
are implicated.

THE SPIRIT HIDDEN IN MATTER

The alchemical process consists of multiple stages but the sought-after
goal is purification. The starting point is *nigredo,* the black state of
chaos and confusion, the heavy "lead" that is ultimately made golden.
Purification is obtained by separating out the elements, distinguishing
the volatile from the fixed, the celestial from the terrestrial.

"Spirits" are celestial and "bodies" are terrestrial. The guiding dic-
tum of alchemy is that "bodies must become incorporeal." The spiritual,
vital essence or soul of matter is separated out by distillation in an alembic, in the same way that the volatile spirit of alcohol is separated from
a fermented beverage (see figure 4.2). Once the process is complete, the
alchemist is left with both the vital essence of a metal—its quintessence—
and its dead body. Once they are distinct, both substances can be further
purified and then later rejoined. In this way, matter is spiritualized, matter and spirit are purified, and both are reconjoined. Since the quintessence is the form-giving soul of a substance, it can also be applied to other
elements to affect their transformation.

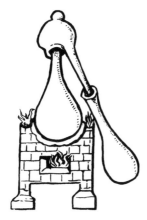

Figure 4.2. The alembic warmed by a furnace, used to separate off the vital spirit from solid matter.

As the alchemists peered ever deeper into the heart of nature, they explored the boundaries where matter and spirit meet. Matter, they discovered, is permeated by a vital spirit, the spirit Mercurius, which is described as fire, water, and the guardian of the alchemical work. Physical mercury is quicksilver. Like a shimmering spirit from a broken thermometer, quicksilver is shiny, animated, elusive, and hard to pin down. Physical mercury is capable of dissolving gold and forming an amalgam with other metals. In this sense it is "the spirit of metals" and a principle of liquidity capable of permeating the most solid bodies. But when the alchemists spoke of "their mercury" as opposed to "vulgar" physical mercury, they were referring to something even more subtle and mysterious—the primordial world-creating spirit revealed in the material depths.

In the old alchemical writings this "philosophical Mercury" was described in dozens of ways. It was an "invisible fire, working in secret."[10] It was identified with the *anima mundi,* the World Soul, and it was "the universal and scintillating fire of the light of nature, which carries the heavenly spirit within it."[11] The "supercelestial spirit" was "conjoined with the light"[12] and identified with both the World Soul and the Holy Spirit as procreator, the "spirit of the Lord who fills the entire universe and in the beginning moved upon the face of the waters."[13] According to another text it "flies like solid white snow" and is the dwelling of the life force, the spirit of the universe upon whom "the motion and fluidity of human nature itself depends."[14]

In a similar vein, Paracelsus spoke of the *Archaeus,* the creative fire hidden in matter. Placed in the heart of the world and the heart of every living creature, the Archaeus is the power of the starry heavens, the astral spirit, which is the life-force present in all things. Like the Stoic Logos, it is artist, the craftsperson, "the inner Vulcan," which shapes and differentiates the prime matter, giving it form.

The psychologist Carl Gustav Jung spent the last thirty years of his life studying alchemical texts and was particularly fascinated by the symbolism of the spirit Mercurius, the spirit hidden in matter. To the alchemists this dream-spirit revealed the secrets of the alchemical process, oftentimes through the most paradoxical and surrealistic images, many of which ornament the old texts as engravings or paintings. Jung was amazed to discover that the images of alchemy—and the entire trajectory of the alchemical process—were reflected in the dreams of his modern patients. Yet his patients had no knowledge of, or access to, the old Latin alchemical writings.

Earlier in his career Jung had discovered the existence of archetypes, or primordial images, that appear in ancient religious texts, the dreams of ordinary people, and the visions of the insane. In one eye-opening instance, Jung was working in an asylum with a paranoid schizophrenic. The patient hallucinated a vision of the Sun's penis. As the penis swayed back and forth, it created the winds. Jung was astonished to discover four years later a description of exactly the same thing in the *Mithras Liturgy,* a highly obscure magical papyrus from the Hellenistic period that the schizophrenic could not have known.[15] As his study progressed, Jung found many other such instances and was forced to conclude that there exists a dimension of consciousness, the *collective unconscious,* of which we are normally unaware. The collective unconscious is a repository of archetypal images like the Great Mother, the Trickster, the Divine Child, and so on. Yet the collective unconscious is transpersonal in the sense that it is not limited to an individual like the personal subconscious but is something common to the entire human race.

Jung discovered that anything unknown becomes a focal point for unconscious projections, attracting them like a magnet. For example, it doesn't take long for any type of strange, unfamiliar phenomenon—

even if it is nothing more than an unreal rumor—to be interpreted by some people as a manifestation of the devil or a sign of supernatural intervention. In a similar way, matter and its processes of transformation were deep mysteries that the alchemists did not truly understand and thus, like a Rorschach test, brought out an entire spectrum of symbolic fantasies and interpretations. In this way, alchemy was "a serious effort to elicit the secrets of chemical transformation," but at the same time an often overwhelming "reflection of parallel psychic process."[16]

For Jung, alchemy was a reflection of the natural process of integration in the psyche, the movement toward wholeness that he called *individuation*. The symbols of alchemy are manifestations of the natural psyche and its own inner dream logic. In this way, regardless of whatever the Hermetic philosophers discovered about matter, Jung discovered the existence of an alchemical process in the psyche—a process reflected via images reminiscent of the alchemical texts and engravings. Life is the seed planted in matter. And the symbolism of Mercurius, the quickening soul of nature, pointed toward the paradoxical aspects of psychic reality, a reality that is material and spiritual—natural and supernatural—at the same time.

Jung found repeatedly that the unconscious produces dream symbolism to compensate for one-sided and unbalanced attitudes of the conscious ego. It was highly significant, then, that Mercurius—the almost pagan nature spirit—should represent the great mystery of the alchemical work. For Jung, Christianity represented a necessary stage in the evolution in consciousness, because the divine image of Christ represented a more unified image of the autonomous human self than did the multiplicity of earlier pagan divinities.[17] Similarly, rather than ensouling nature with vital energy, the Judeo-Christian God-image stood apart from the world, psychologically reflecting and feeding a growing autonomy in human awareness. But this autonomy was also one-sided, for with this increasing sense of self-differentiation came a much greater separation from world. Spirit came to be exalted over nature.

Compared to ancient Greece or the sensate spirit of the Renaissance, Jung felt that the medieval spirit with its overwhelming emphasis on the supernatural devalued the living world of *nature*. While the earlier Greeks had seen the world as animated by divine presences, Christianity led to a desacralization of the cosmos. People's eyes became fixed on the afterlife, and while the world remained a battleground for the supernatural, it was no longer seen as sacred or numinous in its own right. The sacred was only to be found beyond this world or in the sacraments of the Church. In medieval times the spiritual imagination became highly codified, schematized, and restricted at the same time that matter was devalued. The great exception to this was in the underworld of the alchemists, where nature still lived and pulsed with a tangible vitality. As Jung noted, in the vision of the Hermetic philosophers, "It was nature and her particular 'light' that had to be acknowledged and lived with in the face of an attitude that assiduously overlooked them."[18]

THE LIGHT OF NATURE AND THE REDEMPTION OF MATTER

Despite its pagan and naturalistic overtones, after the coming of Christianity, alchemy remained rooted in the Christian worldview. The perfecting power of the Philosophers' Stone was identified with the saving power of Christ and the alchemical process itself was seen as a reenactment of God's work of creation.[19] Alchemy was a comprehensive science that depended upon an understanding of the entire universe, but at the same time it was a science totally permeated by a spiritual view of creation.

Either consciously or unconsciously, the alchemists repeated the old gnostic myth of spirit that had descended into matter. Looking down on the mirror of nature, the primordial spirit of the cosmos became enamored with its own reflection and drew closer. Through an act of allurement and self-forgetting, it became ensnared, submerged, and lost in the confusion of material nature. In various gnostic myths, it is the role of the Gnostic Revealer—identified as Christ or some other divine figure—to descend to the terrestrial sphere. Through the teachings and knowledge bestowed by the revealer, the elect are led to remember their true nature as spiritual beings who originated from the heavenly realm of light. The revealer fans the slumbering spiritual spark in the hearts of the forgetful and, through this awakening, reminds them of their source, essential nature, and heavenly destiny.[20]

As Jung noted, "Nature not only contains a process of transformation—it is itself transformation."[21] Yet such transformation is also a source of pain and suffering. Like the passion of Christ, metals, chemicals, and souls must surrender themselves to a process of suffering, death, and rebirth if they are to arrive at a higher and more refined state. In the unfolding ordeals and painful transformations of life, the golden spark of understanding is kindled only as the base matter begins to become clarified. Spirit is trapped in matter and must be liberated so that matter itself can achieve its true flowering. In the same way that Christ saved mankind, alchemy redeems nature. This redemption is a process of rebirth or regeneration, but it always involves a painful destruction of old forms before the primordial elements can be resurrected in a higher synthesis. As one alchemical text succinctly notes:

Nothing can be reborn to a better state unless it has first died and gone through a period of dissolution and putrefaction of its previous principles.[22]

Or as Paracelsus wrote:

Decay is the beginning of all birth. . . . It transforms shape and essence, the forces and virtues of nature. Just as the decay of all foods in the stomach transforms them and makes them into a pulp, so it happens outside the stomach. . . . Decay is the midwife of very great things! It causes many things to rot, that a noble fruit may be born; for it is the reversal, the death and destruction of the original essence of all natural things. It brings about the birth and rebirth of forms a thousand times improved. . . . And this is the highest and greatest *mysterium* of God, the deepest mystery and miracle that He has revealed to mortal man.[23]

This emphasis on the creative power of decay is a central part of the alchemical work summed up in the motto *solve et coagula,* "dissolve and recombine." The old pattern must come apart and be dissolved before a new synthesis can arise. In a psychological sense, this involves dissolving the brittle psychic armoring that we develop as a defense against life so that the vital spirit of the self can be liberated and released into the world. As Jung noted, neurosis is "an act of adaptation that has failed"[24] and "always a substitute for legitimate suffering."[25] In the same way that spirit is trapped in matter, human vitality gets tied up in rigid structures of self-protection that may have once served a useful purpose but ultimately insulate us from the vitality of life.

Alchemy is a devotional practice in which the Hermetic philosopher experienced firsthand the dynamic processes of natural transformation. Science and spirit, world and self, were not separated, but part of one all-encompassing process. As scholar James W. Jones writes, "The alchemist undergoes the same process of transformation as his chemicals. Alchemy is not an objective science with an experimenter detached from his experiment, but is rather a single process of transformation in which both the chemist and the chemicals are involved together."[26]

In the alchemical work, *laboratory* and *oratory*—a place of prayer—stood side-by-side (see figure 4.3). To guide the work, the alchemist depended on inspiration: not only divine revelation, but direct inspiration from "the light of nature." Mercurius, the light active in matter, helped point the way through image, dream, and intuitive insight. The light of nature is the starry, astral spirit of the heavens that permeates all things, "a secret radiation of nature of that makes possible the discovery of natural mysteries."[27] It is the seat of our inner spirit, the root of both rational and intuitive knowledge. In the words of Paracelsus, "Nothing can be in man unless it has been given to him by the Light of Nature,"[28] and as Jung commented, "The light of nature is an intuitive apprehension of the facts, a kind of illumination."[29]

In the gnostic myth, spirit has fallen into matter and must be liberated. But alchemy itself is a form of creative, natural, and material spirituality. The gnostics wanted to leave the corrupt and anxiety-provoking

*Figure 4.3. Engraving that shows the alchemical laboratory and oratory
(a place of prayer) standing side by side. The alchemist, as natural
philosopher, approached his work as a devotional process that resulted in
both an understanding of nature and a transformation of the self. The
musical instruments on the table represent the living harmony that must
be maintained between theory and practice, art and nature, and work and
prayer. (Heinrich Kuntrath,* Amphitheater of Eternal Wisdom, *1609.)*

world of matter behind and return to the pure, celestial realm of light. The alchemists, in contrast, sought to liberate and purify spirit, but then *return* it to the embodied, material realm, to the unfolding laboratory of lived experience.   bodisatva

As James W. Jones writes,

> Authentic spiritual wisdom comes not from ascetic withdrawal, but by daily intercourse with the physical world. Spirituality arises from matter, and acts back upon it by transforming it; true spirituality is gained and tested in the laboratory.[30]

Rooted in the depths of the world, the alchemical process is a path of transformation, but not a spiritual path that leaves the world behind.

NATURE'S CREATIVE WORK

Led by the light of nature, the alchemists discovered through experience and intuition that all matter is alive, dynamic, and evolutionary. Matter and life is a state of creative becoming. But for the earlier Greek philosophers the world was essentially static. For Plato the focus was on the world of unchanging Being. While Aristotle held a biological and developmental view of natural phenomena, he saw the heavens as being eternal and constant. Similarly, Plotinus held that the celestial bodies were perfect and immutable.

Yet in all fairness, we can't blame the Greek philosophers for thinking that the world has always existed in its present state. Lacking precise instruments to extend their senses and the detailed information necessary to contradict everyday perceptions, it is only natural to assume that the cosmos has always been the way that it is. But if the very recent discovery that the universe is an unfolding, evolutionary event has forever shattered the Platonic vision of "the eternity of the world" and the Judeo-Christian myth of Genesis, it also reestablishes the alchemical perception of a cosmic, developmental process in which we as humans are embedded.

In an uncanny way, it was the alchemists who prefigured the modern scientific understanding that the physical universe is an unfolding, evolutionary phenomenon. Everything that we can see, touch, or feel has unfolded from a primordial state of light, energy, and hydrogen. Through the birth and death of stars, new forms of matter were synthesized which allowed organic life to emerge on Earth and, almost certainly, on countless other planets. The entire history of the universe is a story of alchemical emergence in which the hard work of becoming is driven forward by a creative movement toward higher levels of wholeness and differentiation. In the case of living organisms, the cosmic process has manifested itself in terms of awareness, exuberant creativity, and resounding delight.

Our new understanding of the self-organizing, evolutionary cosmos contradicts the sterile, mechanistic vision of a predetermined, clockwork universe. Computers, ticking clocks, and other closed deterministic systems never give birth to novelty or emergent form. But as Nobel laureate Ilya Prigogine has proven, nature itself is an open, evolutionary system, whose future states can never be determined in advance.[31] While the cosmos may be partially bound by the laws of necessity, it is creativity, freedom, and playful symbiosis that drives the unfolding universe forward.

If our new understanding of the universe is essentially alchemical—in which matter is creative and active, flowering into more complex states—perhaps we will be able to recover the central Hermetic insight of spiritual participation in nature's work as well. In that vision our task is not to mercilessly exploit the Earth as either consumers or producers, but to bring the world-spirit to fruition through creative participation and a sacred art.

Figure 5.1. Tellus Mater *(Mother Earth). Roman bas relief from the Altar of Augustan Peace, Rome, 9 B.C.*

Divine Earth, mother of men and of the blessed gods,
you nourish all, you give all, you bring all to fruition,
and you destroy all.
When the season is fair you are heavy with fruit and
growing blossoms;
and, O multiform maiden, you are the seat of the immortal cosmos,
and in the pains of labor you bring forth fruit of all kinds.
Eternal, reverend, deep-bosomed, and blessed,
you delight in the sweet breath of grass, O goddess
bedecked with flowers.
Yours is the joy of the rain, and round you the intricate realm of the
stars revolve in endless and awesome flow.
But, O blessed goddess, may you multiply the gladsome fruits
and, together with the beautiful seasons, grant me favor.

ORPHIC HYMN TO THE EARTH,
TRANSLATED BY APOSTOLOS ATHANASSAKIS

5

The Lushness of Earth and the Spirit of the Desert

In the story of Genesis, God created the world and he saw that it was good. For Plato, too, the universe was a living reflection of goodness and divine beauty. In the perception of traditional peoples everywhere, humans live in an animated and radiant universe, permeated by the awe-inspiring powers of creation. The common perception is that the Earth and the greater universe are alive. Mother Nature brings forth her fruits and the living Earth nurtures us into existence. If nature was not permeated by the spirit of life and generation, the universe would have never brought forth its exquisite offspring.

The early Greeks were deeply sensitive to the place of humanity in the fabric of the world. Living close to nature, the fecundity of the Earth, and the rhythms of the seasons, their vision was clear enough to perceive the living spirit that animates the landscape. As Plato wrote,

The land is [our] ancestral home and [we] must cherish it even more than children cherish their mother; furthermore, the Earth is a goddess and mistress of mortal men, and the gods and spirits already established in the locality must be treated with the same respect.[1]

Even Socrates, who rarely left the city gates of Athens, was over-come by the living beauty of nature when he did so. In Plato's *Phaedrus,* Socrates and a companion wandered out into the countryside to find a perfect setting for a philosophical conversation on the nature of love. They arrived at a spreading and lofty plane tree set on the banks of a cool stream, surrounded by tall and shady willows. Relaxing in the breezy and charming atmosphere to the summer music of cicadas, Socrates judged the place sacred to the nymphs based on the presence of some nearby statues and figurines. Finally, after a splendid afternoon of lengthy conversation, they got ready to depart, but Socrates wondered if it was not best to pray to the deities of the place before leaving.

His companion agreed and Socrates spoke out:

O beloved Pan and all ye other gods of this place, grant to me that I be made beautiful in my soul within, and that all external posses-sions be in harmony with my inner man. May I consider the wise man rich; and may I have such wealth as only the self-restrained man can bear or endure.[2]

On concluding Socrates asked his friend if anything more was required, explaining that "for me that prayer is enough." His compan-ion responded, "Let me also share in this prayer; for friends have all things in common." And on that they set back for the city.

By honoring the spirits of the countryside, the spirit of the vine—which flows forth as wine—and the fecundity of the Earth ripened in the fall harvest, the Greeks paid homage to a sacramental view of nature. Despite our sometimes too-cozy sense of security, life and health hangs on a thread, which could be severed at any moment. For traditional and tribal peoples, their dependence on the nurturing Earth is not eclipsed by the structures of agribusiness, brand names, colorful packaging, and supermarkets. Rather, in traditional cultures, the thread of life stands visible, immediate at every juncture from field, to slaughterhouse, to public market, to the family hearth. Without the fruit of the Earth and its fecundity we would die, and when directly experienced, this inspires a deep sense of gratitude. While the American holiday of Thanksgiving is an official celebration of gratitude, for people who live closer to the Earth, every single meal affords an opportunity for recalling the generosity of nature, the resourceful mother of all.

THE MONOTHEISTIC
AND POLYTHEISTIC IMAGINATIONS

The universe is one thing but manifests itself in a wide variety of ways. Under the shining stars and the radiance of the heavens, fertile pastures, craggy peaks, and blue-green seas are all laid out. The world contains complex, changing terrains, but the types of life found about the globe are even more various. Oftentimes, we take our natural settings for granted and can only appreciate them as unique when traveling to another land or when exposed to something out of the ordinary.

Like the human personality, the natural world reveals itself through various powers, some peaceful and reassuring, others thundering, awe-inspiring, and overwhelming. If the natural world is diverse, within the human heart we also find a spectrum of powers: love, anger, intelligence and studiousness, and the desires for beauty, physical comfort, and civic participation. Through religion and science, we seek ways of journeying beyond isolation by gazing into and participating in the great mystery of the cosmic tapestry. But in all of these ways and more, life reveals itself as complex, multifaceted, and richly diverse.

This diversity of human experience and the various domains of nature inspired the polytheistic imagination of the classical Greek world.[3] Zeus ruled over the bright skies but was also a powerful storm god, lord of the thunderbolt. Hermes, his quick-footed messenger, was a god of intelligence, communication, and commerce. Aphrodite, the fertility goddess who rose from the sea, inspired love, the greening of meadows, and the fertility of animals. Apollo, the lord of healing and purification, also oversaw music and every art that involved rational clarity. Demeter, goddess of agriculture, protected the ripening of grain, while Dionysus, lord of the grape, was a vital spirit and ecstatic liberator. Hephaistos, lord of fire, was associated with metallurgy and creative craftsmanship. And that is but a small listing. The important point is that the polytheistic imagination offers avenues for celebrating the primordial richness of the world and human experience.

In the polytheistic imagination, the principle of plenitude holds sway. It is almost a case of "the more the merrier." One of my favorite writings is a collection of Greek texts known as the Orphic Hymns.[4] No one knows who wrote these works, but they're a collection of poems addressed to the Greek divinities. Not only are the major divinities included, but so too are other natural powers like the four winds, the stars, and the clouds, and such personifications as Law, Justice, Good Fortune, Dream—and even Death. In the hymns, each dimension of life and the world is touched by the sacred. Our individual experience is imagined in a larger context. We are called back to our senses, to the lushness of Earth, and reminded that the everyday facts of life and nature are themselves profound and meaningful events, rooted in a larger order.

The Greek philosophers and other educated people certainly didn't literally believe in a host of human-like gods and goddesses cavorting through the heavens. But nonetheless, humans are an embodiment of nature—and in humanity nature herself "personifies." Both the forces of nature and the human psyche have their distinct personalities, and when we start talking about personalities we are speaking about representing something in human form. By allowing ourselves to personify, symbolize, and mythologize, we open ourselves up to the creative power of the imagination, which is rooted deeply in both human nature and the cosmic pattern. Perhaps even more importantly, the mythic imagination allows us to speak deeply about the world through metaphor in a way that avoids the deadness of literalism and conceptualization.

People who live in the desert imagine divinity in human terms, but the quality of imagination is different. In the lush, fertile regions where Hinduism evolved, the world is buzzing with energy and spirit. This fertile plenitude of life is reflected in the exuberance of Hinduism's polytheistic imagination, a world populated by vital, colorful deities. In the desert, however, divinity is remote and transcendent. The world itself does not bloom in vivid confusion but is neat and well-divided. Nomadic life, poised beneath the vast sky and amid the ever-stretching sands, is a struggle in an oftentimes-harsh environment. But at night when the oppressive heat of the day finally subsides, the dark sky opens deeply to reveal its transcendent glory. Under the dark night on the desert sands, heaven stands remote from Earth. Huddled in the blackness of night, the tiny human soul stands before the awesome, spine-tingling power of the heavens that brought the world into existence.

If the fertile, irrepressibly blooming regions of the Earth favor the polytheistic imagination, the dry desert region of the Middle East brought forth the three great monotheistic religions of Judaism, Christianity, and Islam. In the desert, the power of divinity is singular. It stands remote from the landscape and the world of human affairs, but rains down from heaven like a distant, commanding voice. In the fertile regions, the spirit of divinity is multiform. Not only is divine power revealed by the heavens, but it flowers forth in the sap of the eternal, resurrecting vegetation spirit and other expressions of life's energies.

I don't want to make a case for either the monotheistic or polytheistic imagination and suggest that one is better than the other. In healthy people both can exist side by side, and both can have their drawbacks. The downside to the monotheistic imagination is a tendency toward one-sided absolutism. It proclaims that there is only one correct way of looking at things, "one true way"—not only to God, but also one true way to envision the world and relate to others. The potential failing of the polytheistic imagination is relativism, the belief that "one thing is as good as another," and that there are no ultimate values worth striving for or embodying in one's life. If people under the spell of the monotheistic imagination can be stern, harsh, and judgmental, people under the spell of the polytheistic imagination can lack focus, be wishy-washy, and be overly experimental. Yet in their positive manifestations, both "monotheistic" and "polytheistic" are necessary, interwoven strands in the fabric of a flourishing life. There are times when single-minded focus and monastic withdrawal from the world are called for, and there are other times when we need to abandon the stern and controlling ego to immerse ourselves in the colorful network and vital, buzzing energies of life.

THE ECLIPSE OF LIVING NATURE

When the sacramental visibility of the world closes down, all things decline to the status of mere objects, opaque and unilluminated. Nothing can be trusted as a receptacle of the sacred.

THEODORE ROSZAK

For the Greeks, nature itself possessed a sacramental, living dimension, but with the coming of Christianity that began to change. On one hand, the Judeo-Christian tradition said that God had created the world and that it was good. Moreover, humanity was made in the image of God. In this sense, both humanity and cosmos possessed a positive evaluation. On the other hand, the Hellenistic period was a time when many people felt a great anxiety and sense of unease.[5] Christianity preached the coming end of the world and contrasted the perfection of the heavenly afterlife with the harsh sufferings of the terrestrial sphere. For the earlier Greeks, human life was more naturally at home in the world. But in early Christianity, individuals withdrew to the desert to purify their souls, renounce the ways of the world, and await the coming kingdom of God.

As Richard Tarnas noted in his book *The Passion of the Western Mind,* during the rise of Christianity the rich pluralism of Hellenistic culture, with its many philosophical schools and polytheistic religions, was replaced with an exclusive monotheism from the Judaic tradition.[6] Moreover, "In Christian understanding, the pivotal role was played by faith, not reason."[7] Because of this attitude, science, philosophy, and attention to the details of the natural world started to go into eclipse. Augustine wrote that it is enough for Christians just to believe that God is the source of all created things; nature itself and the teachings of the philosophers are unimportant. Ambrose wrote that "to discuss the nature and position of the earth does not help us in our hope of the life to come." In the words of the early church father Tertullian, "For us, curiosity is no longer necessary."[8] The study of nature was no longer essential because, compared with the spiritual realm and the anticipated glory of the afterlife, the material world was no longer significant.

While many of the early Christians taught that the world was shaped by the divine Logos and that the Holy Spirit was present in nature, the dualistic and pessimistic evaluation of the cosmos began to predominate with the passage of time. Because of this, the sacramental vision of living nature and the World Soul began to fade. Humanity was no longer at home in the cosmos, a living part of the living world, but pictured as an exile in an alien world awaiting the coming judgment day of salvation. For the Stoics, nature was alive and God was a divine power immanent *in the world*. In the new Christian view, nature was dead and God was a distant reality who didn't belong in the cosmos. Both the Stoics and the Christians held an idea of divine law, and for the Stoics God was the power of cosmic law present *in* nature and synonymous *with* nature. For the Christians, God was pictured as a lawmaker and cosmic architect who existed totally *apart* from nature and built it like a house. But ultimately, if the divine power of God did not exist in the artificially constructed world, humans didn't really belong there either.

This view of a nonliving, constructed universe was best summed up by the early Christian writer Lactanius. After ridiculing pagan ideas about the divinity of nature, Lactanius concluded that

> the world is neither god nor living, if it has been made: for a living creature is not made, but born; and if it has been built, it has been built as a house or ship *is built*. Therefore, there is a builder of the world, even God; and the world which has been made is distinct from him who made it. . . . If, therefore, it has been constructed as an abode, it is neither itself God, nor are the elements which are its parts; because a house cannot bear rule over itself, nor can the parts of which a house consists. . . . For a house, made for the purpose of being inhabited, has no sensibility by itself and is subject to the master who built or inhabits it . . .[9]

As Theodore Roszak noted, with Lactanius "nature is pronounced dead and desacralized."[10] But Lactanius failed to even place humanity in the dead world fashioned by the cosmic architect. Like God, humanity was essentially outside of nature, because

> the world does not produce man, nor is man a part of the world. For the same God who created the world, also created man from the beginning; and man is not a part of the world, in the same manner in which a limb is part of the body; for it is possible for the world to be without man, as it is for a city or house.[11]

For Lactanius, humanity had no essential kinship with nature, the world, or any terrestrial reality. The universe was a house of sorts, but not a true home. Unlike the Greek philosophers who held that all things and creatures are bound together by the harmony of the World Soul in the sacred community of the cosmos, for Lactanius the cosmos was dead, inorganic, and artificially constructed by a distant God who was outside of nature. The universe was built for the benefit of humans alone, who like God were outside of nature. Because of this, nature was a disposable, exploitable resource, unconnected to humanity, unanimated by spirit, and essentially insignificant in the great scheme of salvation. Man, after all, was empowered by God to possess "dominion over the Earth"—an Earth that shall itself pass away come the glorious judgment day of the elect.[12]

While some early Christians like Origen pictured the universe as a harmoniously ensouled cosmic organism, Lactanius's vision of a dead, desanctified universe came to represent the official position of the organized Church in late antiquity and early medieval times. For a while at least, the austere spirit of the desert won out over the lush spirit of the living Earth.

THE DISCOVERY OF NATURE IN THE TWELFTH CENTURY

For around nine hundred years the idea of living nature had laid dormant, slumbering in the depths of the Western psyche. Some medieval writers ridiculed science and the study of nature, devaluing the frailness of the human intellect and its smallness in trying to grasp the great miracles of God. Others, like religious writer Manegold of Lautenbach, ridiculed philosophers for "seeking out the natures of things," suggesting that they were incapable of imagining an existence beyond this world.[13] Because nature had been reduced to a book of allegorical and mystical significances, it wasn't pictured by the medieval mind as an autonomous domain subject to its own laws and coherent patterns of relationship. While the symbolic view of nature had given natural phenomena a moral significance, by codifying the Book of Nature as a catalog of symbolic types—a phenomenon so well reflected in the anti-realistic art of the period—it also blinded the medieval mind to the luscious, sensuous reality of the world that lay before its very eyes.

But in the twelfth century a reawakening occurred. A new group of thinkers believed that the universe was something worthy of study in its own right. These scholars were centered at the cathedral school of Chartres in France and they were all inspired by a fragment of Plato's *Timaeus,* which existed in Latin translation. The *Timaeus,* it will be remembered, was Plato's great cosmological dialogue in which he described the generation of the World Soul by the harmonic ratios of music. Through other channels various Pythagorean ideas about the nature of number, music, harmony, and proportion had reached these medieval thinkers. These were synthesized with the reading of the *Timaeus* and the biblical idea that God had created all things according to number, measure, and weight. As Otto von Simson has shown in his book *The Gothic Cathedral,* these Pythagorean, Platonic, and Christian ideas all congealed to inspire not only an intellectual and spiritual renaissance, but the design of the great cathedrals. Nature was now seen as a Great Chain of Being ordered by the rational principles of number, proportion, and harmony, and the great cathedrals incorporated these natural harmonies into their designs. In essence the cathedrals are Pythagorean models of the universe in which slumbering matter reaches skyward only to dematerialize into light via the sacred geometries of the great Rose Windows. In their own way, the luminous cathedrals embody the proportions of the World Soul and were designed to expose the minds of their inhabitants to the underlying spiritual harmonies of the cosmic pattern.

Some of the names associated with this movement include Thierry of Chartres, Bernard of Chartres, and Bernard Silvestris. Bernard Silvestris wrote an elaborate allegory, the *Cosmographia,* which describes how the World Soul animated nature at the world's creation, fashioning unformed matter according to the ideas and forms existing in Nous, the cosmic mind of God. William of Conches went even further and identified the World Soul with the Holy Spirit. In identifying the World Soul with the Holy Sprit, he was followed by Abelard who was also closely connected with the Cathedral School at Chartres.

The "discovery of nature" at Chartres and the rediscovery of the World Soul were a synonymous event. For as medieval historian Winthrop Wetherbee pointed out, in the renaissance of the twelfth century:

> the discovery of Nature, a power identified precisely with the preservation of life and order, and the obedience of all creation to cosmic law, meant the discovery of a new, more profound meaning in form and order themselves; her autonomy, like the vitality of the world soul, was imparted to all aspects of life in her domain.[14]

This discovery of living nature, which coincided with the emergence of the grail romances, gave humanity more autonomy in the cosmic scheme. It inspired a new interest in aesthetic form, an appreciation of realism in art, and an interest in the symbolic dimensions of myth and classical literature. Under the spell of this awakening, nature and human life became more autonomous, vital, and alive. Soul had always been seen as an intermediary between the distant realm of spirit and the concrete realm of matter, and the rediscovery of the World Soul helped to heal the dualism of medieval thought. God and divine power was brought back into the world and nature was revivified as a manifestation of divine beauty.

Like William of Conches and Abelard, earlier Christians like Clement of Alexandria,[15] Theodoretus,[16] and Basil[17] had identified the World Soul with the Holy Spirit of God. In the twelfth century the World Soul was once again seen as it had been in ancient times, as the ordering and animating principle of nature. Through soul the cosmos has life and through intelligence it has rationality. For fifty years the idea met with great success at Chartres, but the school of Saint-Victor distrusted it and the school of Citeaux denounced it.[18] Yet even Hugh of Saint-Victor who opposed the idea was forced to recognize "a mysterious power of nature which invisibly feeds and fosters all things."[19]

In the minds of the critics, the World Soul invested nature with too much life and divinity. It also threatened the purity of Christian doctrine. Especially dangerous was the identification of the World Soul with the Holy Spirit. By identifying the *anima mundi* with the Holy Spirit, it "reduced the Holy Spirit to presiding over cosmic evolution."[20] Moreover, it had been quite common for early Christian Platonists to identify the One with the Father, the Logos with the Son, and the World Soul with the Holy Spirit. But as Christian theology developed, it became a doctrinal point that Father, Son, and Holy Spirit were *equal*. This could not be said of the One, Logos, and World Soul. While they were all dynamically related as parts of an unfolding chain, they existed in a logical hierarchy and were qualitatively different from one another. Thus, for identifying the World Soul with the Holy Spirit, William of Conches was attacked and forced to confess that he was "a Christian and not a member of the Academy."[21] Similarly, and perhaps more seriously, Abelard's identification of the World Soul with the Holy Spirit was condemned by the Council of Soissons in 1121, and he was forced to recant.[22] Warned by this, other medieval thinkers decided to simply refer to the World Soul as "Nature."

The medieval interest in the World Soul and living "Nature" was short lived. The idea and perception of a spirit animating matter lived on in alchemy, but alchemy was always an underground repository for ideas that didn't fully harmonize with official, mainstream theology. In the thirteenth and fourteenth centuries, the idea of the World Soul once again went into eclipse and the universe was no longer recognized as an animated being.[23] But this was short lived, for in the Great Renaissance of Florentine Italy the world would return to life with a vital exuberance and grandeur that has never perhaps been matched.

6

The Last Flowering

The Rediscovery of Soul in
Renaissance Florence

THE EARTH REBORN

There is no philosopher of any reputation . . . who does
not hold that the world and its spheres are in some way
animated.

GIORDANO BRUNO

With the advent of the Renaissance, an organic vision of living nature returned—a fact reflected in the work of many thinkers.[1] Leonardo da Vinci pointed out that "the earth has a spirit of growth" and went on to compare the structure of the world body to that of an organism.[2] Marsilio Ficino likened the cosmos to an "animal," a living, animated being.[3] Bernardino Telesio taught that there is a divine spark in nature and that all matter is alive.[4] Tomasso Campanella wrote that "the world is a great animal, and we live within it as worms live within us."[5] Giordano Bruno maintained that it is not reasonable to suppose that any part of the world is not without soul and organic structure.[6] Giambattista della Porta wrote that "the whole world is knit and bound within itself," for "the world is a living creature, everywhere both male and female, and the parts of it do couple together, within and between themselves, by reason of their mutual love."[7]

The Renaissance was a time of transformed vision in which nature reappeared with resplendent vitality. *Renaissance* means rebirth. Not only was there a rebirth of classical learning, but the senses opened to the deep beauty and exuberant lushness of nature. Under the spell of renaissance, the world returned, living and ensouled.

Renaissance was a time of rediscovery, a coming back to the senses, a reimagining of what it meant to be human and fully alive in the great tapestry of the world. The rediscovery began in late medieval times. Translations of Aristotle appeared that gave birth to medieval Scholasticism and inspired such great figures as Thomas Aquinas. But under the influence of Scholasticism, philosophy became analytical, hairsplitting, and stagnant. Analytical reason became prized, but it was usually assumed that reason could not contradict the higher wisdom of faith. In this way, philosophy did not embody a spirit of free inquiry, nor was it pursued as an end in itself. The arguments of philosophy were employed to defend the predefined doctrines of the Church, and medieval philosophy had tended to become a frozen system of rules, definitions, and logical syntax.

In many ways the Renaissance was a reaction to all this. With the Italian humanists, an exciting renewal of human culture began to take place—a renewal that could be tangibly seen and felt. New sources of learning and inspiration became available from the past. The humanists rediscovered the great Roman writers, philosophers, and orators and became intensely interested in the legacy of classical civilization. While much of medieval art and literature had followed rigid formulas, the humanists, fueled by the economic prosperity of the Italian city-states, began to emulate the literature, art, and thought of the classical world in new and creative ways. Leading humanists began to focus their attention on the dignity of man and the powers of human creativity. While medieval culture emphasized the importance of the afterlife, the humanists became increasingly concerned about cultivating human potential here, in this world. And central to this entire transformation was the rediscovery of living nature and the *anima mundi*.

SPRINGTIME IN FLORENCE

There is nothing to be found in this whole living world so deformed that Soul does not attend it, that a gift of Soul is not in it.

MARSILIO FICINO

The Renaissance as we know it hinged upon a rediscovery of the Platonic tradition, and behind that rediscovery lay the figure of Marsilio Ficino (1433–1499). Greek scholars in Constantinople had preserved Plato's writings, and with political upheavals they started to travel to the West. In the mid-1400s, manuscript copies and teachers of Greek started migrating to Italy. Cosimo de' Medici, a wealthy banker, statesman, and patron of the arts, encouraged a rebirth of learning and humanistic scholarship. He commissioned Marsilio Ficino to translate the entire body of Plato's writings into Latin. As things would turn out, these translations, along with Ficino's own writings, would help shape both the spirit and art of the Renaissance.

Ficino was a medical school dropout who, since a young age, had been preoccupied with philosophy. His father was a court physician to the Medici family, and thus news of Ficino's early interest in Plato and Greek philosophy reached Cosimo. In 1459, at the age of twenty-four, he was summoned to appear before Cosimo, who asked Ficino to translate all of Plato into Latin. Cosimo assured Ficino's parents that their son would receive handsome support for the undertaking, and told his worried father that "you are a doctor of bodies, but he will be a doctor of souls."[8]

Cosimo gave Ficino a farmhouse near the Medici Villa at Careggi, located on the outskirts of Florence, and the Villa became a meeting place for some of the greatest men of the day. After the death of Cosimo, Ficino was a close friend and advisor to his grandson Lorenzo the Magnificent, who became ruler of Florence at the age of twenty-one. Lorenzo went on to become one of the most gifted individuals of the Renaissance. He possessed a deep love of knowledge and the arts, was successful in war and business, and was perhaps the finest Italian poet of his time. Under his generous patronage, the artists, scholars, and philosophers of Florence flourished to produce their greatest work.

Over the years Ficino translated not only all of Plato, but also the Hermetic writings, the Neoplatonists, and other ancient writers in which the ideas of the living universe and the World Soul figured prominently. Not since antiquity were these writings or their ideas directly available, and now with the invention of the printing press they could be widely disseminated. Through Ficino's translations, it was now possible for all educated readers to gain access to the work of the past masters, and a revivifying breeze of renewal began to radiate outward. As Ficino himself wrote,

> Our century, like a Golden Age, has restored to light the liberal arts that were nearly extinct: grammar, poetry, rhetoric, painting, sculpture, architecture, music, the ancient performance of songs with the Orphic lyre, and all that in Florence. And accomplishing what had been revered among the ancients, but almost forgotten since, it united wisdom with eloquence. . . . And in Florence it restored the Platonic doctrine from darkness to light.[9]

THE FLOWERING IMAGINATION

Ficino's writings and the work of the other humanists gave a new, high status to the faculty of the imagination, giving new form also to the polytheistic imagination of the ancient Greeks. Like the ancient pagan philosophers, it was once again possible to believe in One High God but also in a whole variety of divine powers that animated the cosmos. As long as the ancient divinities were poetic and symbolic, it was perfectly acceptable for Ficino to be a good Christian and playfully fill his writings, talks, and correspondence with allegorical references to Apollo, Bacchus, the Muses, the Graces, and so on. Ficino did not abandon Christianity, but forged a new, individualistic type of Christianity in which the teachings of the Church could happily exist alongside the polytheistic imagination in the same way that Botticelli could paint masterpieces of Christian art and pagan mythology at the same time.

With the flowering of the imagination, the world itself became animated and resacralized. The creative imagination is not something that just dwells in us, but is rooted deeply in the life of the greater world. The creative spirit, the *spiritus mundi,* permeates the stars, growing plants, and all of reality. As nature brings forth its fragrant tapestry of life, the world spirit exhales and blooms forth creatively. The world itself breathes, and we participate in that vital breath. As Ficino wrote, "The world does wholly live and breathe, and we are permitted to absorb its spirit."[10] Thanks to this vital spirit of participation, nature's body came alive to the Renaissance artists, who personally took part in the unfolding of the world's creative energies. Creativity itself is a divine, godlike power. Where the medieval artist was confined to well-established styles and symbolic types, the Renaissance artist broke free of those formulas and was able to encounter the world in a more deeply intimate way. Nature and the living textures of the world could be sensuously experienced in all their richness and vibrant immediacy. As philosopher Henryk Skolimowski notes, in the new resacralization of nature, "it is not the power to observe nature that is so important but the power to worship it. When this power is gone, in subsequent centuries, the power of rendering nature through painting diminishes."[11]

If medieval theology had removed God to a wholly transcendent sphere, to the Renaissance Platonists nature was permeated by life, divinity, and numinous mystery, a vital expression of the World Soul and the living powers of creation. In the words of Richard Tarnas, "The garden of the world was again enchanted, with magical powers and transcendent meaning implicit in every part of nature."[12] For Ficino, the lush garden of the world was animated by love, a force that emanated from God, descended into nature, and returned to God through human desire and the appreciation of divine beauty (see figure 6.1).

Figure 6.1. Botticelli's Primavera. *Commissioned by a friend of Marsilio Ficino, Primavera is an elaborate mythological allegory that illustrates the Neoplatonic theory of love. The soul enters the world in a naive state, is transformed through the power of love, and led to contemplate divine beauty and the source of creation.*

Ficino taught that love is the bond of the universe. It is also another name for humanity, he wrote, for the more we love others, the more we prove ourselves to be humane members of the entire species.[13] Through the power of love, it is possible to be closer to the soul of another person than we are to our own body.

AS ABOVE, SO BELOW: NATURE'S MAGICAL SYMPATHIES

Heaven above, heaven below.
Stars above, stars below.
All that is above also is below.
Grasp this and rejoice.

ATHANASIUS KIRCHER

The whole power of magic consists in love. The work of magic is the attraction of one thing by another because of a certain affinity of nature. But the parts of this world, like the parts of a single animal, all deriving from a single author, are joined to each other by the communion of a single nature. . . . From this common relationship is born a common love; from love, a common attraction. And this is the true magic.

MARSILIO FICINO

Whenever the idea of the living universe has flourished, so too has the idea of the microcosm, humanity as an encapsulation of the entire universe.[14] Running as a common thread through the living universe tradition, the idea of the microcosm goes back to the earliest Greek philosophers and appears in various guises to this very day. Humanity is a compendium of the macrocosm, the all-encompassing totality of existence—and both the little world of humanity and the great world of the cosmos are bound together in organic harmony. In the words of the *Zohar,* a thirteenth-century mystical text:

There is not a member in the human body that does not have its counterpart in the world as a whole. For as a man's body consists of members and parts of varying rank, all acting and reacting upon one another so as to form one organism, so it is with the world at large: it consists of a hierarchy of created things, which, when they properly act and react upon each other, together form one organic body.[15]

Humanity contains all the elements of which the world consists. In the Great Chain of Being, we find material existence in rocks, the power of growth and reproduction in plants, active sensation in animals, and rational activity in angelic and celestial spirits. Yet humanity is a compendium of the entire universe. Placed in the center of the cosmos between heaven and Earth, spirit and matter, humanity alone belongs to the two worlds and is the unifying bond of creation.[16] Because of this, humanity has a special role to play in cultivating the perfection of the universe.

Because of the fact that humanity fully encapsulates the cosmic pattern, human beings possess a deeply intimate bond with all levels of creation. If our inner potential is brought into fruition, individuals possess an almost godlike power to peer into the depths of reality and to participate in the unfolding drama of creation. Aristotle wrote that "the soul is in a sense all things" because by thinking or knowing the universe, the mind actually "becomes" the universe.[17] Similarly, the ancient Hermetic writings maintained that "a human being is a great wonder, a living thing to be worshipped and honored," thanks to the godlike spark within.[18] Humanity cultivates the earth, understands the elements, and "plumbs the depths of the sea in the keenness of his mind."[19] In short, "Everything is permitted him." Even "heaven itself seems not too high, for he measures it in his clever thinking as if it were nearby."[20] Because mankind is a microcosm and contains the divine order within, humanity is drawn toward the highest realities through the bond of love.[21]

While medieval theologians taught that humanity occupies the lowest rung on the cosmic ladder, Ficino, deeply influenced by the Hermetic writings, espoused the dignity of man and the nobility of human nature. He explained that "men are the only beings on earth to have discovered their infinite nature."[22] Through their creative faculty, humans participate in the nature of God; and because humanity embodies the divine, it can never be satisfied with the finite. Ficino wrote that "our minds occupy neither time nor space," for "they can run at once through the entire world."[23]

For Ficino the universe was a living being, a coherent organism, animated by intelligence and reflecting a divine beauty. As he wrote, "In the one living body of the world there is everywhere a single life."[24] And in such an organism there cannot be parts that are unrelated to the whole. As in a living creature, each part of the universe is an organ, each with its particular place and function in the overall makeup of the cosmic organism. Each part is not a separate entity, but a particular mode by which the whole expresses itself.[25]

Love is the cosmic power that circulates throughout the universe and animates the world. Through desire and the magnetic power of attraction, love unites those things that are separated and causes like to attract like. In the same way that the Moon influences the tides and the Sun brings forth the seasons, all parts of the cosmic pattern are bound in vital sympathy. In the same way that the heavens are enlinked with the Earth, the inner is bound with the outer. All are part of one world. The living, sympathetic interconnection between the different parts of the cosmic organism accounts for the efficacy of magic and other enchantments. As Plotinus wrote, "Love is given in Nature" and "the qualities inducing love induce mutual approach."[26] As he explained, like attracts like, and cosmic sympathy arises through the interconnection of all things, since all souls are rooted in one Soul.[27] Thus, if "spells and magical acts in general draw men together and make them share experiences at a distance, this must be altogether due to the one soul. A word spoken quietly acts on what is far off, and makes something separated by an enormous distance listen; and from this one can learn the unity of all."[28]

For Ficino, love, soul, spirit, and humanity were all analogous. He described them all as principles of mediation, "the bond and juncture of the universe" that connects all things together. As he wrote:

The soul is all things together. . . . And since it is the center of all things, it has the forces of all. Hence, it passes into all things. And since it is the true connection of all things, it goes to the one without leaving the others. . . . therefore it may be rightly called the center of nature, the middle term of all things, the face of all, the bond and juncture of the universe.[29]

Like the two-faced Roman god Janus, soul faces in two directions at once. Soul is the bond between spirit and matter. If there was no soul, but only mind and body, there would be no connection between the two.[30] The World Soul flourishes everywhere, but especially through the Sun, "as it indiscriminately unfolds its common power of life" throughout the universe. Like the alchemists, Ficino held that "the power of the World Soul is diffused in all things through the quintessence, which flourishes everywhere as spirit within the world body."[31]

Spirit circulates throughout the world and is especially associated with the lively radiance of the celestial bodies. This radiance may be drawn down to the Earth and concentrated for medicinal purposes, to restore physical and spiritual health. Trained as a physician, Ficino wrote *Three Books on Life,* the third volume of which is titled "On Obtaining Life From the Heavens."

The basic idea behind Ficino's natural magic is simple. Light connects everything in a flash, and spirit is like light, "the bond of the universe." The difference is that spirit circulates throughout nature, connecting the world of the stars with the Earth below. Ficino described this subtle spirit as "a divine influx, flowing from God, penetrating through the heavens, descending through the elements and finishing up in lower nature."[32] But the path of spirit is not a one-way street. The supernatural energy flows from heaven to Earth only to revert from below to above, thus forming one great spiritual circuit.

As the *spiritus* descends to Earth, it carries with it the influences of the seven planets, each one presiding over various moods, emotional states, and physical conditions. By drawing upon such subtle powers as song, light, and scent, coupled with the soul's ardent desire, the Renaissance *magus,* or natural philosopher, was able to pull down, concentrate, and attune his own soul to the appropriate heavenly rays, as through an act of prayer. As Ficino explained:

> Our *spiritus* is in conformity with the rays of the heavenly *spiritus,* which penetrates everything either secretly or obviously. It shows a far greater kinship when we have a strong desire for that life and are seeking a benefit that is consistent with it, and thus transfer our own *spiritus* into its rays by means of love, particularly as we make use of song and light and the perfume appropriate to the deity. . . . For the *spiritus,* once it has been made more akin to the deity by emotional disposition, song, perfume, and light, draws a richer influence from it.[33]

Ever since the construction of Stonehenge, Newgrange, and even before, it has been important for humans to align their lives with the cosmos and draw down the life-giving energies of the heavens. In this respect Ficino's natural magic reflects a primordial desire to fertilize human life with the animating spirit of the greater universe. Yet for Ficino and the other Renaissance masters, the living universe was not just an idea, but something they *experienced.* In the living universe our bodies, emotions, thoughts, dreams, and higher insights are all integral aspects of the larger Cosmic Life in which we participate. The phenomenon of magic, or the power to influence reality through imagination and desire, owes its existence to the World Soul, which links everything together as a seamless whole. All great works of art—itself a magical practice—likewise lure and channel the energies of the *anima mundi.* Thanks to the soul of the universe, the outer world moves the inner and the inner world moves the outer. In some way that is more than metaphorical, nature herself is sympathetic.

NATURE'S VITAL INTELLIGENCE: GIORDANO BRUNO ON THE WORLD SOUL

The vision of the living universe had slumbered underground in medieval times like the alchemical Mercurius, the spirit hidden in nature.

But with the coming of the Renaissance, the rebirth of classical learning, and the rebirth of nature, the Hermetic spirit was released into the greater world. Like a genie released from a bottle, the philosophical Mercury started to work its magic. Despite the difficult social conditions of the time, the world of nature, matter, and the power of the human imagination all turned fertile and vibrant. With the Renaissance, the vision of the World Soul and living nature emerged as an exciting and dominant tradition.

One of the most comprehensive accounts of the living universe is found in the writings of Renaissance philosopher Giordano Bruno (1548–1600), who held that "there is nothing not endowed with life and owning a vital principle."[34] As we gaze at the world fabric we see it graced with beauty, but "there is no beauty which does not consist of some species or form, and there is no form which is not produced by the soul."[35] All things that have form depend upon soul, and the World Soul is the form of the entire universe.[36] As every animate thing develops, it is guided by psyche or life, but soul is guided by intelligence. The World Soul is the seat of the universal intellect, which guides the unfolding life of the cosmos. As Bruno wrote:

> The universal intellect is the innermost, most real and essential faculty and the most efficacious part of the world-soul. It is the one and the same thing, which fills the whole, illumines the universe, and directs nature in producing her species in the right way. It plays the same role in the production of natural things as our intellect does in the parallel production of rational systems.[37]

Our rationality, then, parallels the productive rationality of the universal intellect. Quoting the Pythagoreans, Bruno stated that the universal mind is "the mover and agitator of the universe,"[38] while according to the Magi it was

> most fruitful in seeds, or the sower, since it is that which impregnates matter with all forms, and, according to their type and condition, succeeds in shaping, forming, and interrelating it in such

admirable systems as cannot be attributed to chance or to any principle unable to distinguish and set in order.[39]

The intelligent, unfurling power of soul is most obviously seen in the rational, perfectly coordinated pattern that unfolds in the growth of plants and animals. The power of the soul is not imposed on matter from the outside, but exists in the very heart of the world and animates nature from within. For this reason it is called

> the inner craftsman, since it forms matter and shapes it from within, as from within the seed or root is sent forth and unfolded the trunk, from within the trunk are thrust out the branches, and from within the branches the formed twigs, and from within these the buds are unfurled, and there within are formed, shaped, and interwoven, like nerves, the leaves, flowers, and fruits.[40]

If our own forethought and intelligence are required in the creative arts, such as making a sculpture of a horse, Bruno asks us to imagine "how much superior must we esteem that creative intelligence" that works in the unfolding of living organisms.

In the same way that individual souls aim toward the development of living organisms, the World Soul as a whole aims at the perfection of the entire universe.[41] And ultimately for Bruno, spirit, soul, or life was "found in all things and in various degrees fills all matter."[42] A table as a table is not animated, but all natural things have within themselves matter and form. Even the tiniest particle contains a spark of form or spirit, and "there is not the least corpuscle that doesn't contain internally some portion that may become alive."[43] In modern terms, the table may not appear to be alive, but if we could view it at the atomic level it would be a dynamic, living activity, a furiously dancing pattern of energy. As if anticipating contemporary physics, Bruno wrote that

> spirit is found in all things, which, if they are not living creatures, are still organisms. If not according to the perceptible presence of

animation and life, yet they are animate according to the principle and a sort of primordial activity of animation and life.[44]

THE STAR IN MAN AND
THE CULTIVATION OF NATURE

Imagination is the star in man.

PARACELSUS

Like Ficino, Bruno was a Renaissance magus, a student of living nature and the sympathies and correspondences that unite all levels of the celestial pattern. Magic conceived in this way had nothing to do with sorcery or trafficking with evil spirits but was an essential branch of natural philosophy and one of the main roots out of which modern science developed. Magic was the observational and experimental study of nature's unexplained or hidden forces, and the relations between the macrocosm and the microcosm. God's work of Creation was seen as a divine magic, while the human study of our place in the universe was merely a form of "natural magic." As della Porta wrote, magic is "nothing else but the survey of the whole course of Nature."[45] In the Renaissance, natural magic was an attempt to unify nature and religion—an attempt to unify the natural universe with the world of spiritual experience. According to Paracelsus, magic was a spiritual quest that led to a greater knowledge of God, and rested on the three pillars of prayer, faith, and imagination.[46]

The old Persian word *magus* refers to a priest who is also a scientist.[47] In the Renaissance view, divine wisdom and the investigation of nature's secrets could not be separated. Scientific research and experimentation was seen as a type of divine service, a spiritual quest that would help illuminate the sacred structure of the universe and join the soul to God. In this way the Renaissance brought forth an entire crop of priest-scientists, individuals devoted to understanding the powers of the cosmos and putting them to use in spiritually helpful and therapeutic ways.

One of the greatest such individuals was Paracelsus (1493–1541), a gifted physician who stands out in many ways as the founder of modern medicine. Paracelsus rejected many ancient theories of healing, calling for increased observation and experimentation. Criticizing those who depended mainly on theory and ancient authorities, he called for a more empirical approach. "The patients are your textbook," he wrote, "the sickbed is your study."[48] He pioneered the use of carefully prepared chemical remedies to be administered in controlled dosages. He rejected the application of cow dung, urine, feathers, and other substances to wounds, believing that the body would heal itself if cared for through proper hygiene. "If you prevent infection," he wrote, "Nature will heal the wound all by herself."[49] Yet behind Paracelsus's devotion to medical practice stood a magical philosophy that emphasized a collaboration between humanity and nature in the healing process.

Ficino was both a priest and a physician, and his natural magic was aimed at concentrating the virtues of the celestial bodies in such a way that they could heal both spirit and body. Like magic, true medicine was defined as "the searching out of the secrets of nature."[50] Inspired by Ficino's idea of the priest-physician, Paracelsus envisioned the true healer as a magus who knew the hidden virtues, signatures, and properties of herbs and chemical substances. In the same way that the magus can bring celestial virtues down to Earth, the physician and chemist can extract the virtues of herbs and minerals, concentrating the vital, healing essences in a medicinal remedy. As Paracelsus clearly stated, just as "the magus understands what is in the stars, and nothing remains concealed in the heavens," so too "a physician understands and knows all the virtues in the herbs." And "just as the physician can give his remedy to a patient and cure his disease, so the magus can transfer such virtues to man, after he has extracted them from the stars."[51]

The light of nature assisted the physician in this task. While the light of God was present in revelation, the light of nature was something accessible to all living creatures. The light of nature brings forth an inner illumination and allows us to see deeply into the inner essence of the created world. Ultimately, the light of nature originates from the stars. Like the great world which consists of heavenly and terrestrial regions, humanity consists of two natures: one, an astral or side-real body that constitutes the vital spirit; second, an elemental material body that is perishable. From Earth, man "receives the material body, from heaven his character. Thus the earth moulds his shape, and then heaven endows this shape with the light of nature."[52]

All our rational, psychic, or inner life results from the astral spirit, and for Paracelsus "imagination is the star in man."[53] Because of this, our imagination, soul, and rational faculties are deeply rooted in the life spirit of the world and the greater universe. Because of this dynamic link with the world-structure, a deep, holistic sort of knowledge is possible, for

> everything in which man is subject to the light of Nature comes from the stars. All natural arts and human wisdom are given by the stars, we are the pupils of the stars, and they our teacher. God has ordered everything in the light of Nature, so that we may learn from it.[54]

If the astral spirit of the stars was not active in humanity, no art would have come to man. Logic by itself does not lead to any sort of new knowledge, but only explains its own statements.[55] Something deeper is needed to directly see into the depths of nature, and this vital bond is provided by the astral light which links our inner spirit with the virtues hidden in nature. In this way, Paracelsus held that the astral body

> "teaches man" and is able to communicate with the astral part of the macrocosm, the uncreated virtues or direct emanations of God in the world of Nature. He saw experience as a process of identification of the mind or astral body with the internal knowledge possessed by natural objects in attaining their specific ends. The researcher should try to "overhear" the knowledge of the star, herb, or stone with respect to its activity or function. Science is thus already present as a virtue in the natural object, and it is the experience of the researcher which uncovers the astral sympathy between himself and the object. This identification with an object penetrates more deeply into the essence of the object than mere sensory perception.[56]

Not only can man see deeply into the fabric of nature, humanity was brought forth by God for this very purpose, and to guide nature to a higher form of fruition, so that what is innate in the universe can become fully realized. According to Paracelsus, God's inner wisdom is concealed in the astral spirit, and

> God is moved by such a love to reveal the secrets of the stars, that He created the microcosm, not just to reveal the secret of the stars through the work of man, but to reveal all natural mysteries of the elements. This could not occur without man. And God wishes that those things which are invisible shall become visible. . . . Because God ordained it thus, He does not want man to rest and to be indolent, not to stand still . . . but daily to explore the secrets of Nature. . . . Thus God created man, in order that His invisible works would be visibly realized, that is through man.[57]

In the Renaissance, the vision of the living universe took ever slightly different forms. But in all these visions the world is seen as an organic tapestry in which the vital essences of the cosmic powers are reflected in the exuberant life of nature's garden. As in the Hermetic formula, "As above, so below," the soul of the very heavens is reflected in the heartbeat, rhythms, textures, and tastes of terrestrial life. In the living garden of a world ensouled, plants, flowers, and the human imagination mirror the celestial potencies of the stars and planets made tangible in nature. Whether metals ripening in the earth or grapes ripening on the vine, all of nature is impregnated with celestial spirit, blossoming toward fruition.

Humanity does not stand apart from this process, but as the heart and soul of the world it acts as creative midwife. As Ficino wrote, soul exists "for the bodies of all earthly things and for the earth itself, to cultivate them and further them."[58] Love and creative energy circulates throughout the world, rising up in the living imagination. As Paracelsus taught, God brought forth humanity in order that nature itself could achieve creative fruition. Like the alchemists, the Renaissance magi did not stand apart from the world, but sought to identify with the divine life of the cosmos so that nature itself could be lifted higher through human love, knowledge, and service. By invoking the creative imagination and bringing forth that which is hidden, humanity taps into the deepest essence of things and enters into a vital collaboration with nature. From the perspective of nature transformed through art, both humanity and the world are creatively perfected. Life itself becomes a magical act.

Based on this worldview, the Renaissance could have marked the beginning of a new civilization based on a creative partnership between humanity and nature. But that was not to be. The Protestant Reformation of northern Europe was, in some ways, a reaction against the sensate spirit of the Renaissance; and similarly, the emerging mechanistic worldview of the Scientific Revolution included a reaction against the idea of living, ensouled nature. Rather than the Renaissance view that science was a divine art through which humanity could care for and cultivate the world, the perspective of the coming era could be summed up in the Enlightenment conclusion that "the negation of nature is the way toward happiness."[59]

PART II

THE DEATH OF NATURE AND THE RISE OF ALIENATION

I have described this earth, and indeed this whole visible world, as a machine.

RENÉ DESCARTES

7

The Mechanization
of the World

A CRACK IN THE UNIVERSE

With the Renaissance, the worldview of the medieval Church started to unravel. Suddenly, with the discovery of classical antiquity, it became apparent that humanity's creative and scientific potential had languished during medieval times. As ancient philosophical, scientific, and literary texts began to circulate in great profusion thanks to the invention of the printing press, a new spirit of creative energy was released. Nature became increasingly worthy of human attention, and the dignity and power of man came to be celebrated in both humanistic and scientific circles. It became obvious to the new lights of the Renaissance that they were standing at the end of an era and the beginning of a new one. The great dream of the Middle Ages was coming to an end, and it was at this time that people began to think of themselves as players in an unfolding historical drama. History itself came to be thought of as "ancient," "medieval," and "modern." With this new sense of personal identity, thinkers attempted to differentiate themselves from what they now perceived as the conceptual narrowness of the medieval mindset.

For the Italian humanists, a deepening of culture became possible

through a recognition of the soul's creative power and humanity's digni-
fied role in the cosmic pattern. For the protoscientists, man was charged
to investigate the secrets of nature through rational analysis and experimentation. In some ways the humanists and the protoscientists represented two distinct cultures that were worlds apart, but in another
way they were both united by their joint dislike of Aristotle, the great
philosophical authority of medieval Scholasticism. For many humanists, Aristotle was seen as a pedantic logic chopper whose hair-splitting
analyses failed to feed the soul and deepen their experience of life in
the world. Because of this, they turned to Plato, who left more room
for creative inspiration and the cultivation of the soul. For many protoscientists, Aristotle was seen as a medieval authority figure who reasoned
about the world deductively, but who failed to engage it through direct
observation and experimentation.

A string of new inventions gave further rise to a modern sense of
self-consciousness. The discovery of gunpowder, the magnetic compass,
the printing press, and the telescope all helped to expand the boundaries of humanity. But at the same time Aristotle still held sway in the
universities and provided much of the underlying intellectual scaffolding of the organized Church. In this sense, both Renaissance humanism
and the emerging Scientific Revolution were fertilized by a rich diversity of traditions that were by no means in harmony with one another.[1]
But it was the very tension between traditions that allowed for a great
creativity to emerge.

One of the boldest conjectures of the Renaissance came from the
hand of Nicholas Copernicus (1473–1543), a mathematician and canon
of the Church who suggested that the Earth, rather than resting at the
heart of the universe, orbited around the Sun instead. For the most part
Copernicus's claim was wholly unsupported by observational evidence.[2]
His theory represented a great leap of the imagination, based in part
on the idea of the dignity of the Sun, which according to the ancient
Hermetic writings was a lower image of God and existed in the heart
of the world.[3] Copernicus produced detailed mathematical models to
explain the Sun-centered world system and claimed that they were more
economical and elegant than those of Ptolemy, the ancient Alexandrian

astronomer whose Earth-centered model had held sway for one thousand years. In reality, Copernicus's model used all the same mathematical devices, but merely substituted the Sun for the Earth. Mathematically, it was not any simpler than Ptolemy's model, and pragmatically it gave no better predictions of the planetary positions. Nonetheless, Copernicus's model simultaneously opened a doorway for further study and produced a crack in the medieval worldview. If Copernicus had done little to prove the validity of his theory, he had at least raised an ominous question mark and demonstrated, from a mathematical perspective, that his heliocentric model worked as well as the Ptolemaic system.

The Copernican revolution would take some years to complete, but once his theory had been modified and improved by the likes of Johannes Kepler, the reality of a Sun-centered system became indisputable. When Kepler's theory was able to correctly predict a transit of Mercury across the Sun's disk in 1631, it had to be taken with the utmost seriousness because such a high degree of precision was not possible with any other theory. By 1650, the Copernican revolution was complete, and with it crumbled the geocentric worldview of medieval times based on the authority of the organized Church, which, in turn, had sought support from that infallible authority, Aristotle.

THE ITALIAN REBEL

Science, like religion, has its own saints and miracle stories; and with the exception of Isaac Newton, few figures are endowed with such heroic significance as Galileo (1564–1642), the founder of modern physics. Contrary to popular lore, the story of him dropping weights off the Leaning Tower of Pisa is a fiction, and he did not invent the telescope. Nonetheless, what Galileo accomplished was monumental, even if in a political sense Galileo was his own worst enemy and practically went out of his way to invoke the persecution of the Roman Catholic Church.

The son of a professional musician, Galileo was born in Pisa, February 14, 1564. As a young man he developed a thirst for empirical knowledge and an even larger distrust for authority. He brought his sarcastic wit to bear on the Scholastics, and in his early twenties mocked the followers of Aristotle for lecturing in togas, like little models of their long-deceased hero. He studied medicine, mathematics, and other sciences, inventing experiments and instruments like the thermometer.

Aristotle had held that the heavens are perfect and never change, while all change is confined to the realm below the Moon. The biggest boost to Copernicus's model came not from considerations of accuracy, but from a host of celestial phenomena in the Renaissance that appeared almost like portents to undermine the belief in Aristotle's assumptions. New stars appeared in 1572 and 1604, and observations proved that they lay well beyond the orbit of the Moon. Aristotle had also held that comets are atmospheric phenomena, but when a brilliant comet appeared in 1577, Tycho Brahe proved that it lay at least six times beyond the orbit of the Moon. This placed the comet among the planets. Its unhindered movement through the heavens challenged the common assumption that the planetary bodies orbited around transparent yet solid crystalline spheres.

Equipped with a primitive telescope, Galileo made observations that also undermined Aristotle's theories. Galileo rapturously discovered that the Milky Way, rather than being an atmospheric phenomenon as Aristotle had thought, was composed of countless stars. Turning his telescope to the Moon, Galileo discovered not a body made out of a pure ethereal substance, but a solid world, ravaged by craters and textured with mountains. Further observations showed that Jupiter had four moons, disproving Aristotle's theory that every celestial body revolves around the Earth. While the phases of Venus observed through Galileo's telescope showed it orbited the Sun, these new findings created major difficulties for the old geocentric cosmos, but none of them taken alone or together were sufficient to fully prove the validity of the new Copernican model.

MATTER IN MOTION

While Galileo's astronomical discoveries are well known, more important for our story is his invention of mathematical physics, the assumptions on which it rested, and the human consequences that flowed from it. While the Aristotelians had reasoned about nature from first principles and sometimes reached logical conclusions without tangible evidence, Galileo the experimentalist believed that was the quickest road to error. When it comes to the study of the physical world, he argued that philosophical considerations must be set aside. Experiment, not authority, is the key to understanding. And mathematics alone is capable of revealing the certain truth of nature's regularities. As he wrote in a famous line, "Without mathematics, one wanders in vain through a dark labyrinth."[4]

Galileo put his beliefs to the test in a study of falling bodies. Aristotle had reasoned that a body weighing forty pounds would fall twice as fast as a body weighing twenty pounds. Using a thought experiment, Galileo showed this to be absurd and later demonstrated it experimentally.

More importantly, Galileo conducted controlled, artificial experiments of the acceleration of "falling" bodies using solid brass balls that he rolled down an inclined plane. If the spheres had just been dropped, they would have fallen too quickly to be measured. But by using the inclined plane, Galileo could experimentally slow down the speed of their descent so that it could be carefully timed. If one overlooked the factor of friction (which would be minimal), Galileo believed that the descent of the ball on a plane would correspond with a sphere in free fall, only more slowly.

Using a water clock, he and an assistant began a lengthy series of experiments to test the hypothesis. Not only do all balls regardless of weight descend at the same speed, but they accelerate uniformly to a mathematical pattern. A ball descending the length of the entire plane took exactly twice as long as a ball descending a quarter of the length. In such experiments, Galileo wrote, "Repeated a full hundred times, the spaces were always found to be to one another as the squares of the times."[5] This led Galileo to realize that the speed of an object increased proportionally faster in relation to the distance it fell. This resulted in his law of uniformly accelerated motion. Not only had Galileo proven Aristotle wrong but he had helped to lay the foundation for mathematical physics and modern experimental science.

Perhaps what Galileo could not have foreseen was the effect that his scientific conceptualization of the world structure would have. Either intentionally or unconsciously, Galileo had revived the atomistic idea that the essential nature of the universe consists of matter in motion. In topics of scientific investigation he claimed that the fundamental principles of size, shape, weight, and motion alone are real. These measurable quantities or "primary qualities" have a genuine, objective existence apart from individual observers, while "secondary qualities" such as color, taste, aroma, and sound are merely subjective, because they cannot be measured by mathematics, which is the sole criterion of objective reality. In taking this fateful step, Galileo implied that quantitative mathematics alone provided genuine insight into the objective nature of the world, while our human perceptions of the world are somehow less essential.[6] In so doing, Galileo suggested that the primary nature of the world consists of discrete bits of matter in motion, and the final test of any theory is the quantitative experiment.

For Galileo, physics needed to be separated from philosophy. While earlier philosophers who investigated the world fabric had asked "why?" it was now the job of the physicist to only ask "how?" Yet by taking this decisive step, the new physics planted a seed, and began to suggest that beauty, value, and meaning may not be objectively present in the physical world, but only subjectively present in human observers. In this vision, the world itself, at its most essential level, is disenchanted matter in motion, which can only be modeled and known with certainty through mathematics. If followed to its logical conclusion, our natural, human perceptions of the living universe are misleading. The ultimate reality is matter in motion.

DREAMS OF A UNIVERSAL SCIENCE

What was implicit, lurking in the shadows of Galileo's thinking, became fully realized in the philosophical ideas of René Descartes (1596–1650), who pictured the universe as a giant machine consisting of nonliving matter in motion.

Descartes, like Galileo, was attracted by the power and clarity of mathematics. It was he who invented the famous Cartesian coordinate system, known to every schoolchild, which consists of perpendicular *x* and *y* axes that can be used to plot out the position of any object on a plane. One day Descartes had been lying in bed when he saw a fly crawling around the ceiling. In a creative flash, the coordinate system popped into his mind as a way of plotting out the fly's movement above.

Descartes was a man of leisure, a member of the minor nobility who lived off his wealth. He never held a university position but is considered to be the founder of modern philosophy in the same way that Galileo is the founder of modern physics. A clear prose stylist, he wrote for the common reader and took pride in the thought that his books could be read "just like novels." Like Galileo who wrote in Italian and not Latin to speak directly to laypeople, Descartes' most famous work was written in French. With Galileo and Descartes, both philosophy and science started to come out of the cloistered, medieval world, and began to make a massive impact on the secular world of day-to-day affairs.

Like Galileo, Descartes pictured himself as standing in opposition to the mistaken ideas of earlier thinkers. Descartes believed that human thought had become terribly confused under the spell of Scholasticism. In addition, a spirit of skepticism was sweeping through France. According to the skeptics, truth is relative and absolutely certain knowledge is unattainable. Thanks to the confusion of the Scholastics and the skepticism of his contemporaries, philosophy had reached a state of profound crisis. The only rational solution, Descartes thought, was to make a clean sweep of every philosophical idea that he ever had. Philosophy itself needed to be reborn anew if it was to yield up absolutely certain and unquestionable knowledge.

On November 10, 1619, Descartes had a vision of a universal science of nature in which mathematical reasoning would hold the key. The starting point of this new, world-altering philosophical revelation lay in *doubt*. Descartes realized that he could doubt his perceptions of the world and what his senses were telling him. In fact, he could doubt just about everything. But the one thing that he could not doubt was his own existence. Hence his famous conclusion, *Cogito, ergo sum*—I think, therefore I am.

After establishing the philosopher's own existence, the existence of God naturally followed. The very fact that an imperfect being like Descartes could so powerfully conceive of an infinitely perfect God proved that this perfect idea must have been planted in his mind by nothing less than God himself. This proof was essential for Descartes, for the existence of a perfect God is the only guarantee of reliability in human reason. He realized that humans sometimes do go awry in their reasoning, but only because they accept ideas that are unclear. Should people stick only with absolutely clear and distinct ideas—*clear* and *distinct* being keywords for Descartes—their reasoning will be flawless.

Having established both his own existence and the existence of God, "in whom all the wisdom of the sciences lies hid," Descartes believed that he could establish a truly universal science that would lay claim to "the whole of that corporeal nature which is the subject matter of pure mathematics."[7] In short, Descartes was confident that he could deduce the structure of the entire universe and its laws from the clear and distinct principles of pure mathematics.

While the world of matter and the body is subject to confusion and uncertainty, the purely functioning rational intellect is not. It is, to use the phrase once again, capable of absolutely clear and distinct reasoning based along mathematical lines. This showed for Descartes that the universe itself is composed of two radically distinct substances. The first substance is mind; the second substance is matter. In fact, as philosopher Anthony Kenny quips, "If you wanted to put Descartes' main ideas on the back of a postcard you would need just two sentences: man is a thinking mind; matter is extension in motion."[8] To further clarify, mind for Descartes is an unextended substance that only exists in humans. It does not exist at all in the rest of nature or other creatures. All of nature, all living creatures, and even our own bodies function as mere machines. Nature is made out of dead matter. It possesses no life, intelligence, or spirit of its own, but like a well-crafted clock goes ticking along, following the laws that God laid down at the beginning of the world. Ultimately for Descartes, to be truly human is to be a pure mind that doesn't even exist in the universe.[9]

With Descartes we enter a new era and a new understanding of what it means to be human: a disembodied, rational spectator who contemplates a world that is radically other. As Goethe wrote, commenting on the reaction of his friends when they saw the Cartesian system in print, "It seemed to us so gray, monstrous and death-like that we could hardly stand it; we shuddered as if facing a ghost."[10]

With Descartes the early Christian view of God, spirit, and humanity existing totally outside of nature received its most systematic presentation, but now under the philosophical guise of pure rationality. Yet, as David Abram argues, the new "mechanical philosophy" won the favor of the Church because it continued to keep God and spirit outside of the universe in a clear and distinct way.[11] By contrast, the notion of the World Soul, the workings of the alchemical spirit hidden in matter, and the ideas of the Renaissance magi all pointed toward an animate vision of living nature. These ideas of living nature invested the world with its own creative potential and raised the anxiety-provoking possibility that maybe, in some way, nature could create itself. But in one stroke the mechanical philosophy did away with this disquieting thought and allowed a theological alliance to be established between the organized Church and the emerging Scientific Revolution.

Let there be no doubt about it: Descartes would not tolerate the idea of living nature, cosmic sympathies, or vital resonances between spirit and matter. As he clearly explained, "There exist no occult forces in stones or plants, no amazing and marvelous sympathies and antipathies, in fact there exists nothing in the whole of nature which cannot be explained in terms of purely corporeal causes, totally devoid of mind and thought."[12] And lest there be any confusion about this point, he wrote that by nature "I do not mean some goddess or any other sort of imaginary power. Rather, I am using this word to signify matter itself."[13] Descartes himself was part of a circle of thinkers who wished to discredit the idea of living nature, and in 1623 his friend Marin Mersenne published a massive refutation of Hermetic philosophy and the magical tradition. While the ancient Hermetic writings had claimed that "this great body of the world is a soul, full of intellect and of God, who fills it within and without and vivifies the All,"[14] Descartes would go on to write that "I have described this earth, and indeed this whole visible world, as a machine."[15]

In his time, wealthy individuals filled their gardens with mechanical marvels and automatons similar to the life-sized, animated creatures found today at Disneyworld. For Descartes, human beings are souls with machine-like bodies, which he didn't hesitate to compare with the hydraulic wonders found in the gardens. As he wrote:

> one may very well then liken the nerves of the animal machine I have described to the pipes of the machines of those fountains; its muscles and its tendons to the other different engines and springs that serve to move them; and its animal spirits, of which the heart is the source and the ventricles of the brain the reservoirs, to the water that moves these engines.[16]

The image stuck with Descartes' followers and the other "mechanical philosophers." As Thomas Hobbes wrote, "For what is the heart, but a spring; and the nerves, but so many strings; and the joints, but so many wheels, giving motion to the whole body, such as was intended by the artificer?"[17]

One consequence of the Cartesian view is that since animals are machines lacking a rational, human soul, they cannot in fact feel pain. Because of this, Descartes believed that it is only possible to damage an animal but not to really hurt it. The yelp of a dog is just a mechanical reaction and not a response to felt pain. Because of this, scientific researchers could engage in vivisection and other types of experimentation on animals without feeling any rational pangs of guilt. As Descartes' follower Nicholas Malebranche wrote, nonhuman animals "eat without pleasure, they cry without pain, they grow without knowing it; they desire nothing, they fear nothing, they know nothing" (see figure 7.1 on page 128).[18]

As the father of reductionism, Descartes' analytical method can be summed up by the phrase "divide and conquer." In his *Discourse on Method,* Descartes set forth the analytical technique of scientific reductionism and urged his readers to follow four basic steps:

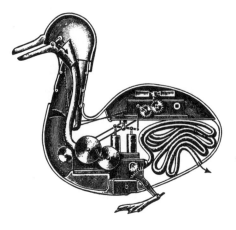

Figure 7.1. An automaton of a duck, inspired by the mechanical philosophy, created by Jacques de Vaucanson in 1783. For Descartes and his followers, animals were only machines that lacked consciousness and the ability to feel pain.

1. To accept as true only that which is so clear and distinct that there is no occasion to doubt it;
2. To divide every problem into as many parts as needed to resolve it;
3. To direct thought in an orderly manner, beginning with the most simply known objects and moving to knowledge of the most complex;
4. To make a so comprehensive review that nothing is left out.[19]

While absolutely invaluable as a scientific technique, reductionism assumes that things are nothing more than the sum of their individual parts. Organisms and living systems, however, operate as whole systems in which the parts represent highly integrated and interrelated functions of the entire system that cannot be "clearly and distinctly" divided from one another. While we can conceptualize the heart as being akin to a machine-pump and the lungs as being akin to mechanical bellows, such crude reductionism overlooks their delicate, intertwined, organic nature, and the fact that lungs and heart are just different faces of one highly integrated, self-regulating organism. But under the spell of reductionism, nature is no longer a living reality—it becomes a mechanized, objectivized, and conceptualized system, mathematically modeled as matter in motion.

Despite these difficulties, Descartes had unbounded faith in the power of his new analytical technique, and it's only natural that such a new approach was to be charged with excitement, attracting the attention of learned minds. But in the same way that the mechanical philosophy had totally eliminated spirit from the world, Descartes' technique promised to remove all wonder and mystery from nature. As he promised the readers of his *Meteorology,* "Those who have understood all that has been said in this treatise will, in future, see nothing . . . whose cause they cannot easily understand, nor anything which gives them any reason to marvel."[20] Descartes was so confident in his method that "given a few more years of life, and sufficient funds for his experiments, he would be able to solve all the outstanding problems of physiology, and learn thereby the cures of all diseases."[21] Under the spell of the new philosophy, the human intellect became deified and infallible. Indeed, in Descartes' own words, the new science promised to render humanity "the lords and masters of nature."[22]

Descartes was certainly an original thinker, but like many great thinkers his philosophical ideas exemplified and brought into focus the spirit of the age in which he was living. With the emergence of the powerful machine metaphor and the techniques of mathematical analysis, the human spirit was becoming more autonomous and self-directed in a rational sense, but was simultaneously distancing itself from the world of living nature.

THE DIVINE CLOCKMAKER

My aim is to show that the celestial machine is to be likened not to a divine organism but to a clockwork.

JOHANNES KEPLER

In a world without gadgets, a clock is a miraculous object. Ticking off the seconds, minutes, and hours all on its own, the clock models the movement of the days and nights, the very rhythms of celestial motion. As science historian Lynn White points out, "Most of the first clocks were less chronometers than exhibitions of the pattern of the cosmos."[23] Without question, the earliest clocks were a reflection of human ingenuity and genius. Moreover, the wonder of a machine that could run on its own possessed an undeniably magical power.

Plato had taught that the regularity of celestial motions is evidence of a divine intelligence, and the first clockmakers must have felt that they were mirroring a similar type of intelligence in their perfectly regular mechanical designs. In the middle of the fourteenth century, the new mechanical clocks captivated the imagination of medieval civilization. As Lynn White notes:

> Something of the civic pride which earlier had expended itself in cathedral-building was diverted to the construction of astronomical clocks of astounding intricacy and elaboration. No European community felt able to hold up its head unless in its midst the planets wheeled in cycles and epicycles, while angels trumpeted, cocks crew, and apostles, kings, and prophets marched and countermarched at the booming of the hours.[24]

Based on the clock analogy, medieval writers began to refer to the universe as the *machina mundi,* the world machine. The fourteenth-century mathematician and Bishop of Lisieux, Nicholas Oresmus, was the first to describe the universe as a giant, mechanical clock, designed and set moving by God so that "all the wheels move as harmoniously as possible."[25] The idea possessed a mythic power and immediately began to capture the imagination. In a medieval illuminated manuscript now in the British Museum, we can see two angels depicted as spinning cranks that move the great wheels of heaven.[26] In 1348, Giovanni de' Dondi created a fabulous device—a cosmic mechanism—that modeled the movements of the Sun, Moon, and five planets. So detailed was this remarkable "timepiece" that it provided for the elliptical orbits of the Moon and Mercury and even accounted for observed irregularities in the motion of Venus.

If the idea of the cosmic clock can be traced back to late medieval times, it is only with the Scientific Revolution and the new mechanical philosophy that the metaphor came to full flower. In the newly emerging worldview, God came to be pictured as a great engineer who designed the universe like a giant timepiece and set it in motion.

Descartes drew on this mechanical image when discussing the nature of the body, pointing out that a perfectly constructed machine would keep running even if there were no mind present in it:

> And as a clock, composed of wheels and counterweights, observes not the less accurately the laws of nature when it is ill made, and points out the hours incorrectly, than when it satisfies the desire of the maker in every respect; so likewise if the body of man be considered as a kind of machine, so made up and composed of bones, nerves, muscles, veins, blood, and skin, that although there were in it no mind, it would still exhibit the same motions which it at present manifests involuntarily.[27]

Similarly, the early scientist Robert Boyle (1627–1691) championed the idea of a mechanical, clockwork universe. The universe functions so perfectly that it appears to be guided by some inner spirit or intelligence, but in reality it is only a clever arrangement of parts. These parts work together and give the impression of continual guidance, when in fact nature itself is dead and unintelligent. It only seems intelligent because, like the workings of a lifeless clock, its parts have been harmoniously designed by an external creator.

This of course points toward a very specific image of God as a thinking, planning, and controlling entity, very much like a Divine Engineer. For Boyle, Descartes, and the other mechanical philosophers, God existed outside of the lifeless universe, but the harmoniously coordinated movements of the cosmic machine revealed the glory of its Creator in the same way that the ticking of a clock revealed the ingenuity of its maker.[28] In this way the new image of God and his perfectly engineered creation aroused human wonder and motivated scientific research. Clearly, the vision of a perfectly designed, mechanistic creation and its omnipotent designer possessed a numinous power for the Enlightenment thinkers, and these highly charged images both mirrored and reinforced humanity's newly emerging self-conception—as a rational, autonomous agent, distinct from the organic world.

⚘

Many of the Greek philosophers, like the Stoics, were *pantheists* who believed that an impersonal, divine power worked from inside the natural world. Others were *panentheists* who envisioned God as existing both inside and outside the world simultaneously. Traditionally most Christians were *theists* who believed in a personal divinity, God the Father, who both created the world and personally intervened in human history. Yet with the emergence of God the Engineer and the clockwork universe, we encounter a new idea of God, that of *deism*. For deists, God is the principle of pure reason, the cosmic lawmaker, who hovers outside the universe. The God of deism designed the cosmic clock, laid down its laws, and set the world machine in motion. Yet after the initial creation, God the engineer pulled back from the universe, which thereafter ran quite adequately on its own accord. In this sense, only God's design was present in nature. The God of deism was a distant, intellectual divinity who had no traffic with the universe. God's intelligence was reflected in the cosmic blueprint, but God itself was emotionally and spiritually distant, accessible only through reason.

The root ideas of God as an architect and divine lawmaker were of course to be found in the Judeo-Christian tradition. But with the new mechanical philosophy, these ideas and a new vision of God came to be amplified. As Descartes wrote to his friend Mersenne in 1630, "God sets up mathematical laws in nature, as a king sets up laws in his kingdom."[29] The idea of "scientific laws" which lie behind the universe is a metaphor indebted to the concepts of Christian theology, but the question remains how nonmaterial laws can effect the movement of bodies in the universe. Regardless of this difficult question, modern physics was born out of a theological tradition, and the Christian idea of God as a lawmaker, external to the universe, may provide the decisive reason why experimental science arose only in Western Europe and no other culture.

Despite the useful benefits that arose from the idea of scientific law, the effect of deism was to reduce God to an exalted image of human reason and to disenchant the living universe, which was increasingly envisioned as devoid of vital, spiritual energy. While the idea of the world machine possessed an exciting, numinous power that was irresistible to the Enlightenment thinkers, in the world of deism we enter an impersonal universe, presided over by an impersonal divinity, and studied by an impersonal intellect—the mechanical philosopher pictured as a detached, theoretical observer. As Theodore Roszak notes, the God of deism was "not experienced, but inferred from the design of nature, a functional postulate in a desacralized universe."[30] For the deists, God existed but did not participate in the universe. Similarly, the emerging rational self existed—"I think, therefore I am"—but did not truly participate in the living energies of the world fabric.

THE PARADOXICAL PROPHET

Nowhere did the ideas of the mechanical philosophy and the deist idea of God the lawmaker find such a powerful synthesis as in the scientific work of Isaac Newton (1642–1727), the inventor of calculus and founder of celestial mechanics.

For Newton, science and religion should not and could not be separated. "The true calling of science," he wrote, "was not to reduce the universe to a machine, but to comprehend the system of causality in such a way that it pointed to the First Cause."[31] Newton's *Principia,* his work on celestial mechanics, was in fact written with the belief that his discoveries proved the existence of God. Nonetheless, Newton never wandered far from the deist conception of God as a divine lawmaker who exists outside of nature. Thus he wrote that God "governs all things, not as the soul of the world, but as Lord over all; and on account of his dominion he is wont to be called Lord God pantocrator, or Universal Ruler."[32] According to Newton, as the supreme architect of the universe, we know God "only by his most wise and excellent contrivances of things."[33] God's intelligence is revealed through the rational design of nature, but not in a more direct or intimate way.

Isaac Newton was a complex personality who worked in many fields. But his most groundbreaking work was on gravity and celestial mechanics. In his *Principia,* Newton set forth three laws of cosmic motion, expressible in mathematical terms, that accurately accounted not only for the motions of the heavily bodies in the solar system, but also for the motion of all projectiles on Earth. In a single stroke Newton destroyed forever the Aristotelian belief that the things of heaven and Earth followed two different sets of laws. Newton did away with Aristotle's cosmic dualism by showing that the universe is one thing—a falling apple and the dance of the planets follow the same laws. As Richard Tarnas points out, "It was Newton's astounding achievement to synthesize Descartes' mechanical philosophy, Kepler's laws of planetary motion, and Galileo's laws of terrestrial motion in one comprehensive theory."[34]

Even more amazing was the fact that Newton's theory allowed for the mathematical prediction of the planetary orbits with astonishing precision. For hundreds of years countless philosophers labored in vain to understand the innermost workings of nature. Now, in what appeared like a divine revelation, Newton had peered into the innermost nature of things with the help of mathematics. Newton wrote, "O God, I think thy thoughts after thee," and his discovery seemed like the ultimate validation of the mechanical philosophy and the power of the human intellect. Voltaire called him the greatest man who ever lived, while Pope wrote that

> *Nature, and Nature's Laws lay hid in Night.*
> *God said,* Let Newton be! *and All was* Light.[35]

Edmund Halley in his "Ode to Newton" exclaimed:

> *Come celebrate with me in song the name*
> *Of Newton, to the Muses dear; for he*
> *Unlocked the hidden treasures of Truth. . . .*
> *Nearer the gods no mortal may approach.*[36]

The mathematician Laplace explained that since the universe only has one set of laws, Newton was the most fortunate man ever, since those laws can only be discovered once. The great statue of Mother Nature at Sais in Egypt bore the inscription, "I am Isis, all that has been, is, or shall be: no mortal man has ever lifted my veil." But in the eyes of many, Newton had finally lifted that veil through the power of mathematical reason. Since Newton seemed to vindicate the mechanical philosophy and the brilliant potential of the human intellect, his discovery was seen as heralding the birth of a new age—the dawning of a rational age of Enlightenment. As Theodore Roszak notes, "In the figure of Newton, the traditional imagery of prophet, poet, sage, oracle, all merge to create a cultural identity of superhuman dimensions" (see figure 7.2 on page 136).[37]

Beneath the surface, however, Newton was not the perfect mechanistic philosopher that he was made out to be. In fact, Newton spent far more time in his alchemical researches than he did studying celestial mechanics. In 1936, when his descendants decided to auction off his manuscripts, the world was astonished to discover that he was obsessed with alchemy, Hermetic philosophy, and related topics. As John Maynard Keynes noted at the time, "Newton was not the first of the age of reason. He was the last of the magicians."[38] In reality, Newton saw himself as a golden link in the Hermetic chain of inspired sages reaching back into antiquity.

Prematurely born on Christmas day in 1642, Newton was not expected to live, and interpreted his survival in terms of divine intervention. According to John Maynard Keynes, Newton saw himself in messianic terms as the divinely chosen inheritor of the Hermetic tradition, a fact amplified by the circumstances of his birth. Yet Newton was a paradoxical prophet and truly a man divided. Not only was his image "cleaned up" after his death, but during his own lifetime he felt compelled to keep the Hermetic side of his personality concealed.[39] On many occasions Newton would make a statement like "we cannot say that all Nature is not alive," only to remove it from a manuscript before publication.[40] In unpublished writings we find Newton making assertions like "all matter duly formed is attended with signs of life"; "nature delights in transformations"; the world is "God's sensorium"; and so on.[41]

If Newton's Hermetic side embraced a vision of living nature, why did he censor it in his writings? A convincing answer is given by historian David Kubrin, who points out that Newton's time was a period of intense social uprisings and revolts against authority among the lower classes. Dozens of mystical sects embraced ideas of utopian socialism

*Figure 7.2. The apotheosis of Newton. This engraving from 1732 shows
Isaac Newton elevated to the heavenly realm.*

and set themselves against the crown. One thing that these numerous "enthusiastic" groups had in common was a belief that matter was animated and that God was present in everything. Any individual, they believed, could have a direct experience of God (thereby dispensing with organized religion), and many of these groups were influenced by Hermetic and alchemical ideas. Many of these radical groups embraced the idea of living nature, and for Isaac Newton—at various times a member of the Royal Society, Parliament, and master of the Mint—to publish similar ideas would have been very dangerous indeed. In the words of Kubrin, "Newton realized the dangerous social, political, economic, and religious implications that would be associated with him should he dare reveal his true thoughts."[42]

As things stood, Newton was having enough difficulty with gravity, which seemed to many like a magical power that acted at a distance. Newton's rival Leibniz described it as "occult," while Huygens called it "absurd." Newton himself had no good explanation for gravity, except for the fact that it worked. He called it "a great absurdity"[43] and honestly confessed "the Cause of Gravity is what I do not pretend to know."[44] Since he had not been able to discover the cause of gravity, Newton simply wrote *Hypotheses no fingo*—"I frame no hypotheses."[45] Thus when Leibniz criticized him for offering no explanation of gravity, Newton replied, "To us it is enough that gravity does really exist, and act according to the laws which we have explained, and abundantly serves to account for all the motions of the celestial bodies, and of our sea."[46] In its own way, gravity could be seen as a hidden or occult property of matter that undercut a strictly mechanistic worldview. It suggested that matter is not entirely passive but somehow active. According to Newton's findings, every body in the universe is simultaneously acting on every other body through a mysterious, unseen force of attraction. For Newton to have gone further and publish his thought that all matter is alive would have suggestively identified him with the radical sects and given his critics a field day.

While gravity may have seemed like an occult force it also raised other difficulties. Assuming that all the planets were influencing each other through the force of gravity as they orbited the Sun, the actual state of the solar system was highly complex and its stability as a clockwork mechanism could not be guaranteed. This forced Newton to reluctantly raise the possibility that God might have to intervene periodically and tune up the clockwork mechanism should it ever get out of alignment. This idea ran against the ideas of both the deists and the mechanists, and caused Leibniz to further ridicule Newton, saying that his God was an incompetent clockmaker. For if God was all powerful, he could certainly build a timepiece that didn't need periodic cleaning and repair.[47]

Due to the stunning success of his theory, however, these difficulties were overlooked and Newton became an international hero. Newtonianism came to be seen as the ultimate triumph of mechanistic philosophy and deism, and Newton viewed his own discoveries as proving the existence of God. In the famous conclusion of his *Principia,* he wrote that "this most beautiful system of the sun, planets, and comets, could only proceed from the counsel and dominion of an intelligent and powerful Being."[48] Yet the mechanistic universe carried with it disturbing implications that Newton himself could not foresee. For if God was a cosmic lawmaker who laid down the inexorable rules of the world machine, what room did that leave for human free will? If every cosmic motion was preordained from the very beginning, how was genuine freedom possible at all? The Newtonian universe was supremely deterministic and caused Voltaire to remark that "it would be very singular that all nature, all the planets, should obey eternal laws, and there should be a little animal, five feet high, who, in contempt of those laws, could act as he pleased."[49]

8

In the Name of Utility

*The Exploitation of Nature and the
Decline of Pleasure*

THE NEW EXPERIMENT:
PUTTING NATURE ON THE RACK

Oh, what world of profit and delight
Of power, of honour, of omnipotence
Is promised to the studious artizan!
All things that move between the quiet poles
Shall be at my command.
        CHRISTOPHER MARLOWE, *THE TRAGICAL*
                HISTORY OF DOCTOR FAUSTUS

I am come in very truth leading to you Nature with all her
children to bind her to your service and make her your slave.
        FRANCIS BACON, *THE MASCULINE BIRTH OF TIME*

The ancient Greeks and medieval people studied nature for enjoyment.
Through the contemplation of nature and the world order, the human
mind expanded. By understanding the universe, humanity achieved

fulfillment of its inner nature and experienced a self-transformation. By understanding the divine order of the universe, humanity experienced a sense of self-completion and identity with the underlying rationality of the cosmic pattern.

While the Greeks wanted to know *why* things worked in a certain way, with the birth of the new scientific mentality that question began to focus on *how*. Galileo, for example, dispensed with all questions of meaning in his investigation of physical principles. At this turning point in human thought, the world started to be seen as a collection of material objects whose interactions could be modeled mathematically.

No one was more harshly critical of the contemplative approach to nature than Francis Bacon (1561–1626), Lord Chancellor of England. If Galileo switched the question from "why" to "how," Francis Bacon went further and maintained that even asking "how" is irrelevant. For Bacon the end of all scientific knowledge was use or utility, and the measure of knowledge was power. Through scientific knowledge, humanity could learn to control nature. For Bacon, the measure of scientific knowledge was its usefulness to the human race in exerting control over the world—the greater the power of control, the greater the measure of knowledge.[1]

Like Descartes, Bacon saw himself as a scientific and philosophical reformer. While Descartes had called for a clean sweep of all previously confused thinking, Bacon called for a "great Renovation of knowledge."[2] Bacon contrasted the "Moderns" with the "Ancients" and looked forward to the future of scientific progress. Bacon became the prophetic voice of scientific and technological progress, a type of progress defined by the control and exploitation of nature as a means to meet human ends. The key to the subjugation of nature lay in the practice of experimentation, the development of technology or the "mechanical arts," and the development of scientific research as a collaborative effort in which human knowledge would become incrementally progressive.

Bacon complained that when "contemplation" and the "doctrinal science" of the Aristotelians began, "the discovery of useful works ceased."[3] Among the writings of the ancients, he wrote, "There is hardly one single experiment that has a tendency to assist mankind."[4] By contrast, nothing in human history has "changed the appearance and state of the whole world"[5] more than the printing press, gunpowder, and the magnetic compass. The key to transforming the world for human benefit lay in a similar application of mechanical technology.

Technology has always possessed a magical, awe-inspiring dimension. In the words of the artist Cecil Collins, "Science and logic are only another form of magic."[6] In hidden or mysterious ways, science taps into unseen power. In legend and myth, wizards use magic mirrors to see or communicate over vast distances. Today we need only pick up a telephone. As Arthur C. Clarke once noted, the technology of a superior civilization would appear to us as magic.

While the Renaissance magicians and alchemists sought to collaborate with the powers of nature in a way that would therapeutically care for both the magus and the world, less scrupulous individuals have always been attracted to the Hermetic arts in the hope that they might lead to the accumulation of personal power and material wealth. In this sense, "natural magic" has often been confused with sorcery, the depraved quest for unlimited power over nature and other people. As Nietzsche once wrote, "Do you believe then that the sciences would ever have arisen and become great if there had not beforehand been magicians, alchemists, astrologers, and wizards, who thirsted and hungered after abscondite and forbidden powers?"[7]

Bacon himself, like the other founders of the Scientific Revolution, was deeply influenced by the magical ideas of "operating on nature" and exerting human power on the world.[8] When seen from a mythological or symbolic perspective, magic and science are closely conjoined. Like the sorcerer drawing a magic circle to ritually purify a space and keep negative influences at bay, the scientist seeks to ritually separate the artificial process of experimentation from outside forces that might contaminate his results. Like the shaman travelling in trance to interrogate spiritual intelligences in the Otherworld, the modern scientist would exert tremendous powers of concentration, mentally traveling into a disembodied, theoretical realm, in which he would discover the hidden secrets of nature. The intricate, geometrical seals of the magician, inscribed with mystic words of power, bear an uncanny resemblance to the mathematical equations of the modern physicist. As Mary Shelley implied in her novel *Frankenstein,* there is a very thin dividing line between the magical power of the necromancer and the modern scientist (or medical doctor) who brings the dead back to life.

While picturing his grand project in the benign light of human progress, for Francis Bacon, careful experimentation, and the technology it gave birth to, would become the sorcerer's apprentice that would ultimately grant humanity power and dominion over nature. Bacon vehemently condemned those false natural magicians who attempted to influence nature through the power of the imagination.[9] He defined magic as that "science which applied the knowledge of hidden forms to the production of wonderful operations."[10] In this way Bacon saw his own experimental philosophy as a reformation of the corrupt magical tradition. Under the spell of the new scientific method, Bacon maintained that "magic," which "has long been used in a bad sense, will again be restored to its ancient and honorable meaning."[11] For Bacon, nature was not to be influenced by imagination and idle fantasy, but was to be forcefully molded by scientific reason and applied technology, which promised to "increase and multiply the revenues and possessions of man."[12]

Like Descartes' search for a universal science, Bacon spoke of a *novum organum,* a "new instrument" of human inquiry that would satisfy humanity's imperial ambitions over the natural world. This new method, he wrote, would apply "not only to natural but to all sciences" and would "embrace everything."[13] The new method of inquiry would allow for universal, objectivized knowledge. It was like an instrument, "a new machine for the mind,"[14] that would infallibly guide humanity to understand the world as it really was. In this process of coming to know reality, Bacon assured us that the mind would not be "left to take its own course, but be guided at every step and the business be done as if by machinery."[15] In this way, humanity would gain infallible knowledge and total mastery over nature.

The key to Bacon's domination of nature lay in the experimental method, and the dividing line between experimentation and domination was never distinct. The only reason for experimentation in the first place was to gain power over the world. As Carolyn Merchant points out, Bacon's guiding image of nature was that of a female waiting to be dominated and violated, and he vowed to his readers that the new philosophy would render nature the very "slave of mankind."[16]

Bacon wrote that "nature exhibits herself more clearly under the trials and vexations of art than when left to herself."[17] In other words, the sure road to understanding was through mechanical experimentation. For Bacon, experimentation was "an inquisition,"[18] in which nature was compelled to offer up her hidden secrets. As part of his professional duties, Bacon was a legal inquisitor involved in the contemporary witch trials, which deeply influenced his language and imagery concerning the domination of nature.[19] During these trials, confessions were tortured out of innocent women laid out on the rack. In similar fashion, Bacon insisted that the mechanical experiments of the new philosophy must approach nature "under constraint and vexed; that is to say, when by art and the hand of man she is forced out of her natural state, and squeezed and moulded."[20] Through experimentation, he believed it would be possible to trick nature into confessing things that she might not under less strenuous testing. But once her secret was out, she could be forced to reveal it again and again. Thus Bacon explained that the scientific researcher needed to "follow and as it were hound nature in her wanderings, and you will be able, when you like, to lead and drive her afterwards to the same place again."[21] Through such experimentation, mankind would be able "to penetrate further," pass beyond "the outer courts of nature," and "find a way at length into her inner chambers."[22]

Since the measure of knowledge was power, the new philosophy aimed at useful discoveries. In this way, Bacon wrote, the mechanical arts do not "merely exert a gentle guidance over nature's course; they have the power to conquer and subdue her, to shake her to her foundations."[23] Since "the dominion of man over nature rests only on knowledge,"[24] the key to man's mastery over the world lay in organized scientific research. In this way, the findings of many researchers would be conjoined in one common enterprise and knowledge would grow incrementally. Bacon called for a united effort, exhorting all men to make peace among themselves so that they may turn "with united forces against the Nature of Things, to storm and occupy her castles and strongholds, and extend the boundaries of human empire, as far as God Almighty in his goodness may permit."[25] The new philosophy would allow the human race to "recover that right over nature which belongs to it by divine bequest"[26] and establish the "Dominion of Man over the Universe."[27] In short, Bacon promised that his new method would lead to genuine progress in every field, usher in the "truly masculine birth of time,"[28] and render nature the "slave of mankind."

IN PRAISE OF UTILITY

> *Utilitarian philosophy is built upon a faith that human beings are perfectible and that they will grow in goodness as they are released from bondage to nature by an increasingly efficient technology. . . . As machines become more mechanically efficient, humans should grow more ethically efficient, gaining in wisdom, judgment, and compassion according to the degree of their relief from drudgery of fear.*
>
> JOSEPH MEEKER, *THE COMEDY OF SURVIVAL*

With the death of living nature the world became radically Other. Descartes envisioned the world as a lifeless machine, grinding on according to eternal laws, which humanity gazed upon from afar as a distant spectator. For Francis Bacon, humanity also stood apart from the world, but the "mechanical arts" provided a way of exploiting nature for human benefit. In the emerging vision, nature possessed no intrinsic value of its own, but was increasingly seen as a "natural resource"—something to be used, "bound into service," "moulded," and put "in constraint" for human consumption. Untouched nature came to be seen as possessing no essential value of its own, but only a means to human welfare. As the Enlightenment philosopher John Locke wrote, "Land that is left wholly to Nature . . . is called as is indeed it is, *waste;* and we shall find the benefit of it amount to little more than nothing."[29]

In Locke's political philosophy, nature only furnished worthless materials that were shaped by humans into things of value. The accumulation of human power was synonymous with the greatest well-being, and such happiness resulted from transforming natural materials into something useful. As Leo Strauss points out, for Locke "the negation of nature is the way toward happiness."[30] With the birth of the mechanical philosophy, the Scientific Revolution, and the Enlightenment philosophers, a new vision of human identity was emerging in which human society was clearly differentiated from nature. While the contemplative tradition of the Greeks had stressed the perfection of humanity through self-transformation, the emerging mechanical philosophy claimed that mankind was perfected through the utilitarian and manipulative exploitation of nature. With the rise of factories in the Industrial Revolution, workers too came to be pictured as "natural resources" and replaceable cogs in systems of economic production and control, a fact humorously highlighted in Charlie Chaplin's film *Modern Times.*

As human society and nature came to be increasingly seen as comprising two separate worlds, the idea that the potential *use* of something determines its essential value began to subtly infiltrate every sphere of human thought—not just in economic matters but even in the ethical philosophy known as utilitarianism. Utilitarians believed that people are hedonistic, seeking pleasure and avoiding pain. Since pleasure set the standard, it was believed that moral decisions should choose that outcome which results in the greatest pleasure for all involved, and the least amount of pain. In this sense utilitarianism involved taking stock of the potential outcomes of any situation, tallying up the pleasure quotient of each, and voting for the outcome with the highest score. In essence utilitarianism was straightforward, pragmatic, and mathematical; it translated ethical decisions into something like an accounting problem.

The British philosopher Jeremy Bentham (1748–1832) was the first to set forth a systematic theory of utilitarianism in his *Introduction to the Principles of Morals and Legislation.* At the beginning of his work,

Bentham declared, "Nature has placed mankind under the governance of two sovereign masters, *pain* and *pleasure*."[31] He went on to explain that "the principle of utility" recognized this fundamental reality and sought to increase human happiness through the joint assistance of reason and law. In short, he believed reason and law should work together to maximize human pleasure and minimize human pain.

But things became problematic when Bentham explained that pleasure and happiness were synonymous with "profit" and "convenience." In the same way that the mechanistic worldview stripped life away from nature, the utilitarian outlook stripped intrinsic value away from the world. By analyzing the potential outcome of any situation or object, things were not important *in themselves,* but only to that which they might lead. As Walter Kerr points out in his charming book *The Decline of Pleasure,* under the spell of utilitarianism *life and leisure are not treasured in themselves, but become accounting or engineering projects geared to yield up the most profitable outcome.* Things are not valued in themselves, but for the result they might bring in the long run—or in the market.

What was implicit in the utilitarian outlook from the start was concretely spelled out later by the British economist, logician, and philosopher William Stanley Jevons (1835–1882), who applied Bentham's ideas to economic theory. Jevons sought to transform economics into a precise, Newtonian science, which led him to a startling conclusion. Writing in his *Theory of Political Economy,* Jevons noted that

> repeated reflection and inquiry have led me to the somewhat novel opinion, that *value depends entirely upon utility.*[32]

While philosopher John Stuart Mill had tried to salvage the idea that things such as art and mental pleasures have some value in themselves, Jeremy Bentham, the founder of utilitarianism, taught that the value of anything depended on the tangible consequences that *followed* from it. As he concluded, utility depends on incidental profit, and as for acts that "rest purely in the understanding, we have not here any concern."[33] From this perspective, a painting or beautiful sculpture possesses no real utility unless it can be sold or used to benefit the owner in some other concrete way.

Picking up on this thread, Jevons maintained that *nothing has intrinsic value in itself;* all value exists outside of things, depending on how they can be used. As he wrote, "A student of Economics has no hope of ever being clear and correct in his ideas of the science if he thinks of value as . . . anything which lies in a thing or object."[34] Jevons maintained that people who talk of intrinsic value speak of a "nonentity," and that utility or use—the true value of something—is that "abstract quality whereby an object serves our purposes, and becomes entitled to rank as a commodity."[35]

As humanity began to see itself as increasingly distinct from nature, the utilitarian imagination began to take hold—and the imagination is a subtle power that can shape the outlook of an individual or entire culture without even being consciously noticed. While most people had never read the utilitarian philosophers, their writings reflected and influenced the spirit of the age. Utilitarian ideas were unconsciously absorbed and began to shape humanity's vision of, and relationship to, the world. Unconsciously, subtly, and pervasively, utilitarianism shaped the trajectory of the modern world. With the eclipse of the idea of the World Soul and the perception of the living universe, the idea that human fulfillment depended on participation in nature's own creative process also went into hibernation. For many, life became less pleasurable and more goal-oriented. Under the spell of utilitarianism, life became a system of mathematical calculations that always sought the best "bottom line." With the new vision of the mechanistic universe, the reduction of nature to a "natural resource," and the emergence of the idea that "value depends entirely upon use," the stage was set for the emergence of the modern world.

THE MYTHOLOGY OF PROGRESS AND
THE DENIAL OF PLEASURE

A purely utilitarian attitude sucks the immediacy and fullness out of life in favor of a conceptual order. And in this conceptual order, everything is analyzed in terms of how it will serve some future interest. Nothing can be enjoyed *in itself,* but only as part of a progressive, ongoing project. Utilitarianism, while ironically defining the highest good as "pleasure," actually reduces everything to an object of use. Rather than encouraging us to take true enjoyment and pleasure in the present moment, it puritanically denies gratification in the name of some future state.

In essence, utilitarianism sacrifices leisure to work. Free time should not be enjoyed for its own sake, but should always lead to a future outcome that can be evaluated and measured. Every dimension of life becomes a "bottom line" situation that is all work and no play. Without the unquestioned attitude of utilitarianism, the mythology of progress never could have taken over the modern world with such fury and "shaken it to its very foundations" (to borrow a phrase of Bacon's). For in the modern, secular world, what we have is never enough. The future beckons. Everything becomes an investment, an opportunity, a leverage point for some future "utopian" state we are promised but which can never ultimately be situated in the world.

Bacon's technological manipulation of nature and utilitarianism went together hand in hand, for they were two faces of the same enterprise. Bacon's "experimentation," rather than being an attempt to understand the deep structure of the world, was a euphemism, in some ways, for what would later be called *manufacturing.* From these underlying premises emerged the commodification of nature, the Industrial Revolution, and the modern consumer society.

Since nature cannot be deeply, sensuously, and passionately enjoyed for what it is, nature must be forcefully dominated and transformed into something else. Because we cannot live in the present, life becomes an ongoing "project"—yet in the endless cycle of denial we are never satisfied. We become numb to the luminous beauty and living depths of the world, which fails to even register as a phosphorescent blip on our computer screens. Nature itself has become dead, disenchanted, and remote—a world machine that possesses less vitality than our cars, appliances, or smart phones. The depressing sense of loneliness and isolation that results from this is all too real, but also too disturbing to face. It is denied and crowded out with ever new goals, projects, and an incessant, manic flurry of busyness.

THE EXCESS COG

While initially sanctioned by Christian theology, the mechanical philosophy began to eat away at the very foundations of Christian belief. Its rigid determinism of eternal law and fixed, mechanistic structure seemed to undermine the possibility of true human freedom. While Newton believed that God had set the planets in motion at the beginning of time, his brilliant follower Pierre-Simon Laplace (1749–1827) proposed an alternate theory, suggesting that the solar system created *itself* by condensing out of a great cloud of gas and dust.

For many religious individuals the mechanical philosophy pointed toward the existence of an intelligent designer. But for others, the fixed and immutable determinism of cosmic law opened up the possibility that the laws of nature had always existed—and thus didn't depend on the wisdom or activity of an initial creator. For these newly emerging secular thinkers, God became an excess cog in the world machine—a cosmic machine that could potentially run itself if the excess cog was eliminated. Thus when Napoleon interviewed Laplace and asked him what role God played in his system of celestial mechanics, Laplace responded, "I have no need of that hypothesis."[36] For not only had the mechanistic philosophy removed life, spirit, enjoyment, and value from nature, it ultimately removed the necessity of a God as well.

PART III

ANIMA MUNDI

Rediscovering the Living Universe

While intelligence treats everything mechanically, instinct proceeds, so to speak, organically. If . . . we would ask and it could reply, it would give up to us the most intimate secrets of life.

HENRI BERGSON

9

Psyche Regained

SILVER VOICES FROM THE DEPTHS

Melody, rhythm, and harmony are the elements of music and also the elements of life. Music is the primordial art, embroidered in the fabric of the world. We respond to music immediately because our own natures are woven from it. As William Blake said, science can describe "discord and harmony" because they are mathematically expressible, but when it comes to melody science has reached a boundary point beyond which it cannot pass. Melody is experiential and pregnant with meaning. It engages us and beguiles the imagination, which resounds with the universe as "a harp struck by a hand divine."[1] As a musicologist friend points out, harmony and the other fundamentals of music can be taught, but melody cannot. It is a gift of inspiration bestowed by the Muses.

I have been writing music since my early twenties, but it's something I have little control over. Sometimes while sitting at the piano, at different times, seasons, and turning points, compositions will announce themselves with a mood. At those moments one must be receptive to the spirit of inspiration and follow it. Through no design of my own I get drawn into a process that is larger than my rational awareness. As the process unfolds, I apply my technical skills and powers of analysis to shape what is emerging, but in the dance of creation, the source of the music lies beyond the scope of my rational intellect. The music unfolds from a deeper part of my own being but rarely ever does it result from a conscious decision. In technical terms we could say that the music comes from the unconscious, but that explains very little. On closer examination, it becomes evident that most of our thoughts, dreams, and inspirations arise from an unknown background source. They are not "willed into being" by the conscious "I," but reflect the silver voices of our inner depths. True creativity can be invoked, courted, and fertilized, but can never be rigidly or infallibly controlled. Creativity, in short, is not an engineering project.

THE UNKNOWN COUNTRY: THE UNCONSCIOUS BEFORE FREUD

The unconscious is really the largest realm in our minds, and just on account of this the inner Africa, whose unknown boundaries may extend far away.

JEAN PAUL F. RICHTER (1763–1825)

When most people think of the term *unconscious* it's only natural that Sigmund Freud (1856–1939) should pop into mind. No one did more to give the idea cultural currency than Freud, and certainly no one did more to popularize a certain vision of the unconscious mind. But despite Freud's involvement, as Lancelot Law Whyte points out in *The Unconscious before Freud,* the idea of the unconscious started to become widely discussed in Europe two hundred years before Freud published his first psychological study.[2] And it is an idea with even deeper roots. As Plotinus pointed out in the third century A.D., the absence of a conscious perception is no proof of the absence of mental activity.[3] Self-conscious reflection is no proof of intelligent activity, which constantly goes on below the surface of conscious awareness. One example is the body's regulation of the heartbeat, metabolism, and every other physiological function. All of these organic processes require an immense amount of intelligent coordination, but happily for us there isn't a little engineer in the brain who is verbally ordering all the shots. If there were, it would drive us insane.

By identifying the mind with the ego and pure mental awareness, it was Descartes who set the discovery of the unconscious in motion. Descartes had claimed that pure mental awareness is clearly and distinctly separate from the animal, machine-like body. For Descartes and many others in the decades that followed, true human nature was identified with the mythic image of a rational, calculating divine engineer, who related to the world with the crispness of mathematical reason. In such a vision, feelings or emotions had no real dignity or cognitive status of their own. Because of this, feelings were reduced to the grit in the wheels of the cognitive machinery. They tended to disrupt the smoothly functioning mental apparatus and contributed little to the project of gaining control over the natural world.

Like other modern philosophers, Descartes was seized by a vision in which a *part* of human nature is mistakenly taken to represent and explain the *whole* of human nature. But whenever this happens, a model of human nature is presented that does violence to our actual experience of the self and the world.[4] As in the case of Descartes, there may be times when our attention is narrowly focused on a technical problem and our analytical reason becomes wholly engaged. Our attention on the body fades away as we clearly analyze premises, inferences, and possible outcomes. But *all* of human experience is not like this. Sometimes the ego or the divine engineer is not as focused. In a state of reverie, moods, feelings, and sensations fill awareness. Useful new insights spontaneously percolate up from the depths on their own, without having to be manhandled or forcefully engineered. The silver voices of creativity speak and unfold. Dreams arise from an unknown source. Descartes' model of human nature left no room for an unconscious, but ironically his entire philosophical project was inspired by a revelatory dream.

By presenting such a one-sided, reduced vision of human nature, the narrowness of Descartes' own model inspired European thinkers to take a closer look at human experience. What they found in the world of actual experience was not a psyche as rigidly structured as Descartes had defined it, but something deeper, more fluid, and more mysterious. For when we reflect on our inspirations, creative process, or the source of our living ideas, it becomes obvious that they are not willed into being. They emerge from another source and are further refined with the spotlight of conscious awareness.

Descartes' acquaintance Blaise Pascal (1623–1662) was also a brilliant mathematician drawn to the crispness of mathematical reasoning. But he was also a man of deep feeling who wrote that "the heart has its own reasons, which reason knows not."[5] Pascal could not bring himself to accept Descartes' starkly dualistic philosophy that reduced human nature to a calculating intellect and left the rest of nature dead and unensouled. Pascal pointed out that there are some people who can only judge by the heart and are unaccustomed to the principles of reason, because they want to understand everything at a glance. But those who are accustomed to reason from principles "do not at all understand the things of the heart, seeking principles and not being able to see at a glance."[6] Pascal was a man of intellect and feeling who could integrate both ways of knowing, but he ultimately deemed the way of the heart to be more profound than the ability to reason mathematically.

After Descartes, the discovery of the unconscious was set in full force. While John Locke had claimed that it is impossible to perceive something without awareness, others disagreed. John Norris (1632–1704), a British philosopher, wrote that "we may have ideas of which we are not conscious" and "there are infinitely more ideas impressed on our minds than we can possibly attend to or perceive."[7] Leibniz (1646–1716) observed that "our clear concepts are like islands which arise above the ocean of obscure ones."[8]

C. G. Lichtenberg (1742–1799), a German mathematician and physicist, was fascinated by the contribution of dreams to self-knowledge and scientific discovery. "I know from experience," he wrote, "that dreams lead to self-knowledge." Lichtenberg saw that his dreams "developed all kinds of ideas that were sleeping in my soul," and concluded that "dreams can serve to represent the spontaneous expression of our entire nature, without the strain of the most elaborate consideration."[9]

Jean Paul F. Richter (1763–1825), a German novelist, wrote that "the unconscious is really the largest realm in our minds," comparing it to the vast, unknown continent of Africa. Moreover, "the most powerful thing in the poet, which blows the good and the evil spirit into his works, is precisely the unconscious."[10] K. F. Burdach (1776–1847), a German professor of medicine, spoke of the "unconscious formative life," a plastic power of nature that shapes all things. He later concluded that "the principle of life and of the mind are not different in essence, but only in their form of expression and stage of development."[11] Ten years before Freud was born, C. G. Carus (1789–1869), a physician, biologist, and philosopher, introduced his work *Psyche* with the declaration that "the key to the understanding of the character of the conscious life lies in the region of the unconscious."[12]

Friedrich Nietzsche (1844–1890) synthesized the ideas of many earlier thinkers regarding the unconscious, and spoke of "the absurd overvaluation of consciousness." For Nietzsche "the great basic activity is unconsciousness" and "every extension of knowledge arises from making the unconscious conscious."[13] While idea of the unconscious was commonly discussed in England and Germany in the late 1800s, Freud had little awareness of the dozens of earlier thinkers who had explored the idea. Freud nonetheless was influenced by Nietzsche and at the suggestion of physician George Groddeck borrowed Nietzsche's term *Id* to denote the impersonal parts of the psyche that are subject to natural law. Freud also borrowed philosopher and scientist Gustav Fechner's analogy that likened the mind to an iceberg: only a small tip points above the surface of the water, while the vast percentage of its structure lies hidden beneath the surface in the unknown depths.

NATURE'S IMAGINATION

Previous to Freud the great explorers and theorists of the unconscious were the Romantic philosophers and poets. The Romantics rebelled against the suffocating reductionism of the mechanical philosophy which taught that the universe was dead and that essential human nature was nothing more than a disembodied intellect. For the Romantics, humanity existed in nature, but *nature also existed in humanity*. The locus and meeting point of human nature and universal nature was the unconscious. While the unconscious itself cannot be visualized, its energies and creative powers can be directly experienced. Through the faculty of the imagination, humanity taps into the creative, form-giving power that shapes the universe and all living phenomena. Nature itself is a dynamic unfolding power, yet it is also a power manifest in the human psyche. Deep within our being, our innermost nature is nature itself. According to the Romantics, the unconscious is the point of contact that links the individual with the creative forces of the universe.

Not only did the Romantic view stand in sharp opposition to Descartes, it also opposed the fundamental dualism of Immanuel Kant (1724–1804), the greatest of the modern philosophers. While Descartes' dualism separated humanity from the world by saying that mind and matter were inherently different realities that could never meet, Kant's dualism embodied a form of intellectual skepticism in which the rational mind could never know the true nature of reality. According to Kant, the world is never given to human perception as it *really is* because the human mind always shapes reality according to preexisting or *a priori* categories of thought. For Kant, there was a clear and sharp distinction between the phenomenal world that we experience and the noumenal world as it really is, which forever lies beyond our grasp. If the Copernican revolution had removed humanity from the center of the universe, Kant's philosophy implied an even greater alienation by suggesting that we cannot even rationally know the true nature of reality.

Yet perhaps in all of this the trouble is with the limited nature of *rationality*. Plato saw reason as a useful tool, but two thousand years before Kant had pointed out its limitations as a way of knowing. Reason holds the world at an arm's length and something higher or deeper is needed to contact and nonverbally experience the world in profundity. While Descartes had stressed the sharp difference between inner and outer worlds and Kant had stressed the unknowability of the world "in itself" apart from the imposed constructions of the mind, the Romantics stressed the congruence of inner and outer reality. Rebuffing the Kantian-like idea of alienation, William Wordsworth proclaimed his "high argument":

> *How exquisitely the individual Mind*
> *. . . to the external World*
> *Is fitted:—and how exquisitely, too—*
> *Theme this but little heard of among men—*
> *The external World is fitted to the Mind . . .*[14]

For the Romantics, we can know and experience the world in deeply intimate ways because "inner" and "outer" are just different aspects of one creative activity. The Romantics revived the idea of the World Soul and the living universe, but enriched it with the new idea that creative imagination is a cosmic power present in both nature and humanity—an understanding foreshadowed by the Hermetic tradition.

For the poet, philosopher, and scientist Johann Wolfgang von Goethe (1749–1832), humanity was not alienated from nature, but an organ of nature's own self-revelation. While Kant had limited knowledge to the faculties of reason, understanding, and sensibility, for Goethe the imagination embodied another way of knowing that allowed humanity to gaze into nature's deepest heart. The poetic imagination is a creative force; the Greek word *poiēsis* itself means "to make." The creative force present in nature is also embodied in the human imagination, for the primary process of nature is a giving birth to form. Goethe described imagination as "pure nature." In the human psyche it operates on its own and has an autonomous existence apart from the ego. As Goethe wrote, it is a gift of nature that operates "involuntarily, even against my will."[15] Ultimately, the imagination is the seat of all psychic activity, whether loving, willing, or thinking. Because the world itself is infinitely deep or multifaceted, we can never sum up reality in a simple formula that corresponds to the world in a one-to-one way, but through the power of imagination we can touch the deepest nature of reality which is itself revealed in our own natures.

Like Goethe, the British poet William Blake (1757–1827) rebelled against the mechanization of the world and the reduction of the mind to the status of a Newtonian engineer. In one of his paintings Blake depicted Newton crouched over geometrical diagrams with a compass, focusing his mind on mathematical abstractions, while the world around grows distant and opaque. Blake wrote of "Satan's Mathematic Holiness"[16] and the deadly, detached purity of the scientific intellect, which robs life from everything it touches:

> *An Abstract objecting power that Negatives every thing.*
> *This is the Spectre of Man, the Holy Reasoning Power,*
> *And in its Holiness is closed the Abomination of*
> *Desolation.*[17]

But if the mechanical philosophy rendered both the universe and humanity one-dimensional, Blake himself spoke of a "fourfold vision" that engaged all aspects of human nature, contrasting it with the "Single vision and Newton's sleep."[18]

The mechanistic worldview had rendered all nature increasingly material and opaque, while the British philosopher John Locke had reduced the human soul to a *tabula rasa:* a blank slate or a passive mirror of mechanical nature, which has no inner life of its own but only receives outside impressions through the senses. For Blake, in contrast, the soul was an active reality, a tablet always writing itself. Nature was not dead and mechanical, but an unfolding creative activity, and the strength of our seeing lay within us. As Blake wrote, "To the Eyes of the Man of Imagination, Nature is Imagination itself. As a man is, So he Sees. As the Eye is formed, such are its Powers . . . To Me This World is all One continued Vision of Fancy or Imagination."[19]

For Wordsworth (1770–1850), the utilitarian spirit that arose from the mechanical philosophy weighs down the soul. "Under a growing weight of vulgar sense," he wrote, we

> *substitute a universe of death*
> *For that which moves with light and life informed,*
> *Actual, divine, and true.*[20]

Science "murders to dissect," as he put it, but in so doing replaces the deeply sensuous nature of life with an abstract conceptual model. Yet in reality, humanity does not stand apart from the world. In each part of nature is an active principle, a spirit active everywhere. The life of the human soul is an extension of the life of the universe, so there is no alienation between humanity and the essential ground of nature, even if this living bond has been ignored by the mechanical philosophers:

> *In all things, in all natures . . .*
> *Spirit that knows no insulated spot,*
> *No chasm, no solitude; from link to link*
> *It circulates, the Soul of all the worlds.*
> *This is the freedom of the universe;*
> *Unfolded still the more, more visible,*
> *The more we know; and yet is reverenced least*
> *And least respected in the human Mind,*
> *Its most apparent home.*[21]

When we realize our unity with the world spirit, humanity also recognizes its distinct nature, which is brought into focus by the experience. For Wordsworth we exist in a collaborative relationship with nature and our exquisitely refined perception works in harmony to bring the World Soul to active fruition. Rather than reducing human nature to a single function as the mechanical philosophers did, human fulfillment depends on bringing the entire person into an active relationship with the whole. Through contemplation we enter into a direct participation with the living spirit of the universe, which is embodied externally in the organic forms of nature and manifested internally in the deepest reaches of the soul.

For Samuel Taylor Coleridge (1772–1834), poet, philosopher, and a friend of Wordsworth, in the mechanical philosophy "everything that is most worthy of the human Intellect strikes *Death*."[22] Thus Coleridge sought to replace the philosophy of mechanism with the realities of "Life and Intelligence." Rather than wondering "what is life?" Coleridge asked, "What is *not* life?" All nature partakes of change, activity, growth, and transformation. For Coleridge, "Whatever *is*, *lives*. A thing absolutely lifeless is inconceivable, except as a thought, image, or fancy, in some other being."[23] In organic life, change and transformation are the most evident, but if our senses could be expanded to survey greater intervals of time, all of nature would be seen in perpetual evolution.

Behind the seemingly multiform world stands a unifying principle of which we catch glimpses:

> In the world we see everywhere evidences of a unity, which the component parts are so far from explaining, that they necessarily presuppose it as the cause and condition of their existing as those parts; or even of their existing at all.[24]

Modern science attempts to explain this unity as the manifestation of a hidden law, whereas the ancients perceived it as evidence of a hidden life. For Coleridge, like the ancient Stoics, mentality or intelligence was manifest in the fabric of the world. If intellect and imagination were not present in nature's fabric, how then would they arise in humanity? As Coleridge noted:

> In the objects of nature are presented, as in a mirror, all the possible elements, steps, and processes of intellect antecedent to consciousness, and therefore to the full development of the intelligential act; and *man's mind is the very focus of all the rays of intellect which are scattered through the images of nature* [my emphasis].[25]

Nature is evolutionary and the World Soul is unfolding, moving toward one dynamic end, which is the increase of consciousness, awareness, and appreciation. But intelligence is present in the structure of the world fabric beforehand and not something merely added later. The underlying reality of the world is not matter, whatever that might be, but nonmaterial patterns of relationship. In a famous passage Coleridge explained how nature's creative power and humanity's creative power are one and the same, for "the *rules* of the IMAGINATION" are themselves "the very powers of growth and production."[26] There is a deep reciprocity between humanity and nature, between the inner and outer worlds, because it is the function of art "to make the external internal, the internal external, to make nature thought, and thought nature."[27]

For Coleridge, "Body is but a striving to become mind" and "Nature itself would give us the impression of a work of art, if we could see the thought which is present at once in the whole and in every part."[28]

Both instinct and intellectual understanding are forms of natural intelligence, but understanding is an "adaptive power" that develops from instinct, grows out of experience, and ultimately leads to abstraction. Because understanding and instinct appear at different poles of a spectrum, "the Understanding appears (as a general rule) in an inverse proportion to the Instinct."[29] Abstraction represents a high development of human understanding, but is concerned only with names and concepts. For Coleridge, through instinct we are united with nature and through understanding we are detached from it, but through imagination we are reunited with it.[30] Abstraction is not to be shunned, but if it is made to be an end in itself we become "a race of animals, in whom the presence of reason is manifested solely by the absence of instinct."[31] In such a situation, human nature is falsified by one-sided "abstract knowledge, or the science of mere understanding," which "leads to a science of delusion."[32]

It is finally with the German romantic philosopher Schelling (1775–1854) that we find the most succinct explanation of the relationship between our own inner spirit and the greater life of the cosmos. Like the other Romantics, Schelling believed that the intellect becomes a spiritual malady if it is made an end in itself. The growth of intellectual reflection introduced a rift between the inner and outer worlds, a rift that was codified by the dualism of Descartes. But if we could penetrate through the remoteness of abstraction to the immediacy of feeling, we would experience our essential unity with Nature. For Schelling, Nature and Spirit—the "objective" and the "subjective" poles—are but different faces of the same underlying reality. For Schelling, nature is "visible spirit," and spirit is "invisible nature." In humanity, nature's slumbering spirit awakens into self-consciousness. But ultimately, *human knowledge is nature's knowledge of itself*, and nature and mind are only different aspects of one unfolding pattern.

For Schelling we are not distant spectators in an alien universe, but living participants in the unfolding of the world fabric. The World Soul manifests itself as inner and outer, Self and Other. In the deeply felt experience of beauty we have a concrete intuition of the underlying unity of these two faces of reality. Art is indispensable because it points toward the living unity of the inner and outer faces of reality. By underscoring the unified nature of the world in a deeply engaging and sensuous way, art provides a direct and tangible experience of unity that philosophy cannot attain by itself.

Schelling contributed to the understanding of the unconscious by pointing out that nature is slumbering spirit, a spirit that becomes awakened in human awareness. A single unconscious energy or will underlies everything and moves toward conscious awareness. Our consciousness is bound with the greater world because a single, organic ordering principle underlies both, but outside of consciousness this principle is not self-aware. As Schelling wrote, "It is impossible to understand how the objective world adjusts to our ideas, and simultaneously how our ideas adjust to the objective world, if a pre-established harmony does not exist between the two worlds. . . . But this pre-established harmony is inconceivable unless the activity which produces the objective world is originally identical with the activity which expresses itself in the will, and vice versa."[33]

For Schelling, in the outer world, the ordering principle of the World Soul unconsciously acts in the determinism of nature; but in the inner world it acts with self-awareness in human freedom. Yet even within our own nature, in the unconscious regions that join our psyche with the greater soul of the world, an active, organic power is at work, maintaining the unity of the organism and the creative, unfolding energies of life.

THE INORGANIC SELF

*If I cannot bend the Gods above, then I will move the
Infernal regions.*

VIRGIL, QUOTED BY FREUD IN
THE INTERPRETATION OF DREAMS

As noted earlier, it was Sigmund Freud, more than any other individual, who put the idea of the unconscious on the cultural map. Freud, a medical doctor, through his careful work with hysterical patients was able to identify and study many types of psychological phenomena including the effects of psychological repression. Freud brought a scientific framework to the study of neurotic symptoms because he felt that there was a cause and purpose for neurotic behavior. Many types of adult neurotic behavior contain elements of reenacted childhood incidents. In a broader sense, neurotic behavior serves a purpose. At some point in an individual's life history, such behavior served to protect a person from suffering, but in later years it becomes a habitual pattern that prevents a person from being fully present to the immediacy of life. Freud's major discovery was that these psychological phenomena follow coherent patterns. In this sense, they were not inexplicable, but capable of being both understood and addressed.

One common phenomenon is that of repression. Many individuals experience hurtful or traumatic events in childhood, saturated with painful emotions. The human organism naturally avoids pain and is also forced to adapt to social expectations and the realities of the outer world. Painful memories and traumatic events are repressed because the smoothly functioning ego feels a need to defend itself against disruption. Neurotic phenomena are often habitual patterns of defense that are reawakened or activated by life situations reminiscent of the original event that gave birth to the defense pattern.

Common to all types of psychic functioning is the phenomenon of dissociation. Whenever we focus the spotlight of attention, something else is left out. Concentrating on my writing, I become oblivious to my surroundings. When focusing intently on a mental problem, awareness of the body fades away. Dissociation is perfectly natural and required for our day-to-day functioning, but it is also the faculty through which painful feelings are split off and held at bay. Through dissociation, normal people become numb and lose a connection with vital energies of their personality—energies that can become unavailable through parental and social conditioning or trauma. In extreme cases, parts of the psyche may splinter off and develop an autonomy of their own, which accounts for cases of dissociative identity disorder, commonly known as "multiple personality."

These patterns of psychic functioning can be observed time and again in the personality development of both healthy and disturbed individuals. But when a painful memory is repressed or vital psychic energy becomes dissociated, where does it go? Freud needed the idea of the unconscious as a repository for these memories and energies that exist below conscious self-awareness. The unconscious was indispensable for explaining the phenomena he was witnessing.

At the age of sixty-nine, Freud wrote that "the overwhelming majority of philosophers regard as mental only the phenomena of consciousness. For them, the world of consciousness coincides with the sphere of what is mental."[34] If applied to such philosophers as René Descartes, John Locke, or those modern philosophers who identify essential human nature with the operations of the strictly rational ego, Freud's statement rings true. But it totally overlooked the writings and ideas of the earlier philosophers who discussed the idea of the unconscious before Freud. Freud was very much a product of his age, in which the idea of the unconscious was something whose time had come. But as noted earlier, Lancelot Law Whyte has pointed out that Freud had little personal knowledge of the many other individuals who had previously discussed the nature of the unconscious and speculated on its functions.

While earlier thinkers had described the life-giving power of the unconscious as a source of creativity and an inner connection with the universal powers of nature, Freud the medical doctor confined his attention to the unconscious solely in its extreme pathological functioning. Rather than being a bond with the greater cosmos and the creative powers of nature, *Freud transformed the unconscious into a personal subconscious.* This subconscious became, to large degree, a subterranean chamber of horrors that served as a repository for all the repressed urges of humanity such as aggression, sexuality, and criminal tendencies. Freud's view of life was tragic and psychoanalysis involved reintegrating these shameful, repressed urges into consciousness so they could be acknowledged and faced in a mature way.

For Freud, the psyche was inherently a house divided and the natural state of civilized man was that of neurosis. The *ego* itself depended on the repression of the psyche's natural urges, and in this process it was guided by the *superego,* a personification of cultural mores and socially appropriate behavior. The *id,* however, was the instinctual part of the personality subject to the functioning of natural law, possessing "the character of being foreign to the ego."[35] By definition, the ego, superego, and id are always in conflict with one another. Civilized man's state is essentially one of self-division and alienation—and even psychoanalysis could offer no hope of curing this fundamental condition.

Freud claimed that his model of the psyche was biological, when in fact it was highly mechanistic and inorganic. Living organisms possess a vital power of self-organization, a formative principle that coordinates the unfolding life pattern in a unified and purposive way, which supports the continuation of life. But in Freud's time mechanistic thinkers had started to suggest that life itself was a freak accident, which had no essential relationship with the cosmic pattern. Life itself was a physico-chemical structure that could be reduced to, and totally explained by, mechanistic principles. Freud's view of the psyche was mechanistic and drew upon hydraulic metaphors in which life energy or libido was treated as a finite, quantifiable substance. Furthermore, life itself was an unnatural phenomenon.

In Freud's time the second law of thermodynamics or entropy taught that the entire universe was running down. Over time, energy becomes dissipated and disorganized. Given enough time, the universe would die a frigid heat death after expending all of its energy. Because life was a physico-chemical phenomenon, Freud believed that death was the most "natural" state. Drawing upon the idea of entropy, he found support for the "death instinct" which he termed "the most conservative instinct." Theoretically, Freud also "obsessed on sexuality to the exclusion of the biological order which sexuality serves, and to which it is normally subordinate."[36] In all these ways Freud's theories were highly colored by mechanistic concepts and failed to be truly biological.

THE UNSEATING OF THE EGO

The awakening consciousness is a danger; and whoever lives among conscious Europeans knows in fact that it is an illness.

NIETZSCHE

While Freud's very real contributions to the understanding of the human psyche cannot be doubted, his reductionist focus on sexuality and belief in the tragic nature of unresolvable alienation became troublesome to many of his closest followers and collaborators. Freud himself took little pleasure in the play of the free imagination, was sternly moralistic, and tended to view the world through rigid theoretical constructs. His theoretical models attempted to minimize complexity, and because human life was tragically alienated, Freud felt that the best response was to face the meaninglessness of life with a realistic stoicism.

One individual who ultimately found Freud's approach to be limiting was Carl Gustav Jung (1875–1961), Freud's closest collaborator. Freud often referred to Jung as the "Crown Prince" and saw him as his successor who would carry forward the mantle of the psychoanalytic tradition. But Jung began to increasingly question Freud's interpretations of sexuality, religion, and his analysis of dream symbolism. When Jung completed a work on "Transformations and Symbols of the Libido" in 1912 (translated into English as *The Psychology of the Unconscious*), he suggested that there was a deeper level of the unconscious mind that was nonpersonal. Jung was in the process of discovering that the same primordial, symbolic images arise in the minds of disparate individuals and exert an influence on human thought. For Jung, this pointed toward the existence of a collective unconscious, which he saw as an important contribution to Freud's theory of a personal subconscious. As Jung himself wrote, for Freud the unconscious "is essentially an appendage of consciousness, in which all the individual's incompatibilities are heaped up. For me the unconscious is a collective psychic disposition, creative in character."[37] For Jung, the human psyche was not merely fixated on sexual concerns, but also reflected a spiritual dimension and yearning for numinous meaning, something that "Freud was so fascinated by but was unable to grasp."[38]

Freud could not accept Jung's extensions to his theory and a split occurred between the two men. Jung never rejected Freud's central insights but went on to develop his own ideas, making significant contributions to the understanding of human nature and psychology. For Jung, Freud had in many ways accurately described the nature of the personal unconscious. But the personal unconscious was itself rooted in a deeper matrix of psyche that linked the individual person to human nature in general and to the long lineage of the collective psyche's historical development. Through the collective unconscious, the individual is bound to the entire spiritual history of mankind and to the spontaneous archetypal images that both shape and reflect that history. Thus Jung could write, "The true history of the mind is not preserved in learned volumes but in the living psychic organism of every individual."[39]

Jung observed that his patients spontaneously produced circular images of wholeness in their artwork and their dreams, often divided into four quarters like the cardinal directions. Jung described these images of wholeness as mandalas, after the contemplative images of Eastern religions. The Sanskrit word *mandala* means "magic circle," and Jung discovered that these circular images were very centering to individuals in a state of psychological stress. This is something I've witnessed personally: my father was a business owner who was frequently under stress, and while he knew nothing about Jungian psychology, he would create spontaneous drawings on pads of paper while making telephone calls. More often than not, his unconscious drawings would take the form of simple mandalas: a circle with crosshairs bisecting the image into quadrants.

This spontaneous appearance of mandala imagery, Jung realized, pointed to a natural compensatory function at work in the psyche. When the psyche is stressed, upset, or confused, it creates images of order and harmony in response. Like the crosshairs of a finder scope, the mandala is a centering image and an archetype of order. Like a thermostat, the psyche has its own metabolism that keeps things in balance. When the conscious attitude of the ego becomes one-sided, the unconscious psyche spontaneously produces dream images and fantasies that serve to bring it back into harmony—especially if they are recognized and understood.

In Jung's thought the psyche itself is like a circle or a mandala (see figure 9.1). The central hub and totality of the circle represents the true self, the totality of psychic reality. Floating at the very top of the circle is the little ego or the conscious self, which incorporates the persona, the outer mask that we wear and show to society. While the ego may become inflated and imagine itself to be the "one true God," the empirical findings of psychology prove that the ego is a frail center of consciousness and not the true seat of the entire personality. As Nietzsche wrote long before Freud, "Consciousness is the last and latest development of the organic, and is consequently the most unfinished and the least powerful of these developments."[40]

Beneath the ego is the personal unconscious which corresponds to Freud's idea of the unconscious. It is the repository of all the parts of the personality that have been split off and repressed due to social conditioning and trauma. Through the study of dreams, Jung discovered that this part of the psyche is often represented by a sinister "shadow"

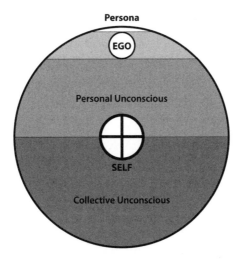

Figure 9.1. C. G. Jung's model of the psyche. The self is both the center and the totality of the psyche, while the ego is a small spotlight of self-reflective consciousness.

figure of the same sex as the dreamer. The shadow is the personification of all the parts of our own personality we do not want to face, and it is often projected outward onto individuals that we have a strongly negative psychic reaction to. Such individuals embody the negative characteristics that we are reluctant to accept as part of our own personality.

At the heart of the psyche lies the true self, which is both the center and totality of the psyche. The psyche itself is not static, but embodies a process of growth or individuation through which the true self comes into being and flowers. Below the individual self in the deepest reaches of the psyche is the collective unconscious in which all psychic reality is rooted. In the Jungian model the collective unconscious is psyche-as-psyche apart from individuality, and at its deepest level is one with the deep structure of the world. Speaking of psyche-as-psyche, Jung described the collective unconscious in the following way:

> If it were possible to personify the unconscious, we might think of it as a collective human being combining the characteristics of both sexes, transcending youth and age, birth and death, and having at its command a human experience of one or two million years, practically immortal. If such a being existed, it would be exalted above all temporal change; the present would mean neither more nor less to it than any year in the hundredth millennium before Christ; it would be a dreamer of age-old dreams and, owing to its immeasurable experience, an incomparable prognosticator. It would have lived countless times over again the life of the individual, the family, the tribe, and the nation, and it would possess a living sense of the rhythm of growth, flowering and decay.[41]

The center of the individual personality is not the tiny ego, but the unfolding power of the self, which the self-aware ego helps to bring into being. Symbolically, the Self is an archetype of wholeness and embodies a miraculous power or divine radiance. It is the fully realized human represented by Christ or other divine figures, or the philosopher's stone of the alchemists—the dynamic synthesis of all conceivable opposites, which can effect astonishing transformations.

While individuation is a natural process, great selves are not born but cultivated. Through self-reflective awareness, it is possible to consciously assist the process of self-realization. The ego is necessary, but it is a helper—not the center of the process. In Jung's psychology, the first and most painful step involves the ego facing and assimilating the personal shadow. Only by first facing this dweller at the threshold can it then journey on to encounter deeper levels of psychic reality. Despite the pain of facing one's own worst traits, the personal unconscious also contains a vast untapped reservoir of vital life energy. By interacting with the depths of the personal unconscious, and the greater depths of the collective unconscious in which all psychic reality is situated, the ego acts like a reflective gardener, fertilizing and nurturing along the process of individuation and the flowering of the true self. For Freud, the ego was permanently alienated. But for Jung, if sufficiently clarified, the ego may become like a transparent window through which the light of the entire self can shine.

Regardless of theoretical orientation, the discovery of the unconscious and the findings of psychology undermined the idea that Cartesian ego was the center or essence of the human personality. The mechanistic philosophy had pictured the rational, human ego as a Divine Engineer—mirroring its image of God. Yet with this identification of humanity as a solely rational entity, the human personality became disturbingly one-dimensional. In the mechanistic worldview, both nature and human beings became radically diminished.

However, as might be expected, a counterreaction set in, and that counterreaction was the discovery of the unconscious. In the mechanistic worldview, everything operates from the outside. Nature has no inner life or reality of its own, but is acted upon by external force. By contrast, *psyche and life unfolds from the inside.* While the mechanistic vision pictured nature as inanimate, for the Romantics the unconscious was discovered as a real but hidden level of life that linked us with the energies of the cosmos. While the mechanical philosophy had cleansed the world of mystery, hidden forces, the unknown, and the spirit of life, through the discovery of the unconscious, psychology rediscovered the vital, hidden forces shaping and inspiring the depths of human nature. Through the discovery of the unconscious—a phenomenon itself rooted in the greater realm of living nature—it was now possible to see that mind and life were not different in essence, "but only in their form of expression and stage of development."[42]

While Freud labored under the belief that life was somehow unnatural and that modern man would forever be alienated, his predecessors (like the Romantics) and his followers (like Jung) did not. The discovery of the unconscious, in fact, pointed toward the promise of a reconciliation between humanity and nature. All human ideation—creativity, fantasy, and inspiration—arises from the unconscious, and at its deepest level the unconscious is one with nature. By attuning ourselves to the voices of creativity from the inner depths, humanity can bring both self and world to living fruition.

THE RETURN OF SOUL TO THE WORLD AND THE GREENING OF PSYCHOLOGY

Living in a repressive Victorian culture, Freud himself clearly pointed out the relationship between madness and civilization. Yet if the repressive, dissociated mentality of the Victorian era was sufficient to provoke a thunderous-enough response from the unconscious depths to bring the new science of psychology into being, Freud himself could not have foreseen the full psychological consequences of urban-industrial society. William Blake spoke of the mechanization of human life and the "Dark Satanic Mills" that were transforming the green pastures of England into an urban-industrial complex, but the culmination of the mechanized lifestyle would only come into its own in the twentieth century.

Standing on the crest of the technological age, we modern people are separated only by a generation or two from a predominantly agrarian lifestyle.[43] But we've become habituated to every new technological convenience so easily, it's hard to understand or remember. Electric lighting was first used in New York City in 1882. The personal automobile went into mass production in 1913. Yet these two inventions alone have transformed the face and atmosphere of our planet. In most human settlements it is no longer possible to enjoy the sight of the stars under the pristine blackness of night. Our satellites at night, gazing down from space above, reveal a glowing planet. Nearly the entire planet is ablaze, dramatically spotlighting the centers and corridors of human civilization. In our own time, Bacon's dream of technological domination has finally been fulfilled.

To illustrate the modern predicament, let me draw on a personal experience. The alarm goes off in the morning and it's time to catch my flight at the airport. I turn on the lights, then switch on the heat. The coffee maker with its built-in timer stands nearby, ready to offer me a freshly brewed cup. After a hot shower, I blow dry my hair. Throwing my bags in the car, I set off down the road, roll up the electric windows, and turn on the radio. On the way to the airport I pass the shopping district. There are hundreds of stores, stretching for miles, and the only way to reach them is by automobile. At this hour, the vast parking lots are empty and the malls look like deserted movie sets, bleakly illuminated by the nauseating glow of sodium-vapor lights. Reaching the airport, I park the car, enter through electric doors, and pass through a metal detector. Once my bags have passed inspection by an X-ray machine, I am allowed to enter the jet, a structure of metal and plastic that flies through the air. As we head down the runway and the speed mounts, I momentarily reflect upon my mortality and hope that the airplane's computers are more reliable than the one I have at home.

The point of the description is simple: *none* of this was here a lifetime ago. We've become so habituated to life in the technopolis that we unconsciously mistake the artificial world of our own creation with reality itself. In the minds of many people, the very idea of Nature has vanished. Instead, with the colorless affect of clinical detachment, we speak of "the environment." That is because the widespread deployment of technology has given birth to a vicious circle of alienation. Technology leads us to live in an ever-more abstract, conceptual world, cut off from the sensuous experience of fauna, landscape, and bird song. This conceptual alienation leads to the creation of more technology and the cycle becomes self-perpetuating. In the end, the utilitarian vision of nature has become complete. A beautiful, irreplaceable forest stand is no longer sensed for what it is, but only seen as a cash investment.

The question is, Under such circumstances is psychological sanity even possible?

In Freud's Victorian culture, a major cause of neurosis was sexual repression. But in the carefree culture of the technopolis, the cause of alienation is mechanization—and a never-before experienced level of distraction and dissociation from the living fabric of the natural world.

If psychology and the discovery of the unconscious pointed toward a recovery of the World Soul and a living relationship with nature, psychology as a cultural reality has done little to heal our relationship with the world. For the philosopher Schelling, the realization of the unconscious spirit slumbering in the self also demanded a corresponding engagement *with the world.* Yet as James Hillman points out in his blistering critique *We've Had a Hundred Years of Psychology—And the World's Getting Worse,* the effect of popular psychotherapy has been to narcissistically oversensitize individuals to their personal plight while the quality of communal life in our fast-paced industrial society continues to decline. The question, of course, has been raised before. If society itself embodies a type of madness, what role should psychology play in such a society? Perhaps neurosis and psychic anguish does not always indicate that there is something wrong with an individual. What if those symptoms indicate that there is something wrong with the entire culture? In this case, professional psychology would err by trying to adjust an otherwise healthy individual to a social system that is itself dysfunctional and crazy-making.

Psychotherapy with Freud and Jung started off in part dealing with the sickness of civilization, but today psychotherapy focuses predominantly on the individual. The individual is supposed to cope, get in touch with his feelings, and, as Hillman contends, become assimilated to a system that is itself pathological and dysfunctional. The effect of psychotherapy's underlying assumptions is to help the individual cope by focusing his energies inward and, in effect, anesthetizing the passions and discontent that could otherwise be directed at the problems of the world.

Psychologist Robert Romanyshyn agrees with Hillman's analysis that after one hundred years of therapy the world is getting worse, but he believes it could not have turned out otherwise "because the therapy room in its inception was already divorced from the world, was already isolated from nature."[44] Psychology treated "the unconscious as only a psychological matter," which precluded seeing psyche as linked to the greater world fabric. As Romanyshyn points out:

> The neurotic, whose symptoms were indicative of a disconnection from nature and the sacred, whose symptoms were colorful and awesome, was imprisoned within the confines of a psychology whose theories of pathology and treatment imagined, and in large measure continue to imagine, psyche, soul, and consciousness as identical with the human. The irony here is that depth psychology, beginning with the profound awareness that psyche is more than ego-consciousness, did not recognize that consciousness is more than human.[45]

As Romanyshyn concludes:

> We need to get beyond psychology or face ecological disaster. The logos of psyche (or psychology) needs to be placed within the larger logos of the earth (ecology), and even within the larger song of creation. We need to struggle toward a *non-human centered point of view,* which terms like the unconscious and psychology—because of their human, all too human ties—prevent us from doing. We need to see ourselves from the viewpoint of the star and the atom, the animal and the stone, the plant and the angel. We need to acknowledge with a sense of awe and humility these other frequencies of consciousness. We need to begin to listen to *them* before *we* begin to speak.[46]

The work of historian and cultural critic Theodore Roszak also points toward the need for a larger framework that he calls an *ecopsychology.* In his book *The Voice of the Earth: An Exploration of Ecopsychology,*

Theodore Roszak explores the relationships between psychology, cosmology, and ecology. His work revolves around the central question, What is the psyche's natural relationship with the world? Roszak points out that in traditional societies madness is seen as an imbalance between humanity and nature. Shamans, or "stone-age psychiatrists," attempted to restore that balance through ritualistic means. With the birth of modern psychology, Sigmund Freud, laboring under the ideas of entropy and the unnaturalness of life, could conceive of no fundamental connection between the psyche and the world, and this disconnect has colored the subsequent development of psychology, which leaves nature out of the equation. Freud himself wrote that "nature is eternally remote. She destroys us—coldly, cruelly, relentlessly."[47] For Freud, the healthy self was the stoic, well-bounded personality, with crisp, well-defined edges. Nature was a cold, lifeless arena, a meaningless backdrop against which the mechanical struggle for existence is enacted. With Freud, "The normally functioning ego was an isolated atom of self-regarding consciousness that had no relational continuity with the physical world around it."[48]

But modern cosmology and the life sciences dramatically undermine Freud's view of nature. The entire universe is now known to be evolutionary and, in Roszak's words, "Even matter has a history." Our own nature is deeply embedded in the cosmic pattern of which all life is an outgrowth. Rather than running down and racing toward a cold, entropic heat death, matter and life have grown more richly complex. The human psyche embodies 3.8 billion years of the living Earth's evolutionary heritage. As Jung said, the deep structure of the psyche is transpersonal and perhaps timeless. Beneath the personal subconscious, we are bonded with the greater life of the planet through what Roszak calls "the ecological unconscious." The ecological unconscious is our biological, genetic, and psychic heritage, the warp and woof of nature's soul out of which we are spun, deeper than even sexuality or archetypes. The very fact that we are so deeply bonded with the planet from which we are evolved is a cause for hope, because the ecological unconscious presumably contains a great store of wisdom that is beginning to speak to us even now. As Roszak notes, rather than asking what we should do about the ecological crisis, perhaps we should ask what the living planet is starting to do about us?

In Roszak's vision of the ecological unconscious, the whole world comes alive and we are an embodiment of that life. Imagination enlivens the world, but imagination is itself, as Coleridge pointed out, an outgrowth of the world process, "the very power of growth and production."[49] By tapping into the ecological unconscious rather than continually dissociating ourselves from the living universe, we may discover the security, insight, and creative power necessary to live with nature in trust and reciprocity.

For Roszak the ecological unconscious is a bond with the living spirit of nature rather than a Freudian chamber of horrors. Our own intelligence arises from the intelligence of nature, and if we carefully listen we can hear the voice of the Earth. In his positive evaluation of the deep psyche and its decisive role in linking us with the cosmic pattern, Roszak's ecological unconscious hearkens back to the insights of the Romantic philosophers and the optimistic, pre-Freudian vision of the unconscious mind. The difference is that Roszak's vision is more inclusive and more deeply grounded in science and modern cosmology than any previous theory. For as modern cosmology forcefully suggests, not only is the entire universe our greater body, it is also the fabric of our very soul.

10

The Mirror of Nature

Modern Cosmology and the Reanimation of the Universe

You may drive out Nature with a pitchfork, but she will always come back.

HORACE

LOST IN STARLIGHT

It's a dark, moonless night in early June. To escape the light pollution of my native town, at least once a year I make the pilgrimage north to the pristine, dark skies of Sleeping Bear Dunes national park on the shores of Lake Michigan. There I rent a cottage at the Shady Shores Resort on the bank of Little Glen Lake and spend the days walking exquisite trails that lead to overlooks hovering hundreds of feet above Lake Michigan. At night I pack up my telescope and head out to a favorite observing site.

Twilight has past and darkness has fallen. Silhouettes of pine trees hug the horizon, illuminated by starlight. They punctuate the skyline and bridge the Earth to the sky, a comforting reminder of where I stand on the face of our living planet. The night itself is vast and laced with mystery, extending off into the trees and countryside, and extending out endlessly into the infinite depths above. It's early in the season so my activity is greeted by the song of some crickets, but not by the full blown insect chorus of the late summer.

In the sea of darkness I seem isolated and exposed, a shuffle of activity making final preparations under the glow of a red flashlight. The telescope itself is large, extremely heavy, and rock solid. Having mounted it firmly on the tripod, I'm making the final electrical connections. The telescope is motorized and has a sixty-four-thousand-object database. Now that it's plugged into my car's electrical system, I need only type a few keystrokes into the hand-controller and the telescope will slew across the sky, center any selected object in the field of view, and emit a beep—a wordless indication that observing can begin.

Before pressing any buttons, I look up and around, amazed by the vista. The luminous band of the Milky Way is reaching upward and thousands of stars pulsate in its folds as if they are alive. As the boundaries separating heaven and Earth melt away, the star stream shines three-dimensional with white clottings and dark rifts, bright enough to illuminate the ground and the trees with a faint, phosphorescent glow. Heaven and Earth are bound together by one luminous glow, the combined illumination of millions and millions of stars in our home galaxy. As I trace the textures and curtains of the vibrant tapestry through binoculars, the boundaries of daylight consciousness dissolve. My soul, my mind, and even my body are adrift, embraced and engulfed by the pulsating star stream. Like the words of the poet Kenneth Rexroth,

> *The stars stand around me*
> *Like gold eyes. I can no longer*
> *Tell where I begin and leave off.*[1]

At this time of year it's impossible not to explore the rich starfields by the constellation Sagittarius. Shaped like a giant teapot, Sagittarius is climbing higher in the south. From the spout of the teapot emerges the hot white steam of the Milky Way, a particularly brilliant and shining star cloud. But more than metaphor is involved here, for right off the tip of the giant teapot is the heart of our own Milky Way Galaxy, some twenty-five thousand light-years away. Encircling this core are the billions of stars that make up our galaxy and through a medium-size telescope you can see endless wonders. The region is rich in star clusters and contains the awesome Trifid and Lagoon nebulae, glowing clouds where new stars are coming to birth. But just as striking are the dozen or so globular clusters that you can see orbiting the central hub of our galaxy. The globular clusters are tightly packed spheres of ancient suns, each one containing between five hundred thousand and a million stars. Through a telescope they are a stunning sight, like countless diamonds huddled together in a sparkling, shivering orb (see figure 10.1).

Figure 10.1. Globular cluster M13 in the constellation of Hercules, containing at least several hundred thousand stars—and perhaps as many as a million. It has a diameter of about 145 light-years and is 25,100 light-years away from Earth. Photograph by the author.

Like the Roman god Janus, technology has two faces. On one hand, technology separates and insulates us from the world. Because of the effects of technology, I am no longer able to experience the profound beauty of the sky and the Milky Way in my hometown. On the other hand, thanks to technology I am able to gaze into the deepest heart of our galaxy from my northern hideaway and actually understand what I'm looking at. Science and the development of technology go hand in hand, and the ever-increasing precision of technology has allowed us to gaze ever deeper into the microworld of the atom and the macroworld of the greater universe. And in the process, our observations and insights have increasingly eroded the premises of the mechanistic worldview. In fact, modern physics has proved that every major assumption of Newtonian science was flawed or incorrect.

It is no exaggeration to say that we are living in the wake of a cosmological revolution, for the most astonishing scientific discoveries of all time have been made only over the last one hundred years. These discoveries, made in astronomy and physics, have completely changed our understanding of the nature of matter and humanity's place in the seemingly infinite cosmic tapestry. While this revolution is far from over, as philosopher E. A. Burtt pointed out, a cosmology or world-picture is a civilization's most vital possession, for our worldviews affect the way that we humans understand our relationship to the world and other people. As he wrote, "In the last analysis, it is the ultimate picture which an age forms of the nature of its world that is its most fundamental possession. It is the final controlling factor in all thinking whatever."[2] If the mechanistic worldview implied that matter was dead and humanity was essentially distinct from nature, that viewpoint had inevitable social and ecological consequences. Now under the spell of the new discoveries, matter itself has returned to life. Nature can no longer be seen as a static, unchanging machine, and we now understand that all living beings are deeply interconnected, having emerged from the unfolding tapestry of the evolutionary universe. By necessity, as this vision becomes more deeply assimilated by society, it will affect the way that we envision human nature and relate to the world in the twenty-first century.

NEWTON'S BOX

For the better part of its history, western physics was undergirded by a conception of matter for which empirical evidence was ever produced. There are no hard balls of ultimate stuff any more than there were, as was once supposed, crystalline spheres holding up the heavenly bodies.

THEODORE ROSZAK

Like every cosmovision, the mechanical philosophy made certain assumptions about the world. While Isaac Newton secretly entertained the idea that all matter is attended with signs of life, in his published writings he upheld the atomistic view that the universe was composed of "solid, massy, hard, impenetrable, movable Particles."[3] In the mechanistic universe, there was a sharp division between matter and energy. Matter itself was dead and inert, acted upon by external forces. Matter possessed no intrinsic life or activity of its own, no hidden affinities or decision-making capabilities. It was inherently noncreative.

The world machine was also pictured as rigidly ordered and deterministic. Like a ticking clock, the movements of the heavenly bodies followed a completely regular order. Newton's follower Laplace summed up the idea of cosmic determinism in a very economical way. According to Laplace, if a superintelligent mind knew the mass, position, and trajectory of every particle in the universe, that superintelligence would be able to calculate any *future* state of the universe. In theory, at least, the universe was entirely predictable, given enough computing power. But in a human sense, this rigid determinism seemed to undermine the possibility of both human freedom and creativity.

Another feature of the mechanistic worldview centered on the role of the observer, who was pictured as being objectively distinct from the world that was under study. Descartes articulated the idea of the Spectator, who was able to distantly gaze upon a totally objective reality—as though the observer was clinically detached from nature, and peering through a glass window or a one-way mirror. In the Newtonian universe, objective reality was a given and would be the same whether or not it was being actively observed. Because of this, mathematics could predict the functions and future states of the world machine in an accurate and precise way.

Yet the only way that mathematics could predict the world involved the assumption that the universe itself was mechanistic, deterministic, and subject to eternal, unchanging laws. Newton pictured space and time as absolute, unchanging realities. In terms of space, the universe was like a giant box that contained everything—an unchanging grid or frame of reference that could never itself expand or contract. In terms of time, it was an objective frame of reference for all observers, for the tick of the cosmic clock was a universal, unchanging metronome against which all movement could be gauged. In this way, the world was essentially static and unchanging. For if the cosmic structure was perfectly regular, no evolution or creative novelty was possible.

Finally, because matter was dead, all creativity and spirit existed outside the universe in the mind of God at the beginning of time. Creation was a one-time event rather than a continually unfolding process, and all creative power existed outside the universe. The laws of nature were forever stamped upon the world by the Cosmic Architect and matter itself was void of all power, creativity, and the ability of self-organization. Yet within the space of three centuries, every one of these primary assumptions would be thoroughly refuted.

THE DEMATERIALIZATION OF MATTER

Since the turn of the century I have lived to see every one of the basic assumptions of science and mathematics set aside.
ALFRED NORTH WHITEHEAD

By radically oversimplifying the world, classical physics contained the seeds of its own undoing. The entire edifice rested on a reductionistic dualism that separated spirit from matter and self from the world. Because of this dualism, the cosmos was not a unified, organic phenomenon in which humanity and life even had a place. For if matter itself was dead and inert, even self-regulating organisms had to finally be pictured as mechanistic constructions. In essence, the mechanistic paradigm banished life and consciousness itself from the world fabric. In the same way that God and divine power did not exist in the world, neither could human life or consciousness. The mechanistic worldview ultimately led to a crushing sense of alienation, for if God itself could be dispensed with as an excess cog in the world machine, human nature could be theoretically explained away too, as the result of purely mechanistic functioning. Then human life could be pictured as a seemingly purposive illusion that should be seen mechanically, or, even worse, as a cosmic accident—or, as one physicist put it, "a disease of matter."[4]

But if matter was really passive and dead, how could life arise in the first place, and what type of continuity did it have with the natural world? The biologist and naturalist Loren Eiseley summed up the question beautifully when he noted that

> if "dead" matter has reared up this curious landscape of fiddling crickets, song sparrows, and wondering men, it must be plain even to the most devoted materialist that the matter of which he speaks contains amazing if not dreadful powers.[5]

Like Loren Eiseley, the Stoics and the alchemists believed that matter was not passive, but animated with amazing and dreadful powers. But only in our own time, through the discoveries of modern physics, has the miraculous fire hidden in matter been so dreadfully illuminated as by the world-shattering explosions of the atomic bombs over Hiroshima and Nagasaki. Matter itself is not passive and dead, but seething with primordial, world-creating energies that flower forth as life—and yet can also spell out world-annihilating, technological destruction.

The mechanistic picture started to come undone in the 1800s with Michael Faraday's exploration of electromagnetic fields.[6] Magnetic fields are seemingly immaterial, yet they extend through space. They are not passive, but active. Nonmaterial fields did not easily fit within a Newtonian framework of dead matter and mechanical causation, but hearkened back to the ancient idea of an animating power that pervades matter. James Clerk Maxwell, a highly gifted mathematician, took up the study of Faraday's fields and in 1864 published an astonishing discovery: electricity and magnetism are just different aspects of a single force, electromagnetism. Light, he also discovered, was an aspect of this force. Maxwell's theory of fields would open the doorway for Einstein's later theories of relativity, and nonmaterial fields were here to stay. For many physicists, fields are now seen as being more essential than the transient "particles" that fill them.

As physicists began their modern-day, alchemical descent into the heart of matter, matter itself started to become more animated and ethereal. In 1897, Joseph Thomson discovered the existence of electrons, extremely tiny particles with a negative electrical charge. Electrical current passed between plates in a vacuum tube gives off glowing rays, and for some time these rays were merely thought to be a type of electromagnetic radiation. Thomson proved that these electrons were in fact particles, but possessed a mass one-thousand-times smaller than that of a hydrogen atom. This suggested that atoms were not the indivisible building blocks of the universe, but composed of smaller, electrically charged particles.

Two years later, in 1899, physicist Max Planck discovered that light was not emitted in continuous frequencies, but in discrete packets, bundles, or *quanta*. Light and other forms of electromagnetic energy travel in waves, but Planck discovered that the waves are composed of packets of energy. Scientists had known for some time that light traveled in waves because, like other types of interacting waves, light creates regular interference patterns just like the bands in a moiré pattern (see figure 10.2 on page 186). The discovery that light also traveled in packets made no sense, but Planck's discovery foreshadowed the birth of quantum physics. In 1905 Einstein published a paper suggesting that not only is light absorbed and emitted in packets, but that it travels in packets as well. These packets are composed of photons or particles, which can hit a surface at a discrete point.

With the discovery of the quantum nature of light, the idea of solid matter was in danger of collapsing, or at least growing incredibly paradoxical. Light travels in waves that cause interference patterns, but a

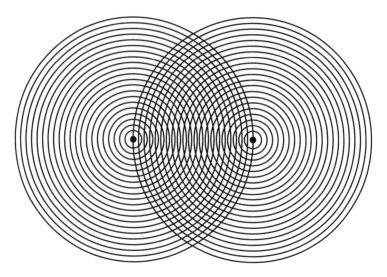

*Figure 10.2. A moiré pattern of interference bands
created by intersecting waves.*

wave is not localized—it spreads out in all dimensions. Throw a rock into a pond and the waves radiate outward. A particle, however, is localized in space like a tiny billiard ball (see figure 10.3). The mechanistic philosophy had strictly divided particles and waves, matter and energy, because waves needed some type of medium to travel through. Waves were seen as energetic fluctuations in a material substance, but pure energy was now shown to be composed of particles. Light could behave like extended waves *or* single particles. The clear and distinct dividing line between active energy and passive matter was coming undone.

A decisive turning point occurred when French physicist Louis de Broglie made a startling suggestion. If the pure energy of light could act both like a particle and an extended wave, what about the tiny, material electrons discovered by James Thomson? Could electrons act like both particles and waves? When put to the test in 1927, de Broglie's hypothesis was confirmed. A beam of electron particles could be made to behave just like light and produce the interference patterns of waves. *From this point on it became apparent that there was no gulf dividing solid matter and pure energy. Pure energy could act like a particle and solid matter could act like an extended wave.* Both matter and energy

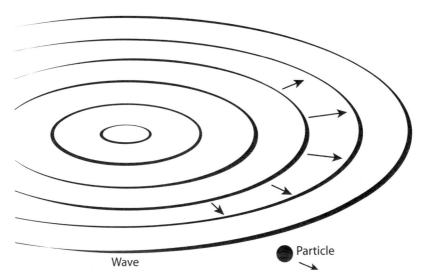

Figure 10.3. Wave and particle. A wave is extended in space while a particle is discretely localized at a particular point.

had two faces, for both exhibited the dual properties of discrete particles and extended waves.

In either case, these subatomic waves or particles are nothing like the inert billiard balls of the Newtonian universe, dead chunks of matter pushed or pulled around from the outside. As our knowledge of physics deepened, it became obvious that the subatomic world is alive, a pulsating tapestry of interwoven symmetries and dynamic activity. Like the larger universe itself, the subatomic world is a glorious pageant of unfolding creativity, not a fixed, frozen, or lifeless reality. As physicist Werner Heisenberg noted, "Atoms are not things." But physicist Max Born put it even better when he wrote:

> We have sought for firm ground and found none. The deeper we penetrate, the more restless becomes the universe; all is rushing about and vibrating in a wild dance.[7]

Near my desk is a statue of the dancing Shiva, the Hindu lord of creation, surrounded by a bright circle of flames. Like the dance of Shiva, the subatomic world is a continual process of dynamic transformation, an ongoing process of creation and destruction. *Matter is an activity,* flashing into existence and then being transformed into energy, according to elaborate symmetries. Even more astonishing is the recent discovery that there is no dead space or perfect vacuum. Arising out of the nothingness of the quantum vacuum, positive and negative particles spontaneously foam out of the abyss, only to annihilate one another and return to the primordial ground of being. Holding in his hand both the drum of time and the flame of eternity, the dancing Shiva spins out the fabric of creation through rhythmic vibration, but also burns away the veil of form to reveal the pregnant void which stands at the heart of the cosmic pattern. If matter is active and self-organizing, and if matter and energy—and perhaps the entire universe—can spontaneously arise from the vacuum of nothingness,[8] then, as philosopher Karl Popper pointed out, through the discoveries of modern physics "materialism has transcended itself."[9] Certainly the dancing Shiva with his rhythmic harmonies and all-consuming flame is a more accurate image of the subatomic world than the dead, mechanical images of Newtonian science.

TAKING THE QUANTUM LEAP

Anyone who has not been shocked by quantum physics has not yet understood it.

NIELS BOHR

In classical physics the universe exists objectively "out there" whether we decide to measure it or not. The same cannot be said about subatomic particles in the quantum realm, where the very act of observation causes the phenomenon to take on a certain characteristic. Quantum phenomena are inherently probabilistic and there is no way to precisely predict where an individual photon will strike a photographic plate. With quantum mechanics, it is only possible to predict likelihoods. If we were measuring a large number of photons as a group, however, their probabilistic nature would average out and an exact prediction would be possible. To use another example, it is possible to calculate the radioactive half-life of a chunk of uranium that contains many atoms. But it is absolutely impossible to predict when any individual atom will decay.

To make things trickier, a quantum phenomenon such as a photon cannot be said to exist in a determinate state *until it is measured.* Until the photon is actually measured, many possibilities are open to it. To use the technical language, making a measurement brings about a "collapse of the wave function," which pins down the infinite possibilities once and for all. *But until the measurement is made, the photon cannot be said to exist in a particular place at all.* In the quantum world, there is no objective reality "out there" until we act as participants and help bring it into being.

If this seems confusing, the best example is the famous two-slit experiment, which illustrates the central mystery of all quantum phenomena. The question is: Is light made up of waves or particles? The answer is: Light acts as neither a wave nor a particle until we take a measurement.

If we shine a light through two slits (see figure 10.4a on page 190), interference bands appear projected on our photographic plate. So far, nothing surprising. Light acts like a wave that is interfering with itself. The light and dark bands represent the peaks and valleys of the interference pattern.

In the next experiment (see figure 10.4b), we close one of the two slits and release one photon at a time. The photons fly through the slit like little bullets and over time form a band of dots where they have struck the photographic plate. In this case, we have asked the photon to behave like a particle and it has responded appropriately. Due to the probabilistic nature of quantum phenomena, we cannot predict where each individual photon will land, but over time the entire group of released photons will sketch out a nice band just as surely as if we kept shooting pellets through the opening. So far, nothing really dumbfounding has occurred.

With our next experiment we begin to encounter the strangeness of the quantum world. This experiment (see figure 10.4c) is a repeat of the first experiment. While both slits are now open, the only difference is that *instead of shining a beam of light through the openings we are now releasing single photons, one at a time.* Each single photon produces a single dot on the photographic plate just like in experiment two, but

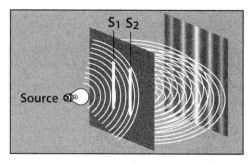

A

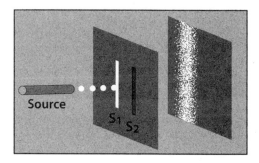

Figure 10.4. Variations on the two-slit experiment.

B

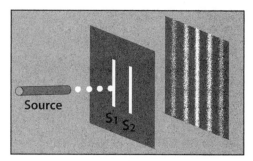

C

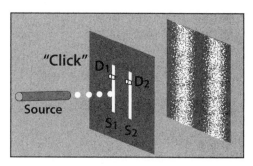

D

this time something else is happening. Instead of getting two bands of dots that build up one by one like we would expect from bullets, we get the interference patterns of *waves. But how can a single, individual photon interfere with itself?* This is one of the great, unanswered questions of quantum physics. Does the single released photon act like a wave, pass through the two slits, interfere with itself, and then transform itself back into a bullet? Somehow the single photon "knows" that two slits are open instead of one.

In the final experiment things become absolutely troublesome (see figure 10.4d). This experiment is exactly the same as the previous one, except for one difference. In this case, both slits are open and single photons are released, but detectors are placed in each slit. "Enough mystery!" we demand, wanting to pin down the wily photon. Now, each time a photon passes through one of the slits, one of the detectors notices its passage and makes a click. But by measuring the photon in this way, we have robbed it of its ability to act like a wave and have forced it to act like a pellet. In this case, over time, no interference pattern builds up. We just obtain two separate bands of dots. The experiment is exactly the same, but by asking the photon which slit it is passing through, we have forced it to act like a particle. *In some inexplicable way, the photon "knows" that it is being measured like a particle, and thus it acts like a particle.* If we were to turn the detectors off, the interference bands would once again build up, one photon at a time. Not only do the photons know whether or not both slits are open, they also know whether or not we are watching them!

The question of whether the photon acts like a wave or particle depends entirely on how we question it. Our questioning and act of observation collapses the wave function in a particular way. Until the question is asked and the observation is made, the photon does not objectively behave like a wave or a particle. At the quantum level, reality does not appear to have a determinate, objective existence apart from our observations. In the famous words of physicist Bernard d'Espagnat:

> The doctrine that the world is made up of objects whose existence
> is independent of human consciousness turns out to be in conflict
> with quantum mechanics and with facts established by experiment.[10]

From the standpoint of classical Newtonian physics, the two-slit experiment is an absurdity—but it has been repeated time and again in countless variations. As Richard Feynman explained in his *Lectures on Physics,* this phenomenon is "impossible, *absolutely* impossible, to explain in any classical way," yet "has in it the heart of quantum mechanics."[11] At the quantum level, the laws of classical physics just don't apply. As Feynman noted, "The 'paradox' is only a conflict between reality and your feeling of what reality 'ought to be.'"[12]

One consequence of "the paradox," however, is that *we cannot observe the world without changing it.* While this is true at the quantum level in the most startling, empirical way, it also applies to daily life. Every worldview or belief involves an interpretive focus. There are no value-free or theory-free data either in science or life. Every action and question already assumes an interpretative framework that renders certain answers possible and excludes other possibilities. This does not mean that everything is relative, but indicates that consciousness is always giving birth to reality in a participatory, co-creative way with the greater universe. In the quantum world, the act of observation collapses the infinite possible states of a photon into the one that we actually observe in a seemingly acausal way. In some way that we do not fully understand, our own awareness, working in harmony with the greater universe, may play a fundamental role in shaping the trajectory and manifestation of the world as it comes into being. Certainly this is true at the quantum level.

NATURE'S SEAMLESS UNITY: THE SPOOKY CASE OF QUANTUM NONLOCALITY

Classical physics, with its mechanical picture of the world, has been used to deny the existence of anything beyond the strictly mechanistic. Quantum physics denies that denial. It hints of something beyond what we usually consider physics, beyond what we usually consider the "physical world."

BRUCE ROSENBLUM AND FRED KUTTNER,
THE QUANTUM ENIGMA

In the mechanistic universe, everything is atomistic and distinct. Descartes and his colleagues wanted to picture the cosmos as a machine, cleansed of marvelous sympathies and hidden links between the inner and outer worlds. For Descartes the universe was a plenum, a materialistic sea in which everything pressed against everything else. Using this idea he tried to explain the movement of the planets as being carried on material vortices, like little bubbles being spun around a whirlpool of water. Any theory was worthy of consideration as long as it didn't involve hidden, nonlocal influences, for those were too closely associated with the idea of the living, sympathetic cosmos of the magical tradition.

To the consternation of the pure mechanists, Isaac Newton introduced the principle of gravity—certainly an example of hidden, sympathetic influence if there ever was one. Nonetheless, if gravity was overlooked as being merely an unknown principle that applied to inanimate matter, an essentially mechanistic worldview could be maintained. For apart from gravity and the mysterious universal laws that shaped the entire cosmos, the individual parts of the universe remained distinct and unconnected. In essence, the theory of dead matter in motion could still be maintained.

But if quantum physics pointed to a renewed sense of living matter, it also pointed to the idea of a radically unified cosmic pattern in which nonlocal influences apply. Specifically, quantum theory implied that any two "particles" which originate from a common system will continue to be entangled and function as a common system instantaneously, regardless of physical distance. Belief in locality requires that no causal influences can travel faster than the speed of light, but quantum theory predicted nonlocal effects that could occur instantaneously—even across the universe.

While Einstein made important contributions to quantum theory, he objected to the indeterminate or probabilistic action of individual particles by insisting that "God does not play dice with the universe." He also objected to the prediction of nonlocality, referring to it as a type of "spooky action at a distance," which violated the principle that nothing can travel faster than light. As he wrote, "I cannot seriously believe in the quantum theory because it cannot be reconciled with the idea that physics should represent a reality in time and space, free from spooky actions at a distance."[13] Einstein's greatness notwithstanding, this is one instance where his genius was wrong. In repeated careful experiments, first carried out in the 1980s by Alain Aspect and later refined by others, nonlocal effects—or spooky actions at a distance— were shown to be operating at the quantum level.

In the quantum realm, particles do not exist in definite times and places, but only show "tendencies to occur" and "tendencies to exist" until they are actually measured and the wave function is collapsed. Going back to the two-slit experiment, the photon exists in a suspended state of indefinite, multiple possibilities, but *only at the point of observation does it take on a definite property.*

The same thing happens with other quantum variables such as the spin or the polarization of a particle. The spin itself remains undetermined and totally unpredictable until the measurement is actually made. Despite the fact that the spin is indeterminate, other laws apply. If you have two particles that originate from a common source, the two particles must have opposite spins. Alain Aspect used this property to test for the existence of nonlocal effects on particles that are "twins."

Using particles that originated from a common source, Aspect measured the spin of one particle of the set. In this case, the experimenter can choose to measure the vertical axis of spin or the horizontal axis of spin (but not both), which will cause it to take on a certain value. At the moment the measurement is made, the twin particle instantaneously takes on the opposite value. The dumbfounding reality is not just that the spin is opposite, but that *the second particle instantaneously knows what axis the experimenter decided to observe.* Even if the particles were millions of miles away, the second particle instantaneously takes on a definite spin according to the axis chosen by the experimenter.[14]

Like the spooky effects of the two-slit experiment, the second particle knows how to spookily respond when the measurement is made. Both particles exist in an undecided, indeterminate state, but when one particle is forced to take on a definite value, the other particle instantly responds regardless of how far away it is. It's like a case of biological twins who always know what is happening to each other once a decision is made.

Quantum nonlocality proves that two particles that originate from a common system are entangled. They continue to operate as a whole system no matter how far apart they may be. Quantum nonlocality does not prove that "signals" travel "faster than light." Rather, it shows that at a deep level of reality the speed of light as a limiting factor is irrelevant because phenomena are instantaneously connected regardless of distance. At the quantum level, space and time are not absolute factors that isolate the parts of a system. The universe is not a collection of discrete, atomistic bits of dead matter floating isolated in space; it is more akin to a dynamic matrix of interconnected "wavicles" that "know" what is happening and "communicate" with one another. Because the entire universe flared forth in the first light of the Big Bang and all of its particles should remain entangled, some physicists have suggested that the entire cosmos is a unified quantum system in which every particle knows what every other particle is doing.[15] In this way, quantum physics suggests the metaphor that the entire universe may be deeply living, knowing, and intelligent—a coherent, unified system in which interconnections are not limited by time or space.

THE FOURTH ADJUSTMENT: LIFE IN THE GALACTIC GARDEN

The heavens are seen to resemble a luxuriant garden,
which contains the greatest variety of productions.

WILLIAM HERSCHELL

If quantum physics has totally altered our understanding of matter at the microlevel, the astronomical discoveries of the last hundred years have similarly transformed humanity's awareness of our place in the greater cosmic pattern.

In the 1800s astronomers debated whether the softly glowing "spiral nebulae" seen through their telescopes were distant "island universes" like our own Milky Way Galaxy (an idea proposed by Kant) or other solar systems in the process of being formed (an idea proposed by Laplace). Because of the great number of spiral nebulae, it seemed impossible that there should be such a large number of other "island universes," and the so-called nebular hypothesis of Laplace won general acceptance.

"The Great Debate" continued into the 1900s, during the time that the actual size and shape of our own Milky Way Galaxy was only starting to become clear. In 1918 Harlow Shapley was able to use Cepheid variable stars as a cosmic yardstick to measure the distance of globular clusters. Due to technical problems he overestimated the size of the Milky Way by a factor of three, but its true shape, structure, and dimensions were coming into focus. We now know that our own spiral galaxy is shaped like a giant pancake with a central bulge in the middle. The central bulge is surrounded by a spherical halo of about 150 globular clusters, each containing over 500,000 stars. The galaxy itself contains around 300 *billion* stars and its disk measures about 100,000 light-years across. Our own solar system sits in a spiral arm, about two-thirds of the way out from the center.

Aristotle, Copernicus, and even Isaac Newton had all assumed that the heavens never change, but the Milky Way Galaxy is a realm of incessant activity. Our galaxy is not a static thing, but a living event, engaged in an evolutionary alchemy. We now realize that the initial state of the universe consisted mainly of hydrogen. In 1920, British astrophysicist Sir Arthur Eddington correctly predicted that "the stars are the crucibles in which the lighter atoms which abound in the nebulae are compounded into more complex elements."[16] For astrophysicists, anything heavier than hydrogen is considered a "metal." The earliest main sequence stars cooked hydrogen and other light elements into carbon, nitrogen, and oxygen. And when these dying stars exploded, they created the heavier elements out of which life and the world are woven. With the exception of hydrogen, every atom within our bodies was created out of nuclear reactions that took place in dying stars. These exploding stars sacrificed themselves so that we might live.

The Milky Way Galaxy is a beautifully spinning and evolving ecosystem, a delicate organism made up of 300 billion cells, pulsating and undulating like a celestial starfish. In human bodies cells may live for only a few weeks, but the overall pattern is maintained. In the galactic body, the star-cells last much longer; but when they die in the brilliant flash of a supernova explosion, they give birth to new stellar formations as the galactic organism creaks, groans, and deploys its unfolding life-pattern over aeons. Like living creatures on Earth, the Milky Way is a self-organizing and self-regulating system with its own distinct metabolism and living pattern.

Only recently, however, did we discover that our own galaxy is not alone. At the beginning of the twentieth century most astronomers thought that the Milky Way made up the entire observable universe. But in February of 1924 American astronomer Edwin Hubble discovered a Cepheid variable star in the great "Andromeda Nebula." By measuring the period of the star he was able to calculate its intrinsic brightness, and this proved that the nebula was over *one million* light-years away. The great spiral nebula was not in our own Milky Way but was, in fact, a distant galaxy or "island universe." The Great Debate had finally ended.

But if the debate had ended, a new, unbelievable cosmic vista had suddenly opened. The Andromeda Galaxy is our nearest substantial galactic neighbor. On a dark summer night its glow can be made out with the naked eye and its shining, oval shape clearly discerned through binoculars. With more accurate measurements we now realize that it lies about 2.9 million light-years away. But beyond the Andromeda Galaxy and the Milky Way, there are at least 100 billion other galaxies at much greater distances. In 1996, using a special camera on the Hubble Space Telescope, the deepest picture of the universe ever taken was compiled over the period of ten days. This photograph, taken of a seemingly "empty" part of space, shows the equivalent area of sky covered by a grain of sand held at an arm's length. And that grain of sand contains no less than 1,500 galaxies. If by the most pessimistic reckoning each galaxy contains only one intelligent civilization, that leaves us with at least 100 billion intelligent civilizations in the observable universe. The actual number must be astronomically higher.

If individual galaxies resemble spinning, metabolic organisms, the entire universe is itself an evolutionary phenomenon. One of the greatest scientific discoveries of our time is the fact that the entire universe is expanding. The expansion of space was originally predicted by Einstein in 1915 but was only proved through observation some time later. In 1929 Edwin Hubble published a paper showing that distant galaxies are speeding away from us. The further away they are, the faster their recessional velocity. As Hubble discovered, the relationship between distance and speed follows a perfect mathematical pattern. A galaxy two billion years light years distant is speeding away from us at exactly twice the speed of a galaxy one billion light years distant. The recessional velocity is directly proportional to the distance. The explanation for this curious fact is that space itself is uniformly expanding between galaxies in every direction on the vast cosmic scale. Contrary to Newtonian thought, space is not a fixed or static reality, but continually rushing into existence. The universe is not expanding into a box or a predefined space, but creating space itself as it expands.

If we were to run the cosmic movie backward, space would be contracting. Rather than rushing away from each other, galaxies would be moving closer together. At some point in the distant past, galaxies would have been very much closer indeed. If we ran the movie back to the very beginning, everything in the cosmos would converge at a single point. This point is the origin of our universe described by the Big Bang theory.

In many ways the actual origin of the cosmic process remains ineffably mysterious since we have little firm idea of what caused the Big Bang in the first place. Nonetheless, using the laws of physics it is possible to describe the early state of the universe, its expansion, its cooling, and the formation of galaxies and stars. In the beginning, the entire universe was much hotter and denser, considerably hotter than the most blazing star. In such an excited state it was impossible for atoms or molecules to hold together. But as the universe started to expand and cool, a process of community building began, for the universe is an unfolding community of beings.

The evolution of the universe is a one-time process of self-organization in which more complex patterns of living "matter" emerge. After the first millionth of a second, quarks combined into protons and neutrons. After the first minute protons and neutrons combined into atomic nuclei. It took a full million years, however, for the fireball to cool sufficiently to allow nuclei and electrons to stabilize into atoms. After a billion years great galaxies began to form. The formation of galaxies is a one-time event in the history of the cosmos and no galaxies have formed since. As the universe continued to cool and stabilize, the primal stars were formed. As the galaxies came alive, supernovas gave rise to second and third-generation stars with heavier elements. As space continued to expand, the galaxies rushed faster and faster away from one another and grew more elegantly organized.

A star went supernova in our arm of the Milky Way Galaxy 4.6 billion years ago. Its shockwaves and elements provided a fertile breeding ground for the birth of our Sun 4.5 billion years ago. 4.45 billion years ago the planets formed. The Earth brought forth a crust, atmosphere, and oceans, but the environment was harsh and cataclysmic. Nonetheless, the oldest known rocks on the Earth are about 3.85 billion years old and already they contain evidence of life that had evolved past the simplest phase. According to the new cosmology, life is a natural stage in the self-organization and community-building power of matter, and it emerged on the ancient Earth at the very earliest possible opportunity.

According to Nobel Prize–winning biologist Christian de Duve, the nature of life is implicit in the cosmic pattern. In his book *Vital Dust: Life as Cosmic Imperative,* de Duve noted that given the physical-chemical conditions that prevailed on the Earth 3.8 billion years ago, "a protometabolism leading to RNA-like molecules was bound to arise along well-defined, reproducible chemical lines."[17] And if it happened here as a natural process, it must have happened on billions and billions of other planets in billions and billions of other galaxies. For de Duve and many other scientists, we inhabit a living cosmos, a universe that is "awash with life."[18] Even a conservative estimate puts the number of living planets in the universe in the trillions. As de Duve notes,

> The Earth is part, together with trillions of other Earth-like bodies, of a cosmic cloud of "vital dust" that exists because the universe

is what it is. Avoiding any mention of design, we may, in a purely factual sense, state that the universe is constructed in such a way that this multitude of life-bearing planets was bound to arise. . . . The universe is not the inert cosmos of the physicists, with a little life added for good measure. The universe *is* life, with the necessary infrastructure around; it consists foremost of trillions of biospheres generated and sustained by the rest of the universe.[19]

Harvard astronomer Harlow Shapley, one of the first to recognize the significance of cosmic evolution, also realized the inevitability of the fact that we inhabit a dynamically living universe—a universe in which living creatures are a rule rather than an exception. In his 1958 book *Of Stars and Men: Human Response to an Expanding Universe,* Shapley wrote that the existence of extraterrestrial life was unavoidable. Noting that "millions of planetary systems must exist, and billions is the better word," Shapley went on to observe that

biochemistry and microbiology, with the assistance of geophysics, astronomy, and other sciences, have gone so far in bridging the gap between the inanimate and the living that we can no longer doubt that whenever the physics, chemistry, and climates are right on a planet's surface, life will emerge, persist, and evolve.[20]

Shapley referred to this new step in human orientation as "the Fourth Adjustment." The earliest people thought that humanity itself was the center of the universe. The shift from humanity to the body of the Earth was the First Adjustment. The Second Adjustment came with the Copernican revolution, which placed the Sun at the center of the universe. Only in our own century did the Third Adjustment dawn when we realized that the Sun and billions of other stars are part of a gigantic system, orbiting the center of the Milky Way Galaxy located in the direction of Sagittarius, some twenty-five thousand light-years distant. "This shift of the sun and earth to the edge of our galaxy," Shapley wrote, "has considerably eroded human pride and self assurance; it has carried with it the revelation of the appalling number of comparable galaxies."[21] The Fourth Adjustment "is ready for the taking," he explained, "if we care to accept that opportunity." This adjustment is the realization that life on Earth is not unique, but part of the larger life-pattern of the living universe. As biophysicist Stuart Kauffman has also suggested, life on Earth—and elsewhere—must not be seen as improbable, but as an essential aspect of the cosmic pattern. As he writes in his book *At Home in the Universe: The Search for the Laws of Self-Organization and Complexity,* "I believe we are entering a new era in which life will be seen as a natural expression of tendencies toward order in a far from equilibrium universe."[22]

The scientific discoveries of the past century may have unseated humanity from the center of the cosmic stage, but they also suggest that life and mind are fundamentally innate aspects of the cosmic pattern. Modern science has overthrown every foundational assumption of the mechanistic worldview, and suggests that we live within the pattern of a systematically unfolding, self-organizing, cosmic organism that is finely tuned for the emergence of life.

11

The Pattern Which Connects

Life and Mind in Nature

Nature proceeds little by little from things lifeless to animal life in such a way that it is impossible to determine the exact line of demarcation.

ARISTOTLE

NATURE'S LIVING SYSTEMS

The universe is a self-organizing, emergent, living system. Earlier thinkers pictured the cosmos as being essentially static, but around the time of Charles Darwin (1809–1882) ideas of geological and biological evolution began to fill the air. The vast age of the Earth was starting to become recognized through the discovery of ancient fossils. A profound revolution in thought was beginning to occur. No longer could the creation myths of the world religions be read literally, for science was starting to offer up its own creation story.

But only in the twentieth century did it become obvious that the universe itself is an evolutionary system. Even at the cosmic scale, there is a creative, self-organizing movement toward greater levels of complexity, sharing, and community building. Through galactic and stellar evolution, even matter has a history and flowers forth into more complex and highly organized forms. Now, at the dawn of the twenty-first century, we are beginning to realize that life itself can only be understood as part of this greater cosmic, evolutionary process— an evolutionary process that possesses its own finely-tuned metabolic pattern.

Fifteen billion years into the evolution of the cosmic pattern, our human minds stretch back to the mystery of the beginning and try to grasp its source. The great mathematician Kurt Gödel proved that no system of mathematics can ever be complete, and this implies that no formal mathematical theory of the entire universe will ever be possible. While the Big Bang theory may take us back to *nearly* the very beginning of cosmic time, it only describes the process of the expanding universe and the increasing evolutionary complexity of matter. Despite its elegance, coherence, and empirical triumphs, the Big Bang theory hardly explains the precise, initial state of the universe or what set the process in motion. Going back to the very beginning, we enter a universe of extreme conditions in which the laws of relativity break down and quantum effects become very prominent. But if the universe itself is evolutionary, it is impossible to prove that the present-day laws of quantum mechanics applied to the universe in its very earliest state.

Despite these inherent limitations to human knowledge, there are many things we do know about the structure of the unfolding cosmic pattern. The universe itself consists of systems within systems, and these systems are evolving and self-organizing. Even at the level of the tiniest molecules and single-celled organisms, we encounter self-organizing and self-maintaining activities that reflect the rudiments of awareness or mentality. The deployment of form in time and space depends upon the power of selection; for example, the growth of a crystal involves the proper arrangement of more than ten billion molecules a minute. Matter itself is active and self-organizing, and the molecules of the crystal "know" how to bond in harmony with one another to create a highly coherent structure. In its own way, the growing crystal is an intelligent, self-regulating organism, but not one with a biological, self-reproducing metabolism.

In her book *The Unfinished Universe,* Louise Young pointed out that self-organization occurs at all levels of the cosmic pattern from galaxies, to solar systems, to the unfolding of reproductive life. "The phenomenon of organism," she wrote, "must not be limited by size or complexity. Each self-organized unit possesses the innate tendency to preserve and extend its own existence, thus increasing the total amount of Form as measured in space and time."[1] As she noted, all organisms, whether living or nonliving, spontaneously act in three ways to increase the generation of Form in space and time.[2] These activities include the synthesis of smaller units into larger units; selection, which facilitates the creation of new organisms; and self-preservation and regeneration, which actively maintains form and increases the average lifespan. The laws of our universe are rigged from the beginning to create form, and *synthesis, selection,* and *self-preservation* are cosmic powers that act at all levels of the world fabric.

The example of the self-organizing crystal illustrates the active powers of synthesis and selection, and all organic entities display a power of self-preservation. A molecule, for example, "arranges its component parts to achieve a state of maximum stability in its environment, and when this arrangement has been disturbed by external forces it restores the original configuration as rapidly as possible."[3] Self-preservation and regeneration are creative forces that are characteristic of natural organisms, but not artificially constructed structures like buildings, computers, or machines. Long before the first living cell was formed and Darwinian natural selection could operate, self-preservation and regeneration were at work shaping and molding the world fabric: "The atom recaptures its lost electrons, the crystal restores its fractured shape, the molecule discards the disturbing energy forced upon it by random encounters."[4] Certainly at the conscious level of the self-reflective human mind, the powers of synthesis, selection, and self-preservation are indicative of self-purpose. This led Young to note that "self-preservation would not be possible without a sense of self. Perhaps consciousness, like integration and the ability to

act, is present (in a very rudimentary sense) even in the most fundamental organisms."[5] Even simple bacteria sense and respond to heat,
light, and sources of nutriment. Some are able to sense and respond
to the presence of magnetic fields. As biochemist Daniel Koshland
wrote:

> "Choice," "discrimination," "memory," "learning," "instinct," "judge-
> ment," and "adaptation," are words we normally identify with higher
> neural processes. Yet, in a sense, a bacterium can be said to have each
> of these properties.[6]

The presence of mind and memory in bacteria, and the characteristics of self-preservation in even nonbiological organisms, raises the
question of how far "mind" can be traced back in the cosmic pattern
before the emergence of self-reflective consciousness in human beings.
Astronomer Harlow Shapley, the first modern scientist to fully grasp
the fact that the universe is an evolving, hierarchical system of systems, touched upon the question in his 1930 book titled *Flights from
Chaos: A Survey of Material Systems from Atoms to Galaxies.* As the
title implies, rather than winding down into an entropic heat death,
the overall development of the universe represents a "progress toward
order." At the farthest edge of complexity we discover the human
mind, but how could the human mind originate in a universe devoid
of intelligence? This led Shapley to wonder, "If Mind appears at all,
might it not possibly enter every class and subclass" in the vast hierarchy of systems that is the universe?[7] The same year, astrophysicist
James Jeans wrote his classic work *The Mysterious Universe,* in which
he claims that "the universe begins to look more like a great thought
than a great machine."[8] Modern science, in its own way, supports the
ancient Stoic idea that the universe and matter itself is intelligent and
knows how to self-organize, and that our own human intelligence is
rooted in the mind of the greater cosmos. Biological evolution is a
natural outgrowth of cosmic evolution, and we are able to think only
because our own minds and thoughts are woven out of the intelligent
patterns of the greater universe.

DARWIN'S MISSING LINK:
THE POWER OF SELF-ORGANIZATION

Life on Earth is a self-organizing phenomenon driven by the energy of the Sun. Five billion years ago when it was born, the Earth was a lifeless planet ravaged by cosmic collisions and volcanic explosions. Yet as soon as the environment stabilized sufficiently, life in its glory started to emerge. In the beginning, not a speck of organic life existed on the planet. Today, life irrepressibly permeates the surface of the Earth and survives in the most hostile environments. The proof of biological evolution is a fact revealed by our very existence. But what shapes evolution?

Charles Darwin's theory of natural selection represents a milestone in scientific and cultural history. In many ways it looked forward to and sanctioned the emergence of a process-oriented, ecological worldview. After Darwin, nature itself was seen as being in a state of creative change. The fixed categories between the species were not so fixed after all. Given enough time and pressure from the environment, new species could emerge from the process of natural selection. Most importantly, humanity's kinship with other living creatures was reinforced. Despite its anthropocentric presumptions, humanity did not exist apart from the world, but was an embodiment of nature and the entire evolutionary process. Human beings did not come into the world as strangers, but emerged from the biosphere itself. The Earth itself is not a house, but our home, and like the ancient Greek myths said, humanity ultimately sprang from the body of the Earth itself.

Despite these developments, Darwin's theory of natural selection did not offer a comprehensive theory of life and the development of biological form. In the same way that Freud's theory of the unconscious was not truly biological, Darwin's thinking was colored by the mechanistic worldview of Newtonian physics. In order to make his theory seem scientifically credible, Darwin framed it in Newtonian terms and presented organic creatures as "things" acted on by external "forces." In the same way that Newton portrayed gravity mechanistically, Darwin pictured natural selection as the outcome of abstract principles and mechanical interactions. In the words of his contemporary Samuel Butler, a believer in biological evolution, Darwin had "taken the life out of biology."[9]

In short, Darwin tended to represent evolution as a mindless, mechanical affair. Darwin's theory of natural selection reduced the complexity of evolution to just three principles. The first principle, variation, states that all individuals are slightly different. The second principle, fecundity, states that all creatures tend to produce more offspring than the environment can support. The final principle, natural selection or natural preservation, states that the differences between individuals, coupled with environmental pressures, will determine which individuals will survive longer and pass on their characteristics through reproduction. The "fittest" will tend to survive, because they represent the best "fit" with their environment.

Natural selection as described by Darwin undoubtedly occurs, but his theory only represents part of the story. That is because in order for selection to occur, you need living organisms to begin with in the first place. Yet Darwin's theory never said much about the inner nature of *life,* its dynamics, or how it arose. His major allusion to the origin of life occurred in a letter from 1877, where he wrote that one could "conceive [of] some warm little pond, with all sorts of ammonia and phosphoric salts, light, heat, electricity, etc.," a chemically formed "protein compound . . . ready to undergo still more complex changes."[10] As far as the theory of natural selection goes, there is little that is biological about it. It details how one form is replaced by another, but says little about the nature of living organisms.

In all fairness to Darwin, no one today knows precisely how life arose on Earth. But new discoveries in the study of complex, self-organizing systems are helping to round out the theory of natural selection and point toward a more comprehensive understanding of biological life and its emergence.[11] Biological life is a dissipative system that exists far from chemical equilibrium. Dissipative systems take in matter and energy and expel them. We eat, excrete, and give off heat.

A state of chemical equilibrium is inactive, a state of death. Our own state of disequilibrium ensures that matter and energy will continue to flow through us.

Life in this sense is like a flame or a whirlpool. The flame cannot exist without oxygen and fuel. A whirlpool cannot exist without a continuous supply of water. Imagine that you have a bathtub full of water and suddenly open the drain. There is a mad rush of water down the drain that enters into a chaotic state. In chaotic systems, feedback occurs, and a tiny difference can produce dramatic effects like a microphone held next to a speaker that begins to squeal. But when a system enters into a state of chaos, *the feedback in the system can cause it to self-organize and emerge from the chaos at a higher level of order.* The water rushing down the drain is in chaos, but feedback is happening: one part is beginning to act on other parts, and this is looped back and reinforced through feedback. Suddenly, spontaneously, through chaotic feedback, a state of closure is attained. The self-organized system of a whirlpool suddenly emerges from chaos and feedback. Like life, it exists in a precarious balance of flowing matter and energy far from static or dead equilibrium; but as long as the water continues to flow through the system, the life of the whirlpool will be perpetuated.

The new science of complexity studies how systems at the edge of chaos spontaneously self-organize. Feedback makes circular systems highly excited because they are folded back on themselves. Like the microphone held in front of the speaker, tiny differences can have exponentially large effects because of the circular pattern of amplification. Tiny movements of the microphone, since they are circular and folded back on themselves, can greatly affect the squeal of feedback. As signals race through the system again and again, they can become more amplified on each pass. Similarly, a tiny movement of the microphone can help to quiet the squeal. As the science of complexity shows, systems that enter into chaotic feedback can spontaneously self-organize and emerge transformed at a new, higher level of order.

When systems like the whirlpool emerge in the bathtub, one characteristic is their *holism*. Rather than just being a collection of water molecules, the whirlpool emerges as an organic entity greater than the sum of its parts. It exhibits the characteristics of synthesis, selection, and self-preservation that we mentioned earlier. It acts as a whole, not as a collection of parts. Life, too, is an emergent, self-organizing, holistic phenomenon. Living organisms consist of parts, but the parts are always subordinate to the greater, self-regulating power of the whole. As the philosopher Immanuel Kant pointed out, in a machine the parts exist *for* each other to perform a predetermined function. In an organism, the parts also exist *by means of each other* because they produce each other. Organisms are self-created, emergent unities that are coherently folded back on themselves through a process of self-regulating feedback and metabolism. In evolutionary history, our lungs influenced the development of our heart; our heart influenced the development of our lungs.

Circular feedback gives rise to the organic forms of fractal geometry. The Mandelbrot set is a visual image of a chaotic feedback equation that is folded back on itself and can be infinitely magnified on a computer (see figure 11.1 on page 210). The most interesting and complex region appears at the boundary between stability and change. Zooming in along the edges, in different parts of the set we discover a host of organic forms reminiscent of the natural world: rivers, coastlines, flashes of lightning, crystals, leaves, and patterns that look like simple organisms. But the most amazing thing of all is that no matter how greatly the magnification is increased, the spaceship-like shape of the "mother set" continually reappears. Such scaling and self-similarity is characteristic of the living forms of the natural world: the part is a model of the whole at a different level of scale. In the fractal model of a fern reproduced in figure 11.2 on page 211, the leaf is a model of the branch, and the branch is a model of the entire fern. As Plato said in his description of the World Soul, the universe is a living harmony of Sameness and Difference united through Proportion. In the fractal geometry of nature, the same pattern is repeated at different levels of scale.

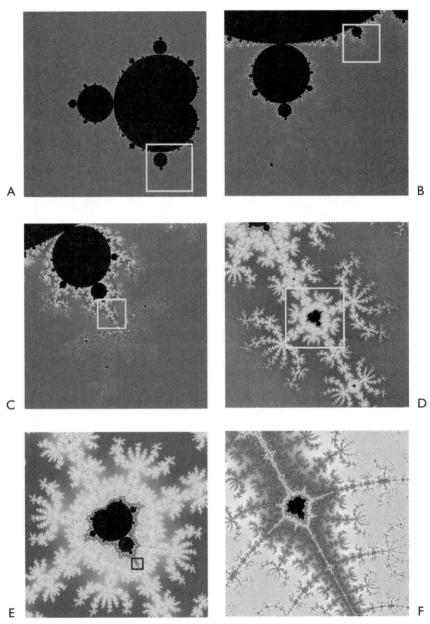

Figure 11.1. A short voyage into the infinite depths of the Mandelbrot set.
Each successive illustration is an enlargement of the highlighted area
in the previous illustration. Created through a feedback equation
that is folded back on itself, the Mandelbrot set is infinitely complex
but displays a holographic self-similarity at all levels of magnification.

Figure 11.2. Fractal model of a fern. The leaf is a model of the branch and the branch is a model of the entire fern.

LIFE AS KNOWING

Mind, or the intelligent power of self-organization, is not something that just exists in our own skulls, but is reflected throughout the entire fabric of nature. Aldous Huxley described the universe as "Mind at Large" and the biologist Gregory Bateson spoke of "mind in nature." For Bateson, mind is a metapattern. It is, in his famous words, "the pattern which connects" living things into an organic unity. Bateson described mind in its simplest expression as a "circular or more complex system of parts in which information flows that makes a difference."[12] Like the circular feedback of the self-organizing whirlpool or the circular feedback patterns that give rise to fractal geometry, mind is a self-recursive system. Processes like ecosystems can be said to possess mind. Through varying combinations of negative and positive feedback within a system, minds can freeze to a halt, be self-regulating, or spin wildly out of control on a runaway course. In healthy organisms, societies, and ecosystems, there is some type of self-regulating dynamic at work; otherwise, these types of minds would self-destruct or cease to exist. Assuming that such minds can pass on their characteristics through time, the evolutionary unfolding of further complexity becomes possible. For Bateson, life and mind were essentially synonymous, for "mind is the essence of being alive."[13] Or as the ancient Greek philosopher Epicharmus of Kos noted 2,500 years ago, "All that is alive is intelligent."[14]

Bateson's ideas are reflected and developed in the work of the Chilean biologists Humberto Maturana and Francisco Varela.[15] Maturana and Varela describe all forms of biological life as *autopoietic* or self-regulating systems. The Greek word *poiēsis* means "to make," and living organisms make and maintain themselves through self-regulation. But self-regulation only occurs in circular systems with feedback and involves a process of cognition. In all living systems, some type of self-knowledge or self-cognition is implied. A metabolism *knows* how to regulate itself. This knowledge may exist below the level of conscious awareness, but it is knowledge nonetheless. Even the simplest bacteria know how to do very complex things. Our own conscious knowledge and self-awareness may be a manifestation at a more complex level of the deep levels of knowing that exist in all biological structures, from the simplest cells on upward. Life is a process of cognition in which organisms act meaningfully in their environments. Moreover, life is a self-organizing learning phenomenon. All living systems—whether single-celled organisms or the ivy plant outside my backdoor—had to *learn* their life-functions and make a considerable number of responses, or adaptations, to get to where they are today over the course of their evolutionary history. Our own capacity to learn and remember is rooted in the fact that all life is capable of learning and decision making at some rudimentary level.

The evolutionary universe rewards excellence. Those living forms that embody sufficient stability and powers of self-regulation are sustained through natural selection. But without the primordial power of self-organization, natural selection could never operate in the first place. If we look at evolution as a learning phenomenon, it becomes obvious that mind and memory exist in all living organisms, even the smallest bacteria. Living organisms are not mindless machines, but coherent, self-organized entities that are open to their environment and capable of further growth and transformation. Not only are autopoietic organisms self-regulating, they have the power to heal themselves in almost magical ways. If you cut your hand, your body literally knows how to repair itself. If flatworms are cut into pieces, they will grow new heads or tails—or even both—to rebuild the living whole.

Self-organization is dynamic and thus occurs at the edge of chaos. In order to truly live, an organism cannot become too static or frozen. Natural forms embody stability, but too much stability is death. In order for us to grow as human beings, we mustn't become too frozen or controlled. Only by entering into unpredictable situations can life truly be lived. Only by coming undone in the dynamic flux of chaos can we enter into a higher level of self-organization through the soul-forging power of feedback and knowledge. In the self-reflective human mind, all the creative, developmental powers of evolution, self-organization, and learning can be deeply tasted and engaged in a single lifetime.

LIFE AS COMMUNITY

In the biological universe no organism is an island. The universe is not a collection of mechanical cogs, but a community of beings. Through self-organization, parts come together to form organic, emergent, and autonomous entities. This community-building process began immediately after the Big Bang, when quarks combined to form atomic nuclei. It has continued ever since in the emergence of galaxies, solar systems, living planets, and biological organisms.

In the process of self-organization, each part maintains its identity at one level, but is folded into a larger organism at another level. Author and philosopher Arthur Koestler referred to complex organic systems as holarchies (as opposed to hierarchies). A *holarchy* is a community of individual parts that he called holons. Each holon has two faces. One face is self-assertive, for such self-preservation is necessary to maintain its identity. The other face is integrative, and this integrative tendency binds it into the self-organizing community.[16] A holarchy is a structure of integrated yet individual parts. An animal is made up of organs, organs are made up of cells, cells are made up of molecules, and molecules are made up of atoms. At each level the individual holons remain, but the total organism is an emergent whole that is more than the sum of its individual parts.

In the same way that Darwin emphasized the mechanical aspect of evolution and overlooked the power of self-organization, he also emphasized the competitive aspect of evolution over the integrative tendency that brings living communities together. But in the evolutionary process, beings depend on one another for their very survival. The most important reflection of this underlying reality is found in the coevolutionary phenomenon known as *symbiosis*. In symbiotic relationships, organisms evolve together in collaboration and depend on one another for their continued existence. One symbiotic relationship exists between bees and flowers, who emerged together about a hundred million years ago and have been closely intertwined ever since. Bees depend on flowers for their food, and flowers depend on bees for their pollination. A more dramatic relationship is seen in the case of lichen, which is a fungus that assimilated green algae. The fungus shelters the algae and the algae make food for the fungus. Such a relationship is a form of *endosymbiosis,* in which one organism absorbs another to form a more complex living structure.

The most startling example of endosymbiosis is found in the human cell—and *all* nucleated cells. Microbiologist Lynn Margulis has proven that all nucleated cells are prehistoric *mergers* of ancient bacteria.[17] The mitochondria in our own cells possess their own strands of DNA apart from those of the cell nucleus. In the primordial oceans of the living Earth, simple bacteria assimilated other bacteria to symbiotically create more complex organisms. The mitochondria in our "single" cells used to, in fact, be *separate organisms*. In the unfolding community of life, patterns of sharing, relationship, and cooperation are as important as competition for survival. "Individual" cells, "single" organisms, more complex ecosystems, and the entire biosphere are all examples of symbiotic, coevolutionary communities.

Figure 11.3. The Earth seen from the Moon.

Viewed from the distance of the moon, the astonishing thing about the earth, catching the breath, is that it is alive. The photographs show the dry, pounded surface of the moon in the foreground, dead as an old bone. Aloft, floating free beneath the moist, gleaming membrane of the bright blue sky, is the rising earth, the only exuberant thing in this part of the cosmos. If you could look long enough, you would see the swirling of the great drifts of white cloud, covering and uncovering the half-hidden masses of land. If you had been looking a very long, geologic time, you could have seen the continents themselves in motion, drifting apart on their crustal plates, held aloft by the fire beneath. It has the organized, self-contained look of a live creature, full of information, marvelously skilled in handling the sun.

LEWIS THOMAS, *THE LIVES OF A CELL*

GAIA: VISIONS OF THE LIVING EARTH

I compare the earth and her atmosphere to a great living being perpetually inhaling and exhaling.

GOETHE

Through Gaia theory, I see the Earth and the life it bears as a system, a system that has the capacity to regulate the temperature and the composition of the Earth's surface and to keep it comfortable for living organisms. The self-regulation of the system is an active process driven by the free energy available from sunlight.

JAMES LOVELOCK

One of the most unpredicted outcomes of the space program was the Gaia hypothesis, the theory that the biosphere itself works to regulate the temperature and chemical content of the Earth's atmosphere. According to Gaia theory, life is a planetary-wide phenomenon that alters the environment on a planetary scale.

In 1961, atmospheric scientist James Lovelock was hired by NASA to study the detection of life on Mars. Lovelock looked at the atmospheres of Venus, Earth, and Mars, and he concluded that the presence of life on any planet would be reflected by chemical changes in the atmosphere of that planet. What Lovelock saw was straightforward but startling (see table on the following page). The atmospheres of Venus and Mars contain over 95 percent carbon dioxide with only trace amounts of oxygen. By contrast, the atmosphere of the Earth contains 21 percent oxygen with only a trace amount of carbon dioxide. The average surface temperature on the Earth is 55° Fahrenheit, because the carbon dioxide level is so low. But without the presence of life on Earth, carbon dioxide would make up 98 percent of the atmosphere and the average surface temperature of the planet would be somewhere between 464 and 644° Fahrenheit. Without the presence of life, the climate of the Earth would be incredibly inhospitable.

When the Earth was formed billions of years ago, the atmosphere

PLANETARY ATMOSPHERES: THEIR COMPOSITION

		PLANET		
Gas	Venus	Earth without life	Mars	Earth as it is
Carbon dioxide	96.5%	98%	95%	0.03%
Nitrogen	3.5%	1.9%	2.7%	79%
Oxygen	trace	0.0	0.13%	21%
Argon	70 ppm	0.1%	1.6%	1%
Methane	0.0	0.0	0.0	1.7 ppm
Surface temperatures °C	459	240 to 340	–53	13
Total pressure, bars	90	60	0.0064	1.0

Planetary atmospheres table after James Lovelock, *The Ages of Gaia.*

was almost entirely made out of carbon dioxide, just like Mars and Venus. But with the emergence of blue-green bacteria and photosynthesis, carbon dioxide became a life-giving food. In the alchemy of Earth's primordial oceans, the living metabolism of bacteria transmuted carbon dioxide and other elements into an expanding tapestry of life. The metabolic activity of the first bacteria started to give birth to a planetary-wide physiology. These first blue-green bacteria removed carbon from the atmosphere, which cooled down the planet, and gave off oxygen as a waste product. But around two billion years ago, the process gave rise to a planetary crisis—an "oxygen holocaust"—when too much oxygen had accumulated. Oxygen itself was highly toxic to the first bacteria.[18] This planetary-wide crisis provided a window of opportunity, however, when a new type of blue-green bacteria finally learned to synthesize oxygen into life-energy. Over immense periods of time, the biosphere transformed the atmosphere into its present composition. The atmosphere so composed was an atmosphere friendly to life, both in terms of its content and its stable, hospitable temperature.

While other planetary scientists had supported a "Goldilocks theory"—assuming that the temperature and atmospheric composition of the Earth had been "just right" for the emergence of life by chance—Lovelock showed that life itself had altered the planetary environment. Lovelock proposed that "the evolution of the species and the evolution of their environment are tightly coupled together as a single and inseparable process,"[19] a claim that was supported by his colleague, the microbiologist Lynn Margulis. Moreover, Lovelock and Margulis claimed that Gaia was a testable, scientific hypothesis.

During the past 4.5 billion years, solar luminosity has increased by at least 10–30 percent.[20] But the Gaian superorganism has successfully maintained a steady temperature through its metabolic processes. When critics complained that Lovelock's theory smacked of teleology or design, he created a simple computer model called Daisyworld. Daisyworld contains two types of daisies, white and black, that naturally live in a certain temperature range and absorb different levels of heat. If the temperature is low on Daisyworld, the black daisies flourish because they absorb more heat. This causes the planet to warm up. If the temperature is high on Daisyworld, the white daisies flourish and reflect heat back off into space. Even if the luminosity of Daisyworld's sun increases substantially, Daisyworld itself maintains a constant temperature—until the environmental conditions caused by the solar warming become just too extreme for the biota to regulate. Lovelock proved that life can act like a planetary thermostat, and more complex models with twenty shades of daisies produced the same result.[21]

In addition to holding the temperature constant by reducing carbon dioxide, life has regulated the amount of oxygen in the atmosphere. Right now oxygen makes up 21 percent of the atmosphere, a level that must have remained constant for over 300 million years. If the concentration of oxygen was just a few points higher, devastating forest fires would engulf the planet. But if the oxygen level was a few points lower, animal life would perish.

As biologist Lynn Margulis points out, "Life does not exist *on* Earth's surface so much as it *is* Earth's surface. . . . Earth is no more a planet-sized chunk of rock inhabited with life than your body is a skeleton infested with cells."[22] Gaia's radical challenge to traditional Darwinian biology is that *life influences the environment*. For Darwin, life was essentially passive, a process that was forced to adapt to a specific environment. Gaia theory shows that life and environment evolve as a single, coevolutionary process. On Earth, all life is an embodiment of the planetary environment, but the planetary environment is also a product of life. Gaia theory and the new biology both embody the circular, metabolic logic of life. The universe brings forth life and mind—but life and mind work to shape the universe. Life and environment are folded back on themselves in a self-referential, evolutionary spiral. Gaia is not a single organism, but a superorganism. Like the single organisms of which it is comprised, it is self-regulating and autopoietic. Like my own body composed of many individual cells, Gaia has its own metabolism. As we breathe and exhale, we participate in the life-breath of the entire biosphere. Gaia theory is strongly supported by the science of complexity, which shows how complex systems with feedback loops spontaneously self-organize and develop metabolic patterns. From the Gaian perspective, our own lives are totally inseparable from the life of the larger planet.

THE FITNESS OF THE COSMIC ENVIRONMENT

The more I examine the universe and study the details of its architecture, the more evidence I find that the universe in some sense must have known that we were coming.

FREEMAN DYSON

Gaia theory shows how life and the environment are but two faces of a single evolutionary unfolding. But what is the likelihood that life should emerge in the cosmos at all? What precisely determines the fitness of the cosmic environment? According to the ancient Hermetic philosophers, human nature, as microcosm, is an embodiment of the entire cosmic pattern. In a similar sort of way, modern physicists have asked what the presence of human observers reveals about the nature of the universe itself. This question is known as "the anthropic principle" and has established itself as a hotly debated topic in modern cosmology.

The basic problem of the anthropic principle revolves around this issue: how do the initial conditions of the universe relate to the conditions needed to produce life? It seems certain that not just any conceivable physical conditions would allow life to form. Thus, according to anthropic theorists, the very fact of our existence should limit what possibilities can be considered.

First proposed by American physicist Robert Dicke in 1961, the *weak anthropic principle* states that life can arise and flourish only during a certain epoch of our universe. Because of this, the size of the universe that we can observe is limited by biological factors. Ultimately, there is nothing controversial about the weak anthropic principle. Only when the universe had expanded to a certain size and cooled down sufficiently, was it possible for life to emerge in the first place. Our own existence, in a roundabout way, thus limits the type of universe we can observe, and the type of universe we can exist in. Put another way, it was not possible for life to emerge in our universe before the universe itself possessed a certain size, temperature, and complexity.

The *strong anthropic principle,* first proposed by Australian physicist Brandon Carter in 1968, states that only for a special kind of universe could life arise at all, at any epoch. Proponents of the strong anthropic principle point toward the recent discoveries that the fundamental physical constants of nature itself seem "finely tuned" or even "rigged" for the emergence of life and evolutionary form. There are many fascinating examples of these finely tuned constants of nature. For example, a variation in the strength of gravity by *one part* in 10^{40} would eliminate all main-sequence stars from the universe, leaving only blue giants (if larger) or red dwarfs (if smaller).

Even more remarkable is the unimaginably fine balance between the expanding force of the universe and the power of gravitational attraction at the beginning of time. If the expansive force had been just slightly stronger, matter would have dispersed outward in such a way that galaxies and stars could have never formed. But if the gravitational force had been just slightly stronger, the universe would have fallen back on itself and collapsed. The actual balance of forces is so incredibly precise that a difference of one part in 10^{60} would have pushed the universe either way. If thought of in terms of accuracy, this is the precision needed to aim a bullet at a one-inch target twenty billion light-years away.[23]

This incredible balance of forces is almost beyond human comprehension. As cosmologist Freeman Dyson put it,

> I conclude from the existence of the accidents of physics and astronomy that the universe is an unexpectedly hospitable place for living creatures to make their home in. Being a scientist, trained in the habits of thought and language of the twentieth century rather than the eighteenth, I do not claim that the architecture of the universe proves the existence of God. I claim only that the architecture of the universe is consistent with the hypothesis that mind plays an essential role in its functioning.[24]

Different readings of the anthropic principle and its significance abound. Some liken it to the eighteenth-century argument for God's existence by design, while others see in it something more like a *post hoc* logical fallacy. But once all of the verbiage and debate has been sifted through, the remarkable fact of nature's finely tuned constants remains. As philosopher Errol Harris noted, "The unity of the universe and the exact nature of the organizing principle that governs its order and structure are clearly not indifferent to the emergence and the existence of life and mind."[25]

In this sense, the anthropic principle does reveal significant features about the universe we inhabit. Even if the universe has no "designer" in the traditional theological sense, the cosmos itself appears to be the embodiment of an *exquisitely sensitive* and self-consistent design that allows the beauty of the cosmos and conscious life to flower forth. As cosmologist Brian Swimme put it,

> The universe thrives on the edge of a knife. If it increased its strength of expansion it would blow up; if it decreased its strength of expansion it would collapse. By holding itself on the edge it enables a great beauty to unfold. The Milky Way also thrives on the edge of a knife. Decrease its gravitational bonding and all the

stars scatter; increase the gravitational bonding and the galaxy collapses on itself. By holding itself in the peace of a fecund balance of tensions, it enables planetary structures and living beings to blossom forth.[26]

Ultimately, the anthropic principle suggests that *we must look at the unfolding of the universe as a single, highly coordinated event.* Our existence in the universe is not an accident, but the reflection of a finely tuned cosmic pattern that was present and friendly toward the emergence of life from the start. In this sense, the anthropic principle points toward the idea of a living, biocentric universe.

Plato wrote that "the cosmos is a single Living Creature which contains all living creatures within it."[27] While the anthropic principle cannot prove the existence of an external creator God, it does point toward the traditional metaphor of a living, intelligent cosmos that is both divinely beautiful and divinely ordered. Like any organism, the cosmos is a self-coherent entity. The universe as a whole is a self-consistent system with its own life pattern and internal metabolism. But contemporary cosmology shows just *how* finely tuned the metabolic patterns of the universe are. Because of these exquisitely balanced parameters, life as we know it is able to unfold and develop. The anthropic principle expresses the fact that we are rooted in the greater life of the cosmos and participate in its deep structure and beauty. In this sense, we are truly meant to be here.

PART IV

A WORLD WITH A FUTURE

Cultivating Life in a Global Community

The creation . . . is not an event which happened in the remote past but is rather a living reality of the present. Creation is a process of evolution of which man is not merely a witness but a participant and partner as well.

THEODOSIUS DOBZHANSKY

12

The Turning Point

Returning Home in the Space Age

The collective psyche seems to be in the grip of a powerful archetypal dynamic in which the long-alienated modern mind is breaking through, out of the contractions of its birth process, out of what Blake called its "mind-forg'd manacles," to rediscover its intimate relationship with nature and the larger cosmos.

RICHARD TARNAS

VOYAGING INTO SPACE

In 1957 Sputnik, the first artificial satellite, was catapulted into space. Not much larger than a basketball, the shiny metal sphere gave off a steady electronic heartbeat, and its regular, metallic sounding beacon was tuned into by amateur radio operators around the world. With Sputnik's successful Earth orbit, the door of the space age opened.

Born in 1961, the first year that a human orbited the Earth, I am a child of the space age. Late at night in my parents' bedroom at the age of eight, I sat enraptured with my family in front of a Zenith color television, which was encased in a finely crafted wooden cabinet. Like millions of others we watched and participated in a moment of planetary history when Neil Armstrong first stepped onto the lunar surface. Like millions of others, it is a moment I will never forget. Leaving our planet behind and setting foot on another world was an event that changed our world forever. Later in my childhood I built a model of an Apollo spacecraft as a science project, and once I witnessed the arching vapor trail of an Apollo space launch on the coast of the Gulf of Mexico, a couple hundred miles away from Cape Canaveral in Florida. But now, no matter when you were born, we are all inhabitants of the space age.

Only within the last generation did our understanding of the large-scale structure of the universe start to open up. Only around 1920 did we start to understand the shape and dimensions of our own Milky Way Galaxy. Today we know that it is a vast spiral galaxy of 300 billion stars; we understand its shape, and the location of our own solar system along a spiral arm. Only in 1924 did we first start to realize that there are billions of galaxies other than our own. Yet that was just the beginning. In 1929, we discovered that the entire universe is expanding. That was followed by the more recent discovery of cosmic evolution, the understanding that matter and the entire universe has an unfolding history. For many years most astronomers believed that other stars had planets, but only recently has this been proven. Today, using both the Hubble Space Telescope and ground-based telescopes, we can now actually see protoplanetary disks— or solar systems in the making—forming around other stars.

Historically, the cosmological impulse, which springs from wonder, has provided the deepest inspiration for humans to understand the nature of the greater universe. The human intellect, charged with passion, is prepared to make almost any sacrifice necessary to understand its deeper relationship with the cosmos. In one famous example, the Renaissance astronomer Johannes Kepler filled nine hundred pages with mathematical models and equations until he could finally understand the orbit of Mars and the laws of planetary motion. Yet this same driving passion to understand the world can also take us away from being present with the world of everyday experience. In the course of human development, however, separation is often necessary before a fuller union can be achieved. Following the Scientific Revolution, the tenor of the modern mind came to be increasingly characterized by detachment, estrangement, and the lack of a felt, living connection with the whole. But we are living in a transitional time when this sense of estrangement is beginning to break down.

In this sense, perhaps the trajectory of the modern world is best symbolized by the figure of the astronaut. In the development of the human personality, each individual needs to forge an autonomous identity—or crystallize an ego—which separates that person from the world by making the world into a distinct "other." With the emergence of the Scientific Revolution and the mechanistic worldview, the image of God also shifted in that direction. The God of deism was a Divine Engineer, a distant spectator, who possessed no contact with the universe but looked upon it from afar, mirroring the detached, theoretical ethos of the scientific spirit. Similarly, no figure could be more clearly and distinctly separated from the living Earth than the astronaut. Floating high in space above the clouds of his home planet, totally encased in metal, plastic, and a hermetically sealed space suit, the astronaut cannot touch the Earth, but only gaze down upon it through a porthole. The astronaut's mechanical umbilical cord is not connected to another human being or to a nurturing mother, but bound to a technological life support system. With the astronaut, it seems as if we have attained the most complete break between humanity and living nature possible. But fortunately, the story does not end there.

RETURNING TO EARTH

Paradoxically, only when we had left the world behind in the most complete way was it possible for us to reawaken and more deeply sense the cosmic bond between humanity and our home planet. Only with the hermetically sealed astronaut, riding aloft in a self-contained bubble at the greatest moment of separation, was it possible to gaze down upon the glorious epiphany of the entire Earth as a whole. Only in the space age could we look back at our home planet from afar and thus realize the fragile and beautiful nature of the living Earth, which is a unique, one-time endowment in the history of the universe.

The experience of seeing the Earth from space was a profoundly transformative event in the lives of many astronauts. One thread that runs through their accounts is the direct perception that the Earth is an organic unity. Spinning above our planet in an orbiting spacecraft, the first thing one notices is that the Earth's political boundaries are arbitrary and man-made. Eugene Cernan, a veteran of many spaceflights and the last man to walk on the Moon, described the exquisite beauty of our spinning blue planet with its lakes, rivers, and carpets of green:

> You quickly fly over changes in topography, like the snow-covered mountains or deserts or tropical belts—all very visible. You pass through a sunrise and a sunset every ninety minutes. . . . You look back "home" . . . and don't see the barriers of color, religion, and politics that divide up this world.[1]

Russell Schweickart, a lunar module pilot who made the first space walk without an umbilical, made a similar point:

> You look down there and you can't imagine how many borders and boundaries you cross, again and again and again, and you don't even see them. There you are—hundreds of people in the Mid-East killing each other over some imaginary line that you're not even aware of, that you can't see. And from where you see it, the thing is a whole, and it's so beautiful. You wish you could take one in each hand, one from each side in the various conflicts, and say, "Look. Look at it from this perspective. Look at that. What's important?"[2]

Returning to the Earth from the Moon, astronaut Edgar Mitchell gazed upon our home planet and then off into the depths of the cosmos, only to experience "a startling recognition that the nature of the universe was not as I have been taught. My understanding of the separate distinctness and the relative independence of movement of those cosmic bodies was shattered. There was an upwelling of fresh insight coupled with a feeling of ubiquitous harmony—a sense of interconnectedness with the celestial bodies surrounding our spacecraft."[3] What hit Mitchell was a profoundly personal insight into the nature of cosmic evolution. There he was, hanging in space, realizing that his body, the bodies of his colleagues, the spacecraft, and the entire solar system were all forged out of the remains of ancient stars, created over billions of years of cosmic evolution, just like the stars shining around him. At this moment he experienced and overwhelming realization:

> Our presence here, outside the domain of the home planet, was not rooted in an accident of nature or in the capricious political whim of a technological civilization. It was rather an extension of the same universal process that evolved our molecules. And what I felt was an extraordinary personal connectedness with it. I experienced an ecstasy of unity. I not only *saw* the connectedness, I *felt* it and experienced it sentiently. I was overwhelmed with the sensation of physically and mentally extending out into the cosmos. The restraints and boundaries of flesh and bone fell away. I realized that this was a biological response of my brain attempting to reorganize and give meaning to information about the wonderful and awesome processes that I was privileged to view from this vantage point. Although I am now more capable of articulating what I felt then, words somehow always fall short. I am convinced that this always has been and always will be an ineffable experience.[4]

Despite the ineffability of such events, many astronauts have felt called to bring their remarkable experiences back to Earth and to share them with their fellow humans. As Rusty Schweickart explains, it's almost like an astronaut becomes a sensing element or representative for the rest of humanity, who cannot have the experience directly:

> You look down and see the surface of that globe that you've lived on all this time, and you know all those people down there and they are like you, they are you—and somehow you represent them. . . . And somehow you recognize that you're a piece of this total life. And you're out there on that forefront and you have to bring that back somehow. And that becomes a rather special responsibility and

tells you something about your relationship with this thing we call life. So that's a change. That's something new. And when you come back there's a difference in that world now. There's a difference in that relationship between you and that planet and you and all those other forms of life on that planet, because you've had that kind of experience. It's a difference and it's so precious. . . . It's life that has had that experience.[5]

THE VIEW FROM ABOVE: LIVING LIFE FROM A COSMIC PERSPECTIVE

As we saw in chapter 3, the ancient Stoic philosophers viewed the world as a *cosmopolis,* an all-inclusive community encompassing the cosmos, our planet, and all living things; and in this community there is a brotherhood of humanity because of the common reason or intelligence that unites us. The ancient Greek philosophers knew that the Earth was a globe or sphere, and hundreds of years before we could actually look back and see the Earth from above, beautiful engravings from the Renaissance illustrated our living blue planet, with continents and oceans, floating through space (see figure 12.1).

Figure 12.1. Renaissance engraving from 1618 of the Earth and its shadow, floating in space.

Seeking to live in harmony with nature and cosmic reason, the Stoic philosophers practiced a spiritual exercise, now called "the view from above," in which they imagined themselves high up in space, looking down on the Earth below. In the words of Marcus Aurelius:

> Watch and see the courses of the stars as if you were running along-side them, and continually dwell in your mind upon the changes of the elements into one another. . . . When you are reasoning about mankind, look upon earthly things below as if from some vantage point above them.[6]

The goal of this exercise was "to relocate human existence within the infinity of time and space, and the perspective of the great laws of nature" and to see "the mutual implication in each thing in everything else."[7] In this way, viewing things from a cosmic perspective, the philosopher would see the world as it really is; and seeing life in a cosmic context, he would not be psychologically troubled by the small disturbances that cause such a large amount of suffering for much of humanity.

As philosopher Pierre Hadot wrote:

> Philosophy in antiquity was an exercise practiced at each instant. It invites us to concentrate on each instant of life, to become aware of the infinite value of each present moment, once we have replaced it within the perspective of the cosmos. The exercise of wisdom entails a cosmic dimension. Whereas the average person has lost touch with the world, and does not see the world qua world, but rather treats the world as a means of satisfying his desires, the sage never ceases to have the whole constantly present to mind. He thinks and acts within a cosmic perspective. He has the feeling of a whole which goes beyond the limits of his individuality.[8]

While this kind of sublime experience was available to only a tiny number of people in the ancient world, thanks to the images of the space program now readily available on the Internet, the transformative experience of seeing the Earth from space is now available to many

Figure 12.2. The Earth's atmosphere as seen from above, showing a towering thundercloud, as the Sun sets over the Pacific Ocean. Photo taken from the International Space Station, July 21, 2003.

(see figure 12.2). Recently, a short, stunning documentary about the transformative effect of seeing the Earth from space, *Overview,* was created especially for distribution on the Internet by a group of young filmmakers, the Planetary Collective.[9] Others have produced astonishing time-lapse photography of the Earth's surface and atmosphere using high-resolution images from the International Space Station.[10] As Stewart Brand, founder of the *Whole Earth Catalog,* wrote, "Those riveting Earth photos changed everything. For the first time humanity saw itself from outside. . . . Suddenly humans had a planet to tend for."[11]

THE NEW COSMOPOLIS: REDISCOVERING OUR PLACE IN A GLOBAL COMMUNITY

After more than two thousand years, only now do we live in a world that once again approximates the global civilization of the Hellenistic world and the "global village" of ancient Alexandria, where the entire world was on tap. Each day in our own time, the world becomes smaller and smaller, due to the nearly instantaneous travel provided by global airlines, the instantaneous communication provided by the World Wide Web, and a globalized, interconnected economy.

But is our globally connected civilization really a *cosmopolis,* a world community, as envisioned by the ancient philosophers? In other words, what is the difference between a global civilization and a global community?

While recently exploring these questions in a talk about the ancient and modern meanings of global community held in Alexandria, Egypt, I concluded that three things are needed to consciously live in a cosmopolis as it was understood by the old philosophers:

1. A real, felt sense of our bond with the transcendent order of which we are a part
2. A vision of living nature and an appreciation of nature's intelligence
3. An ethical concern for society based on our intrinsic kinship with others[12]

Interestingly, when ordinary people see the stunning images of the Earth taken from space, they are inspired to immediately and intuitively grasp these three points *just by seeing*. Even the ancient Stoics, who routinely practiced "the view from above" in their spiritual imaginations, would be utterly astonished by the sublime beauty of our home planet seen from space. Viewing the Earth from space is more powerful than any philosophical argument or scientific theory, because it touches our inner emotions and awakens our larger sense of self-identity in a visceral, poignant, and transformative way.

In a cosmopolis, there is a living, felt sense of our bond with the greater, transcendent order of which we are a part. The most fundamental fact of our existence is that we are all part of a greater life, a cosmic life. While that reality is continually being eclipsed by the distractions of life in our technological society, the vision of the Earth from space immediately reminds us. Seen from space, the Earth is one living organism that encompasses all living creatures within it. In the famous words of author Lewis Thomas, the astonishing thing about the Earth seen from space "is that it is alive . . . it has the organized, self-contained look of a live creature, full of information, marvelously skilled in handling the sun."[13] The image of the whole Earth shows that all human beings—and all living things—belong to one grand community. As noted earlier, in the words of Lynn Margulis, "Life does not exist *on* Earth's surface so much as it *is* Earth's surface."[14] The ancient idea of the cosmopolis is not just an abstract concept, but something we can now see.

This new vision of the living Earth communicates immediately the central fact that our own lives and the life of the biosphere are inextricably intertwined. And like some kind of providential gift, this understanding arrived at exactly the right time as we humans are struggling to integrate our own needs with the needs of the greater biosphere. Now, being able to view the Earth from space, we can also see the tangible traces and scars we have left on the surface of our planet, the way our cities illuminate the Earth's skies at night, and time-lapse movies of deforestation and climate change.[15]

Without question, the single most serious problem human beings face at the beginning of the twenty-first century is that of crushing overpopulation, and the simple fact that "unlimited growth" is simply not possible in a closed system of natural resources (see figure 12.3).

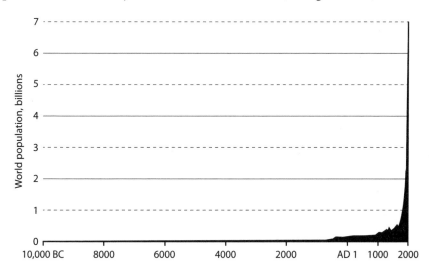

Figure 12.3. Graph of world population growth from 10,000 B.C. to A.D. 2010 from data of the U.S. Census Bureau. The figure highlights the exponential growth in human population that has taken place since the eighteenth century.

As biology writer Janine Benyus notes:

> We are still beholden to ecological laws, the same as any other life-
> form. The most irrevocable of these laws says that a species cannot
> occupy a niche that appropriates all resources—there has to be some
> sharing. Any species that ignores this law winds up destroying its
> community to support its own expansion. Tragically, this has been
> our path. We began as a small population in a very large world and
> have expanded in number and territory until we are busting the
> seams of that world. There are too many of us, and our habits are
> unsustainable.[16]

After the Black Death in 1350, world population stood around
370 million; it now exceeds 7 billion. During the entire history of our
planet, human population never exceeded the level of 1 billion people
until around 1800. And before recent times "no one ever lived through
a doubling of the entire human population. But during the twentieth
century human population *quadrupled*. Experts dispute how many people the Earth can support, but no one seriously proposes that the Earth
can sustain another population doubling."[17] Right now, our human
ecological footprint exceeds the natural, long-term, sustainable carrying capacity of the planet by about 50 percent. What this means is that
each year we are unsustainably drawing too much from our planet's
long-term reserves, resulting in "ecological overshoot." It now takes the
Earth 1.5 years to regenerate what we use in a single year and to reab-
sorb the carbon dioxide we release.[18]

As economist Hazel Henderson reflects:

> The stage that we're really at now is that the planet is teaching us
> directly. It's as if we really are coming up to graduation time, as
> Bucky [Buckminster Fuller] always said, and that the planet has all
> of the positive and negative feedback signals, which, if we can hear
> them, are the signals for us to change our belief systems and our
> value systems.
>
> For me, the metaphor was really Gaia, the living planet. People

are beginning to realize that we humans do not manage this planet; and so it was an excessively anthropocentric view, which could have gotten us into a tremendous amount of trouble. So I think that [without] having a more correct view of our place in nature, and realizing that we are part of an orchestration of species, and that unless we think of the entire planet as a living system, we will not be able to survive and keep our place in it.[19]

Future generations, I believe, will clearly understand that seeing the whole Earth from space was both a symbolic and historical turning point for the human race. Like a child seeing and consciously recognizing the face of its mother for the first time, seeing the Earth wasn't a detached intellectual experience for anyone; it was a vital awakening to the nature of life on our home planet and the living bond that connects us all. This vision and gift of authentic perception marked a turning point—and a shift away from the disconnected gaze of the Cartesian spectator.

When we see the living Earth from above, no one can remain a detached spectator any longer. Both emotionally and aesthetically, we immediately sense our connectedness with the entire web of life, in which we participate. In the words of poet Archibald MacLeish, "To see the earth as it truly is, small and blue and beautiful in that eternal silence where it floats, is to see ourselves as riders on the earth together, brothers on that bright loveliness in the eternal cold—brothers who know now they are truly brothers."[20]

In the living world, we are participants, not spectators. And in the New Cosmopolis of our global community, wherever we might live, and whatever tribes we might belong to, we are all now planetary citizens.

13

The Alchemy of Engagement
Working in Collaboration with Nature

The question of the century is: How best can we shift to a culture of permanence, both for ourselves and for the biosphere that sustains us?

EDWARD O. WILSON

ECOLOGICAL DESIGN AND BIOMIMICRY: LEARNING FROM NATURE'S INTELLIGENCE

In order for human life and nature to both really flourish far into the future, a new relationship between them is needed. This requires new ways of thinking about our connection with nature and nature's intelligence, ways of thinking embodied in the new sciences of ecological design and biomimicry.

Nature's intelligence is not just an abstract concept but a dynamic, regulating power embodied in all living creatures and living systems. Life on Earth has a 3.8 billion year history, and this is a history of creative problem solving. As biologist and writer Janine Benyus likes to point out, "We live in a competent universe . . . we are part of a brilliant planet . . . we are surrounded by genius."[1]

236

Most of the problems that human beings face have already been solved brilliantly by other living organisms. This is the basic premise of *biomimicry:* that nature is a vast storehouse of creative intelligence, which we can learn from and apply to solve our most pressing problems. "What's happening now in this field of biomimicry is that other organisms, the rest of the natural world, are doing things very similar to what we need to do. But in fact they are doing them in a way that has allowed them to live gracefully on this planet for billions of years."[2] In other words, the ideas present in nature's design intelligence are not only proven and tested over long periods of time, they are by definition ecologically sustainable.[3] Biomimicry and ecological design draw on the genius of nature so that nature's intelligence can be applied to solving human problems.

In her book *Biomimicry: Innovation Inspired by Nature,* and her well-illustrated talks, Janine Benyus describes dozens of scientific breakthroughs and new technologies directly inspired by the study of nature's intelligence. The most famous example of biomimicry is the invention of the airplane, inspired by generations of humans studying the flight of birds. Velcro was inspired by the way in which burs from plants securely attach themselves to fur and human clothing. A new kind of paint called Lotusan creates self-cleaning building exteriors, reproducing the self-cleaning designs found in lotus leaves and butterfly wings. Noting that shark skins do not carry bacteria, one inventor followed nature's blueprint of the shark-skin solution when creating a surface covering for hospital use. The covering is designed to help keep surfaces sterile without the use of antibiotics. The list goes on.

Ultimately, all the energy on the Earth comes from sunlight falling on the surface of our planet. Billions of years ago, plants learned how to capture and make use of this energy, which made life on Earth possible. Today we can directly make electricity from sunlight by using photovoltaic cells and solar panels, but these are created using toxic substances and vast amounts of energy. By contrast, plants are 90 percent more efficient at converting and storing solar energy. Imagine what breakthroughs might be possible if we could approximate the energy-gathering capabilities of plants, by learning from their design intelligence. In fact, one California-based company, OneSun LLC, is working on this very project. Imitating the way a leaf uses the sun, their "thin film 'panel' is water-proof, 90 percent recycled and 100 percent recyclable, it can be installed completely flat (as opposed to tilted to face the sun), it can make energy from any kind of light, including moonlight, and a 75W panel only weighs 3 pounds."[4] OneSun seeks to produce solar energy for less cost than coal, which has a 60:1 return on the initial energy invested. OneSun's solar technology has a return of 200:1.[5] As architect and ecological design pioneer Sim Van der Ryn has noted, "In many ways, the environmental crisis is a design crisis."[6]

In her book, Benyus defines biomimicry as drawing on three key principles:

BI - O - MIM - IC - RY
[From the Greek *bios,* life, and *mimesis,* imitation]

1. *Nature as model.* Biomimicry is a new science that studies nature's models and then imitates or takes inspiration from these designs and processes to solve human problems, e.g. a solar cell inspired by a leaf.

2. *Nature as measure.* Biomimicry uses an ecological standard to judge the "rightness" of our innovations. After 3.8 billion years of evolution, nature has learned: What works. What is appropriate. What lasts.

3. *Nature as mentor.* Biomimicry is a new way of viewing and valuing nature. It introduces an era based not on what we can extract from the natural world, but on what we can learn from it.[7]

While green building design is becoming quite mainstream in the United States and elsewhere, ecological design goes far beyond a quest for greater energy efficiency and better materials use. In its deepest sense, *ecological design represents a new kind of science (and knowing) in which humanity consciously enters into collaboration with nature to create a better, more flourishing world that is mutually beneficial to all life-forms.* To understand what ecological design can represent in its deepest sense, and what a real, ongoing collaboration with nature can involve, we now turn to examine the award-winning work of biologist John Todd. One of the great visionaries in the field, Todd's "living machines" or "eco-machines" embody a new kind of collaboration between humanity and nature.

A DIFFERENT KIND OF SCIENCE: WORKING IN COLLABORATION WITH NATURE

Ecological design and ecological engineering is about as radical a discipline as you can get. Because what it says, at the very outset, is that human beings are going to be partners with other life-forms.

JOHN TODD

Trained in marine biology, John Todd began his ecological design work as a cofounder of the New Alchemy Institute, a research center based on Cape Cod, Massachusetts, devoted to "the creation of ecologically derived human support systems," including renewable energy, agricultural aquaculture (growing fish for food), and energy-self-sufficient, ecologically sustainable architecture. Inspired equally by the ecological spirit of the counterculture and the rigorous use of scientific testing, the New Alchemists conducted pioneering research between 1969 and 1991 in how to apply nature's design intelligence to meeting human needs.

One key milestone in the work of New Alchemy was the development of the bioshelter, a solar greenhouse that is a self-contained ecosystem. What makes a bioshelter different from a conventional greenhouse is the presence of clear or translucent above-ground aquaculture tanks that contain algae, fish, other aquatic organisms, and floating hydroponic crops. These tanks are connected so water flows between them, replicating the patterns of connection and the cycling of nutrients found in natural ecosystems. Like the oceans of the planetary biosphere, the solar algae tanks in a bioshelter absorb solar energy and heat during the daytime and then release it back into the environment over long periods of time. In this way, the solar algae tanks provide a way of heating the

Figure 13.1. Solar-algae tanks in an early, experimental bioshelter at the New Alchemy Institute. Like the Earth's oceans, the aquatic tanks absorb heat from sunlight and release it back into the environment over long periods of time.

bioshelter year-round, even in winter climates, without the use of fossil fuels (see figure 13.1).

Bioshelters can be used for a variety of purposes, including the year-round production of food and the elimination of conventional heating systems. During the New Alchemy years, Todd designed two large-scale bioshelters called "Arks," which also included areas for living and working. With a tropical-like, indoor climate in the middle of winter, Todd knew that the Ark built on Prince Edward Island in Canada was a success when, during one winter blizzard, he saw the people inside working in shorts—all without the use of any fossil fuels.[8]

Over the course of decades, Todd's work evolved from the New Alchemy Institute into even more promising directions with the development of Living Machines (later to be called Eco-Machines, because of a trademark issue). A Living Machine is a type of bioshelter specifically designed, in collaboration with living organisms, to solve a particular problem: for example, turning sewage into pure water or eliminating carcinogens in polluted lakes.

As Todd explains in a lecture, for some time ecological designers "have been trying to decode what a forest knows. Or decode what a prairie knows. Or decode what a lake knows. By that I mean we are trying to tease out the hidden language of nature, which is really a legacy over several billion years old."[9] As he notes:

> For over several billion years, life has been organizing itself in concert—experimenting, evolving, changing, adapting—[and] inherent in the magnificence of this life is a deep set of instructions. And if only we could decode these instructions, we could then begin to design human systems which are as wise as they. And the thesis goes, if we could design human systems, say as wise as the forest, we could do great things based primarily on sunlight, using efficient interactions between life forms, and carry out the tasks of society without the current negative impact on the natural world. The thesis here goes that it is possible, if we truly look to nature for our instructions, that we could reduce the negative human imprint on this planet by as much as 90 percent.[10]

During the New Alchemy years Todd discovered that it is possible to draw on nature's intelligence to solve pressing human problems, leading him to conclude that ecological design is "the intelligence of nature applied to human needs," and that "ecological design is one way of forming a new partnership between the ecological needs of the planet and humanity."[11]

One of his key findings from this period is that living technologies begin to work—and to produce amazing results—when three separate ecologies are brought together in a living machine. For example, figure 13.2 on page 242 illustrates three separate ecosystems, placed within a greenhouse: in the foreground, a pond; in the middle, a marsh; and in the background, clear-sided tanks, filled with water and aquatic organisms.

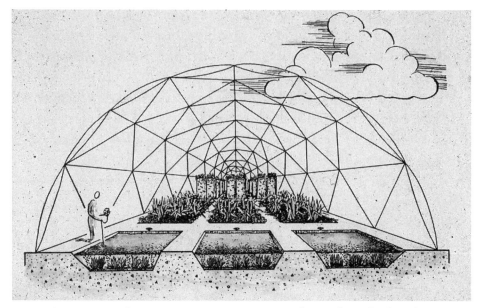

Figure 13.2. Three separate ecosystems—a pond, marsh, and solar-algae space—linked together in a greenhouse to form a living technology.

As Todd explains:

By putting those inside the greenhouse, the ecological engineer or designer brings into that structure three different kinds of intelligence: the intelligence of the pond, the intelligence of the marsh, and the intelligence of what is called a solar-algae space. And then if you combine those three and have water or waste flow between them, what happens inside is that a kind of meta-intelligence forms; and inside there, the living ecology, made up of those three systems, then has an uncanny ability to self-organize, self-design, and self-repair. Therefore, the human being can put into that [system] compounds that are considered noxious or dangerous, and by the interactions that take place, have that compound be transformed into something that is useful and beautiful.[12]

In one of the earliest experiments conducted with Living Machines, a system using twenty-one solar-algae cylinders, linked with a constructed marsh, was set up to treat chemically laden toxic waste near the town of Harwich on Cape Cod. It took about ten days for the waste to flow through the system, with astonishing results: 99 percent of the ammonia and phosphorous were removed from the effluent, and so too were heavy metals, fats, and grease. Fecal coliform bacteria were largely eliminated, and nitrite levels were reduced to a tenth of those considered to be safe for well water. But most amazingly, "of fifteen volatile compounds listed as carcinogenic by the EPA contained in the septage as it entered the first tank, *fourteen had been completely removed by the aquatic ecosystem. The remaining substance was ninety-nine percent removed.*"[13] And when the fish residing toward the end of the system were analyzed for PCBs, dioxin, and other related toxins, they were found to be free of all contaminants.

In conventional wastewater treatment plants, chemically hazardous substances are used, and the wastewater treatment industry is itself a significant polluter, creating toxic sludge, using large amounts of energy, and producing nothing in the way of economically useful by-products. But by using Eco-Machines, John Todd discovered a way to bypass all of these problems. Bacteria and other organisms in the system recognize toxins and produce enzymes to break down their chemical bonds, turning the toxins into food and less harmful substances.

Ecological design attempts to replicate the flows and networks of living systems. In the natural world, there is no such thing as unreclaimable "waste." In nature, waste is food for other organisms or used in another way by living systems. Eco-Machines can create pure water from human sewage in under three days, but they have also been used on extremely poisonous toxic waste sites. What Todd discovered is that "given the right conditions, purification cycles which are measured in centuries in the wild can be speeded up so that purification can be achieved in weeks and months."[14]

One Eco-Machine in South Burlington, Vermont, treated the wastewater of 1,200 residents (see figure 13.3 on page 244). The linked ecosystems broke down the toxins in the wastewater, transformed them into food, and, in the end, produced water cleaner than that produced by traditional treatment facilities. Because they are pleasant environments, an Eco-Machine could be placed anywhere. Walking inside, you see a beautiful, peaceful garden, hear water trickling like the sound of

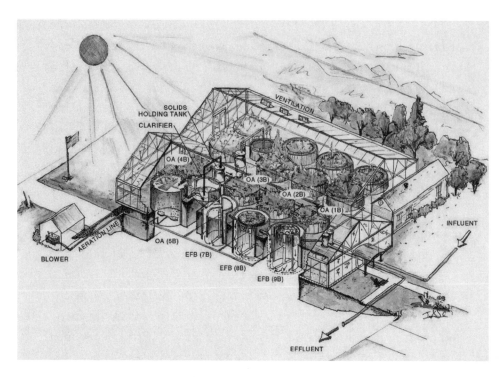

Figure 13.3. This large-scale Eco-Machine in South Burlington, Vermont, treated 80,000 gallons of sewage per day, transforming it into water cleaner than that produced by traditional treatment plants.

a tiny creek, and sense the aroma of citrus, ginger, and growing tropical plants. It's a world far removed from that of industrial waste treatment plants, and more like a garden or terrestrial paradise.

THE ALCHEMY OF ENGAGEMENT: NATURE AS TEACHER, NATURE AS PARTNER

What biomimicry offers us, in learning from nature instead of just about nature, is the opportunity to feel a part of, rather than apart from, this genius that surrounds us.

JANINE BENYUS

As author and environmentalist Paul Hawken notes, today we have "resources," but not "nature"; "human resources," but not "people"; and we talk about "producing energy" rather than "extracting" it.[15] I've often noticed how people talk about "the environment" with clinical detachment, as though nature is not alive, and not really our home, but more like a sterilized hospital room or laboratory setting into which we were placed by accident. This language usage unconsciously reflects the heritage of the Cartesian/Newtonian worldview, in which nature was seen as a collection of dead objects rather than living subjects. Today we should know better—but our society is still, for the most part, half asleep, unconsciously living and sleepwalking in a Newtonian universe.

As cosmology writers Joel Primack and Nancy Abrams observe, the Earth is a planet "integrated into the cosmos, but our current thinking about it is not, and therein lies the root of many problems."[16] They also suggest that we humans don't see the long-term consequences of our actions because "the still-dominant Newtonian cosmology implies that humans are of no particular significance in the universe."[17] "We need," they say, "to experience the universe from the inside."[18]

A new worldview is needed in which both we and the world come alive *experientially*. We humans would then see ourselves not as spectators, but as active participants in a living, dynamic universe, on a living, dynamic planet. We need to experience the universe from the inside once again, and realize that we are *participants*—co-creators in the unfolding fabric of life. As Nancy Jack Todd writes, "A shift from our inherited Newtonian/Cartesian acceptance of the natural world as mechanistic and malleable at will to human manipulation to a Gaian cosmology is a vast leap of mind—and heart. This constitutes a change of mind-set—of worldview—as profound as any in the past. Yet, as Einstein once pointed out, only when we change the way we think will we change the way we behave."[19]

In his book *The Participatory Mind,* philosopher Henryk Skolimowski wrote about the three Western projects. In the first Western project of the ancient Greeks, knowledge was seen as a tool of self-transformation and enlightenment. In the second Western project, which gave birth to the modern world, knowledge was seen as a way of exerting power and control over nature. This would lead to the perfection of humanity and the ability to control nature with mathematical precision. Now that the second Western project is a myth in decline, a new worldview is emerging that is ecological in nature. While the details are yet to be worked out, this new third Western project is holistic, spiritually inclined (without invoking any organized religion), and stresses our place in, and evolutionary collaboration with, the living, natural world.[20] Once again we are coming to see the world and living nature as not just a utilitarian object to be used up, but as something to be treasured and appreciated in itself.

In the new worldview's scientific dimensions, the world is not static, but evolutionary. Life and the universe are not strictly deterministic, but embody an interplay between structure and openness. Like an ecosystem, the cosmos as a whole is not made up of isolated, atomistic bits, but patterns of interdependent entities bound together in mutual relationships. Rather than consisting of pure spirit and dead matter, the world is multileveled, creative, and self-organizing. Rather than picturing the universe as a machine, we can now see it as being a community. What the outcome of this shift will be is hard to predict, but science, worldview, and culture are intimately related. As our visions of nature, life, and the universe change, so too will the ways that we relate to the world and other people.

The emblem of our new worldview will be, I believe, the fragile and arresting beauty of our living planet, seen from space. And if the human species is to have a flourishing future, the ethos of our new worldview will be based not on the idea of control, but on *collaboration with nature and nature's intelligence.*

As I've tried to show in this book, the idea of learning from nature and collaborating with nature is part of our Western heritage. Many philosophers have seen nature as "teacher and guide," and the Stoics taught that all of nature is animated with intelligence. It was the alchemists who taught that humanity collaborates with nature and participates in nature's work as part of the Magnum Opus, or Great Work, which aims to lead the world to deeper fruition. Similarly, the Hermetic philosophers of the Renaissance, like Paracelsus, sought to be directly inspired by "the light of nature" (that is, nature's intelligence), and sought to participate with nature in a collaborative, creative, and therapeutic relationship.

These spiritually profound ideas were pushed underground with the mechanistic worldview, in part for a very simple reason: if nature is a machine, you can only learn *about it.* But now that we can again see nature as a living repository of intelligence, we can once again learn *from it.* Along with the "New Alchemists" and the ecological designers, we can once again start learning from nature's design intelligence—not only to solve our human problems, but to create a more beautiful, flourishing, and satisfying world.

As Janine Benyus notes:

> In the process of meeting their needs, organisms manage to fertilize the soil, clean the air, clean the water, and mix the right cocktail of atmospheric gases that life needs to live. . . . What life in ensemble has learned to do is to create conditions conducive to life. And that's what we have to learn. Luckily, we don't need to make it up. We need only step outside and ask the local geniuses that surround us. The key question for a biomimic is "What would nature do here?" And that's a rare question, even for ecological designers.[21]

As in any other field, there are "shallow" and "deep" forms of ecological design. Someone trying to emulate one of nature's design strategies to solve a simple problem is at the shallow end. At the deeper end is the effort to collaborate with the intelligence of multiple ecosystems in an ongoing partnership. I have focused here on the work of John Todd because his work is philosophically deep and engaging, and it vividly illustrates to what degree a real collaborative partnership with nature is possible. As he says, "Ecological design is one way of forming a new partnership between the ecological needs of the planet and humanity."[22]

In our experience of human collaboration there must be openness, trust, and a willingness to listen, to work together, and to leave room for the unexpected. When we are involved in a true collaboration, we must have faith that it is possible to work together and that needed solutions will self-organize and emerge. This, too, is the kind of logic followed by living systems, but it is not the kind of precise, mathematical control aimed at by Newtonian science. In a living collaboration, we must be willing to listen, learn from others, and engage in an ongoing dialogue. In its deepest sense, ecological design is an ongoing collaboration with nature's intelligence.

In creating an Eco-Machine to fulfill a particular purpose, the designer will know, based on past research, what kinds of organisms might be right for the job. But the designer is not trying to engineer a solution through control. Rather, in collaboration, the designer relies on nature's intelligence to participate in finding a working solution. As John Todd explains in an interview:

> One of the things that we find about designing these systems is that we can't know a fraction of what they know. That's why I call it a true partnership. I mean, they know more than we do. Say the organisms for waste treatment . . . when you set up the Living Machine, you don't know which organisms will recombine in the presence of the waste. So you get thousands of species of organisms from all kinds of different aquatic environments, and you seed them—preferably every season, or four times a year—and they begin to recombine in ways to adapt to your waste. It can be as deadly as hell—*they'll* figure it out. You can't. But you must honor the system by ensuring the cast of characters is there.[23]

Ecological design, at its deepest, he says, is "a deliberate and consciously evolving partnership with the natural world."[24]

BEYOND SUSTAINABILITY:
THE POWER OF REGENERATION

The old part of the city where I now live, Sarajevo in southeastern Europe, is one of the most beautiful cities on Earth, especially if you love architecture and a tangible sense of the past. A meeting place between East and West, Sarajevo is like a kind of Alexandria, where different cultures came together and intermingled. Located in a valley surrounded by mountains, Sarajevo was the northern boundary of the Ottoman Empire, the southern boundary of the Austro-Hungarian Empire, the eastern boundary of the Roman Catholic Church, and the western boundary of the Eastern Orthodox Church. For about five hundred years, Christians and Muslims lived a common life together in harmony, until the terrible and pointless siege of Sarajevo, lasting from April 1992 to February 1996, during the breakup of the former Yugoslavia. During that period, hundreds of artillery shells rained down on Sarajevo each day from the hills above, great damage was inflicted on the city and its heritage, and 11,500 Sarajevo residents lost their lives—while the rest of the world sat by and watched without intervening for years.

Since the war ended, and perhaps against great odds, the city has come back to life. While scars remain, the ancient buildings have been repaired, the city is alive with a vibrant café culture, and Sarajevo is once again one of the most beautiful places on Earth. Each day you can hear church bells ring and the call to prayer echo out from minarets. The nearly miraculous power of regeneration exists in all things; and living systems, even if damaged severely, can be incredibly resilient.

Like the city of Sarajevo, the living systems of the Earth have been under attack, too, as human population has skyrocketed and our ecological footprint has expanded exponentially. During this same period, we have found ever-more efficient ways of turning nature's gifts into human commodities on a vast, industrial scale. We live at a unique point in the Earth's history when, in the words of Paul Hawken, "During the last fifty years every living system on earth has been in decline, and the rate of decline has been speeding up."[25] At the same time this is happening, our human demands on the biosphere are increasing exponentially, even faster than population growth. Just a short list of key statistics[26] helps to make clear what is happening at our point in time:

- Between 1975 and 2000, total material consumption in the United States grew at more than twice the rate of population growth.[27]
- During the past 50 years, humans have consumed more resources than in all previous history. Between 1970 and 1995 alone, worldwide consumption of raw materials (not including food and fuel) doubled.[28]
- Human beings currently consume 40 percent of all organic matter produced by photosynthesis on Earth, leaving what remains for other species.[29]
- Habitat destruction has contributed to species disappearance at rates about a thousand times faster than normal.[30] Once a species is extinct, it is gone forever.
- Due to human activity, forest cover has been reduced by at least 20 percent and as much at 50 percent worldwide.[31]
- Half of the world's wetlands are estimated to have been lost in the twentieth century.[32]
- Globally, vertebrate populations were on average one-third smaller in 2008 than they were in 1970.[33]
- Freshwater fish and amphibians are under threat around the world. In the United States, for which good data exists, 37 percent of freshwater fish species and 40 percent of amphibians are threatened or have become extinct.[34]
- 24 percent of all mammal species face extinction in 30 years.[35]
- 70 percent of biologists believe that we are in the midst of the fastest mass extinction in the Earth's history, and the only one due to human activity; they also believe that this loss of species diversity poses a threat to human life over the long term.[36]
- "Ecological overshoot" means that it now takes 1.5 years for the Earth to regenerate the renewable resources that people use, and to absorb the CO_2 waste they produce, in a single year.[37]
- If everyone on the planet lived like an average resident of the

United States, a total of four Earths would be now required to regenerate humanity's annual demand on nature.[38]

Ecological *sustainability* was first defined in a 1987 report of the World Commission on Environment and Development in the following way: "Sustainable development is development that meets the needs of the present without compromising the ability of future generations to meet their own needs."[39] While "sustainability" is perhaps a starting point, this bland and unimaginative definition can also be used as a way of maintaining the status quo. Taking a look at some of the statistics highlighted above, and all of the damage that has been done, no one in their right mind should want to *maintain* this level of environmental degradation for future generations, but to *reverse it,* helping to restore our damaged ecosystems to flourishing health. *What we need is ecological restoration and regeneration, not "sustainability."* Given the damage that has already occurred, each generation should now aim to leave our planetary biosystems in a better and *healthier* condition for the generations that follow.

Regenerative ecological design is not only possible, but proven. As the work of John Todd shows, we already possess the knowledge needed to restore poisoned lakes and rivers, to bring dead bodies of water back to life. We already know how to create homes that require no fossil fuels for heating. Located at Snowmass, Colorado, high in the Rocky Mountains, the superefficient and superinsulated home of Amory Lovins is solar-heated, with a built-in tropical greenhouse to store solar energy (see figure 13.4 on page 252). Not only does the home stay comfortable when the outside temperature is −40 degrees Fahrenheit, it also produces banana crops, even in the dead of winter. Each year, the building saves at least $7,100 in energy costs, or about $19 per day—"economically equivalent to the output of a barrel-per-day oil well; but unlike oil, it doesn't pollute, can't be interrupted, and won't run out."[40] Ultimately, the energy savings will pay for the entire cost of the building. This is regenerative design in action, the type of design now being championed by the Living Building Challenge, in which buildings must capture their own energy, clean their own water, promote health and human well-being, and be beautiful and

Figure 13.4. The tropical greenhouse in the home of Amory and Judy Hill Lovins, located high in the Rocky Mountains, in Snowmass, Colorado. The stone surfaces absorb the Sun's warmth and provide the home's heating even during harsh, subarctic winter conditions.

Figure 13.5. Certified by the Living Building Challenge, this cob house constructed by Ann and Gord Baird in Victoria, British Columbia, Canada, is an example of regenerative design. The home collects all of its water, generates all the electricity it uses, and is beautifully integrated into the landscape from which it seems to emerge.

inspirational, leading us to higher levels of awareness and action.[41]

Finding fault with the notion of "sustainability," ecological designer and architect Sim Van der Ryn speaks instead of *surpassability,* describing four different kinds of buildings: Standard, Green, Restorative, and Regenerative (see figure 13.5). Green building reacts to standard construction, seeking to utilize more efficient systems and materials, to limit the impact of constructed environments on nature, but doesn't fully draw on nature's intelligence. Restorative Buildings seek to reestablish the connection between buildings and natural processes, while Regenerative Buildings:

reconnect humans with the community and environment. Long-term human needs are valued over short-term expedience solutions.

Occupants feel empowered to regenerate their community and build interconnected relationships with their neighbors through active participation with government and society. Buildings suggest growth and rebirth while contributing to the community's energy supply rather than depleting it. Spaces inspire justice, uplift spirits, calm stress and comfort pain.[42]

Not only is regeneration possible in the human sphere, it is possible in the biosphere. Thousands of years ago, the Sahara desert had a lush, tropical climate, with trees, lakes, grasslands, wildlife, and a human population. Using ecological design principles, even arid desert areas can once again become fertile. While species loss is forever, as John Todd's work shows, with a helping hand from humans, the natural world can regenerate itself in much shorter periods of time than anyone thought possible. This regeneration occurs not through a process of technological control, but through a living partnership in which we are able to hear, learn from, and actively collaborate with nature's intelligence and the living world.

As we have learned, when we gaze upon the world from a distance and objectify it as if we were distant spectators, it becomes an object of exploitation. But when we relate to the world with a spirit of engagement, both we and the world are transformed through a spirit of creative collaboration.

CULTIVATING NATURE AND THE RESTORATION OF PARADISE

Hundreds of years ago, some of the first travelers to reach Sarajevo described it as resembling a terrestrial paradise. They were particularly impressed by the myriad fountains, to be found in public places and the inner courtyards of private homes. As one writer reported in the 1600s, in the city

> are a hundred and ten fountains of running water, and there is besides abundant running water, and in the surroundings are

twenty-six thousand gardens of paradise adorned with water, fountains, arbors and summer houses.[43]

Writing about the same time, a poet also noted, "Here it seems one could live long, for in a thousand places around Sarajevo flow fountains from the spring of immortality."[44]

While some of those fountains still remain, many have disappeared. In their place we come upon something beautiful—roses. From springtime through the first frosts of winter, public spaces and small private gardens in the old neighborhood districts are unexpectedly ablaze with roses. Despite the beautiful architecture here, city streets can be harsh and gritty. Coming upon a stand of roses in a private garden, a schoolyard, or the courtyard of a mosque (where they are always found), makes the grittiness of urban life fall away. This encounter transports the mind, arresting it, and invites us to contemplate the beauty of nature, in which we participate, and which extends far beyond us too. In some sense, the roses and the mountains are the saviors of Sarajevo, keeping the city from becoming too disconnected from nature.

If the image of the entire living Earth seen from space is an emblem of our new worldview, I hope another image of our relationship with nature will be that of the garden. Not surprisingly perhaps, since the entire focus of alchemy was on "cultivation" and "working in collaboration with nature," one of the common symbolic images of alchemy was "the rose garden of the philosophers." Similarly, in the desert-born monotheistic religions of Judaism, Christianity, and Islam, the garden was an image of paradise—the Garden of Eden—and the word *paradise* itself comes from an old Persian word meaning "a walled garden or orchard."[45] In our human experience, perhaps paradise represents a type of preconscious wholeness or perfection, in which everything feels just right, just the way it's supposed to be.

In his beautiful book *Gardening as a Sacred Art,* philosopher Jeremy Naydler discusses the history of gardening as a way of understanding the changing qualities of human consciousness and our changing relationship with nature. In very ancient times spirits, and for the Egyptians, the gods, were present in the landscape. For the Egyptians, "The garden was truly where the human and divine worlds met."[46] Later in medieval times, the *hortus conclusus,* the "enclosed" or "walled" garden that became popular in the twelfth century, was "meant primarily as a place of spiritual contemplation, and this was because its features . . . intended to recall Paradise to those who stepped inside it."[47] As many people instinctively realize, to be in a garden is one way to taste the sacred, to experience a memory of paradise.

Regardless of what modern people may think about God (which has for many become a concept), I think it is very important for us modern people to understand and embrace the experience of *the sacred,* which, at its core, is not a concept, but a human experience of belonging to a larger reality that transcends our limited selves. The experience of the sacred takes us beyond ourselves, linking us with the experience of other people in all times and places. Going back to their deepest, most central meanings, the ancient root of the word *divine* means "to shine," while the ancient root of the word *holy* gave birth to other common words, too: *whole, heal, health,* and *wholesome.*[48] When we experience the sacred, we sense the luminous nature of reality, a divine light shining into human life, connecting us with a greater whole. By definition, that which is sacred or holy is "worthy of veneration," and *veneration* is love. If we are unable to sense the sacred in nature, we will have no love for the world; and without love, the world will not be worth saving. And without the devotion and dedication engendered by love, nothing else is worth doing either.

During the course of my life, there have been many times I've experienced a taste of paradise in the garden of nature, sitting outside, either alone or with a friend. On many occasions I've meditatively played a musical instrument outside, only to have the birds, frogs, and crickets respond. Together, we created music—a magical back-and-forth collaboration with nature's symphony.

In the experience of paradise, we immediately appreciate our own presence in the sacred radiance of nature's beauty, savoring the completeness, wholeness, and perfection of life at that very moment. Sensing the world as it is, and our deep kinship with this reality, there is no felt need to transform it into something else, which is why such moments feel perfect. When we are wholly present to the beauty and vitality of the living world, we appreciate it fully for its unique, irreplaceable value.

As Jeremy Naydler shows, during the period in which the Cartesian and Newtonian worldview began to emerge, there was a major shift in the design of gardens, reflecting humanity's changing relation with nature. Vast formal gardens, like the gardens at Versailles in France, became highly geometrical and imperial enterprises, designed not to highlight or to enhance nature's beauty, but to illustrate humanity's glory and power over nature. Later in the Romantic period, a significant shift occurred in which some gardeners began to see themselves working in collaboration with nature's creative spirit, to cultivate nature, and to help its beauty shine forth. One of these pioneers of gardening as a sacred art was William Robinson (1838–1935), who also introduced the idea of *the wild garden,* human gardens that enhance and blend into the natural landscape (see figure 13.6 on page 258).

As Naydler notes, discussing the wild garden at Heaselands, Sussex,

all this beauty has been achieved not by unaided Nature, but also through creative human involvement. It is only through the co-operative effort of human beings with Nature that this kind of Paradisal environment can come into being. We notice, too, that this wild garden is outside the borders of a garden as conventionally understood. Robinson believed there was no need to restrict gardening to conventionally demarcated garden areas, because for him the whole world was a garden. Thus the beauty of fields, meadows and woodlands could all be enhanced through such sensitive human participation.[49]

As both a symbol and a reality, a garden represents the meeting point between humanity and nature. Through a garden, humanity is brought in relationship to nature; nature is consciously brought in relation to humanity; and humanity and nature emerge as co-creators in a work of divine beauty.

While the garden may remind one of the timeless, intoxicating beauty of paradise—the sound of trickling water, birds singing, and the perfume of flowers—it invites us to experience that divine beauty here

Figure 13.6. The wild garden at Heaselands, Sussex, in which human collaboration with nature aims to enhance nature's glory and beauty.

on Earth, in the here and now, as it shines through and enlivens the fabric of our lives. Similarly, as a garden cannot exist without human care, it invites us to enter into a living, collaborative relationship with both nature and society.

If we could see the entire Earth as a garden—as a living but damaged paradise, worthy of love and admiration—we could then act as gardeners, working in collaboration with the soul of the world. In this role, we could creatively participate in the cultivation of all life, and help to restore nature's beauty, fertility, and resilience where it has been lost.

Acknowledgments

Since this book was written over a long period of time, beginning in Michigan and ending in Sarajevo, there are too many friends and colleagues to thank for their assistance, but at least a few must be singled out.

Special thanks to Theodore Roszak for his inspiring body of writings, for encouraging my work, and for his willingness to serve on my doctoral committee. Thanks also to Richard Tarnas, Ralph Abraham, Joseph Meeker, Joel Primack, E. C. Krupp, and Robert Romanyshyn. Special thanks to Roger S. Jones, for carefully reviewing the sections on physics, and to Gwendolyn Faasen for her editorial feedback on the manuscript.

Thanks to poet Kathleen Raine for her many years of encouragement; to my lifelong friend Arthur Versluis for so many stimulating conversations; and to my astronomy friend Andy Harwood, who was there when I began writing, and with whom I spent many memorable nights observing and photographing galaxies, globular clusters, and two astonishing comets. Thanks to my family, Almira and Benjamin, and the people, mountains, buildings, and roses of Sarajevo, which make my life beautiful. Finally, thanks to the staff at Inner Traditions, for the work they put into publishing this book.

Illustration Credits

Figure 1.1: Drawing after Alexander Marshack, "Lunar Notation on Upper Paleolithic Remains" (1964).

Figure 1.4a: Photo courtesy of the National Library of Ireland.

Figure 1.4d: Drawing after the plan of Newgrange by Jack Roberts.

Figure 1.4e: Photo from Martin Brennan, *The Stones of Time: Calendars, Sundials, and Stone Chambers of Ancient Ireland* (Rochester, Vt.: Inner Traditions, 1994); reproduced by permission of Inner Traditions (www.InnerTraditions.com).

Figure 1.5: Triple spiral after photo from Martin Brennan, *The Stones of Time.*

Figure 2.1: Polychord, author's collection.

Figures 2.3b–c from Michael Barnsley, *Fractals Everywhere* (Academic Press, 1988); reproduced by permission of Michael Barnsley.

Figure 2.3d: Author.

Figure 4.1: Jan Baptista van Helmont, *Opera Omnia* (1682).

Figure 4.3: Heinrich Kunrath, *Amphitheatrum sapientiae aeterna* (1609; original edition 1595).

Figure 5.1: Photo by Chris Nas, courtesy of Wikimedia Commons.

Figure 6.1: Courtesy of Wikimedia Commons.

Figure 7.2: Engraving by George Bickham, 1732; author's collection.

Figure 10.1: CCD photo of M13 by the author, Concord Grove Observatory.

Figures 10.3–10.4: Diagrams after Kafatos and Nadeau, *The Conscious*

Universe: Part and Whole in Modern Physical Theory (New York: Springer-Verlag, 1980).

Figure 11.1: Mandelbrot set sequence by the author.

Figure 11.2: Barnsley fern, courtesy of Rodd Halstead.

Figure 11.3: NASA.

Figure 12.1: Engraving by Theodore de Bry in Michael Maier, *Atalanta Fugiens* (1618).

Figure 12.2: NASA.

Figures 13.1–13.3: Reproduced with permission of Nancy Jack Todd, Ocean Arks International.

Figure 13.4: Photos copyright by Judy Hill Lovins.

Figure 13.5: Photo copyright by Ann Baird.

Figure 13.6: Photo by Tony Evans from Jeremy Naydler, *Gardening as a Sacred Art* (Edinburgh: Floris Books, 2011).

Notes

INTRODUCTION

1. Eliot, *The Rock: A Pageant Play,* introductory lines to part I.
2. Wilson, *The Future of Life,* 22.

CHAPTER 1. STARLIGHT AND COSMOVISION

1. Plato, *Timaeus* 47A.
2. Einstein, "The Cosmic Religious Feeling," 14.
3. Aristotle, *Eudemian Ethics* 1.5.1216A, in John Robinson, *An Introduction to Early Greek Philosophy,* 191.
4. Diogenes Laertius, *Lives of the Eminent Philosophers* 2.7.
5. Bernard Silvestris, *Cosmographia,* quoted in Davidson, *Sky Phenomena,* 122.
6. Plato, *Theaetetus* 174B.
7. Plato, *Timaeus* 90A–C.
8. Clark, "Ancient Philosophy," 4.
9. See E. C. Krupp's article on "Archaeoastronomy" in John Lankford's *The History of Astronomy: An Encyclopedia,* and Frank Durham and Robert Purrington, *Frame of the Universe,* chapter 3. For late Upper Paleolithic lunar tally marks on a fragment of bone from the Dordogne region of France dated circa 28,000 B.C., see Alexander Marshack's *The Roots of Civilization: The Cognitive Beginnings of Man's First Art, Symbol and Notation,* 43–49. Marshack's book contains many other similar examples from Paleolithic times. For a short summary of his findings, see his work "Lunar Notation on Upper Paleolithic Remains."

10. Plato, *Seventh Letter* 341D, in *Plato: The Collected Dialogues, Including the Letters*, 1589.

11. Goethe, *Goethe on Science: An Anthology of Goethe's Scientific Writings*, 33.

12. Science is inherently open-ended because the complete validity of any formal system, including a scientific one, cannot be proved within the system itself. In other words, every system depends on certain a priori premises, but those premises that are taken for granted by the system cannot be proved within the system itself. This was demonstrated in 1931 by mathematician Kurt Gödel's second incompleteness theorem.

13. On the relationship between science and the other ways of knowing in the search for an inclusive worldview, see Fideler, "Science's Missing Half: Epistemological Pluralism and the Search for an Inclusive Cosmology."

14. See Campbell, *Myths to Live By*, 221–22, and *The Power of Myth*, 31.

15. Abraham, *Chaos, Gaia, Eros*, 175.

16. Ibid., 175.

17. Krupp, *Skywatchers, Shamans, and Kings*, 17.

18. Watkins, editor, *American Heritage Dictionary of Indo-European Roots*, 69. Similarly, the Greek word *temenos*—the sacred precinct in which a sanctuary is located—originates from the same root as *templum*.

19. Corbin, *Temple and Contemplation*, 386.

20. See Lockyer, *The Dawn of Astronomy*. Lockyer discovered that the great temple of Amon-Ra at Karnac was exactly oriented toward the setting sun on the summer solstice, the longest day of the year. For a recent study and evaluation of the solar alignment of Egyptian temples, see E. C. Krupp, "Light in the Temples."

21. See North, *Stonehenge: Prehistoric Man and the Cosmos*.

22. North, *The Norton History of Astronomy and Cosmology*, xxv.

23. In this description of Newgrange and its structure, I am indebted to the account of E. C. Krupp in his work *Shamans, Skywatchers, and Kings*. The interpretation of its spiral symbolism is my own.

24. Watkins, editor, *American Heritage Dictionary of Indo-European Roots*, 3.

CHAPTER 2. BEAUTY, DESIRE, AND THE SOUL OF THE WORLD

1. Guthrie, *A History of Greek Philosophy*, 1:4.

2. That at least was Aristotle's interpretation in *De Anima* 1.411.A7. See Guthrie, *A History of Greek Philosophy*, 1:65.

3. For a discussion of the idea of the living universe in Greek philosophical

thought, see Collingwood, *The Idea of Nature,* chapter 1. See also pp. 3–4.

4. For discussion, see Armstrong, editor, *Classical Mediterranean Spirituality,* 307.

5. On the human love of nature, and need for nature, explored from a biological and evolutionary perspective, see Wilson, *Biophilia,* and Kellert and Wilson, editors, *The Biophilia Hypothesis.*

6. Bateson, *Mind and Nature,* 18–19.

7. Goethe, *The Maxims and Reflections of Goethe,* 171.

8. Blake, *The Marriage of Heaven and Hell,* plate 14, in *The Complete Poetry and Prose of William Blake,* 39.

9. For an in-depth discussion of the ideas of *kosmos* and *harmonia* in Pythagorean thought, see Fideler, introduction to Guthrie, *The Pythagorean Sourcebook and Library,* 19–54.

10. Plato, *Gorgias* 507E. This Pythagorean-Platonic idea, I believe, is the origin of the Stoic idea of the cosmopolis discussed in chapter 4.

11. Sextus Empiricus, *Against the Professors* 9.127, quoted in Guthrie, *A History of Greek Philosophy,* 1:278.

12. Or, as Plato put it, "The philosopher through association with what is divine and orderly (*kosmios*) becomes divine and orderly (*kosmios*) in so far as a man may" (*Republic* 500c).

13. Einstein quoted by Vallentin in *Einstein: A Biography,* 24. (Vallentin cites Einstein's "Physics and Reality," 1936.)

14. Quoted by Ferris, *Coming of Age in the Milky Way,* 301.

15. Emerson, in *The Works of Ralph Waldo Emerson,* 4:40.

16. Henri Bergson, *Creative Evolution,* 182.

17. Thus in Plato's epistemology described by the divided line of *Republic* book 6, the type of thinking or discursive analysis that rests upon a subject–object duality (*dianoia*) is a lower form of cognition than *noēsis* or direct knowledge. This central epistemological idea was later developed in considerably more detail by the Platonic philosopher Plotinus.

18. Rowe, *Rediscovering the West,* 11.

19. Nelson, "The Theology of the Invisible," 198.

20. Ibid., 199.

21. Plato, *Phaedrus* 265B.

22. The following discussion in this section is indebted to Rowe's work, *Rediscovering the West.*

23. Cushman, *Therapeia: Plato's Conception of Philosophy,* xvii.

24. Ibid.

25. Moline, *Plato's Theory of Understanding*, x.

26. Collins, *Meditations, Poems, Pages from a Sketchbook*, 26.

27. Rowe, *Rediscovering the West*, 90.

28. For the idea that the universe possesses infinite depth and that multiple ways of knowing are required for a more complete vision of the world, see Fideler, "Science's Missing Half: Epistemological Pluralism and the Search for an Inclusive Cosmology."

29. James, *A Pluralistic Universe*, 260.

30. This myth appears in Plato's dialogue on love, the *Phaedrus*.

31. Plato, *Phaedrus* 251C.

32. Plato, *Symposium* 211D.

33. Hillman, "Concerning the Stone: Alchemical Images of the Goal," 236.

34. Plato, *Timaeus* 92C.

35. Ibid., 33A.

36. Ibid., 30D3–31A1.

37. Ibid., 32C.

38. Ibid., 36E.

39. Emerson, *The Works of Ralph Waldo Emerson*, 3:190–91.

40. Ibid., 3:193.

41. Plato discussed this connection in the *Philebus*, where he concluded that "the power of the good has taken refuge in the nature of the beautiful; for measure and proportion are everywhere identified with beauty and virtue" (*Philebus* 64E).

CHAPTER 3. LIFE IN THE COSMOPOLIS

1. For a study of Apollo, Hermes, and Jesus as personifications of the Logos, see Fideler, *Jesus Christ, Sun of God: Ancient Cosmology and Early Christian Symbolism*.

2. Clement of Alexandria, *Exhortation to the Greeks* 6.

3. In *Timaeus* 30C Plato described the *kosmos* as a Living Creature endowed with soul (*psychē*) and reason—literally, with mind (*nous*). For the qualities of the cosmic soul, see also *Laws* 897 and following.

4. Clark, "Ancient Philosophy," 36.

5. Toulmin and Goodfield, *The Architecture of Matter*, 105.

6. Plato, *Gorgias* 507E.

7. In Plato's political philosophy, the philosopher should strive to understand the eternal and divine order, beauty, and harmony of the cosmos, which he

will then follow as a model in both personal and communal life. See *Republic* 500c–e.

8. Seneca, *Epistle* 28.5.

9. Colish, *The Stoic Tradition from Antiquity to the Middle Ages*, 1:36.

10. Seneca, *The Stoic Philosophy of Seneca*, 170.

11. As contemporary philosopher Thomas Nagel notes in a similar fashion, "Even though the manifestations of mind evident to us are local—they depend on our brains and similar organic structures—the general basis of this aspect of reality is not local, but must be presumed to inhere in the general constituents of the universe and the laws that govern them" (*The View from Nowhere*, 8).

12. Marcus Aurelius, *Meditations* 7.9.

13. Ibid., 5.30.

14. Ibid., 3.11.

15. Ibid., 5.16.

16. Ibid., 9.23.

17. Ibid., 7.13.

18. *Corpus Hermeticum* 11.4, "Mind to Hermes," translated by Yates, in *Giordano Bruno and the Hermetic Tradition*, 31.

19. *Corpus Hermeticum* 12.21, "Hermes to Tat on the Common Intellect," translated by Yates, in *Giordano Bruno and the Hermetic Tradition*, 34.

20. See Plotinus, *Enneads* 5.9.13: "For the sense-world is in one place, but the intelligible world is everywhere." As Michael Hornum notes in his introduction to *Porphyry's Launching-Points to the Realm of Mind*, in the Neoplatonic philosophy of Plotinus the incorporeal nature of Real Being is invisible, placeless (hence omnipresent), and extensionless: "Since the incorporeal is not subject to spatial or temporal separation its relation to the corporeal is one of immediate presence. Our higher self does not reside within us as if some internal organ or hover somewhere about the galaxy, but is present to each of us with an intimacy far closer than any corporeal thing can have" (15).

21. Armstrong, "Psyche, Ourselves, World-Soul, and Gaia in Plotinus," 117.

22. Emerson, *The Works of Ralph Waldo Emerson*, 4:53.

23. Plotinus, *Enneads* 1.6.8 (Armstrong translation).

24. Ibid., 2.3.7 (MacKenna translation).

25. Ibid., 2.1.7 (MacKenna translation).

26. Ibid., 1.6.9 (Armstrong translation).

27. See Plotinus, *Enneads* 2.9.1, 3.8.8, and 5.1.5.

28. Plotinus, *Enneads* 4.4.32 (Armstrong translation). Plotinus here quotes Plato, *Timaeus* 30D3–31A1, as he does on many occasions.

29. Plotinus, *Enneads* 4.4.32 (MacKenna translation).

30. Ibid.

31. Ibid., 3.3.6 (MacKenna translation).

32. Ibid., 1.8.14 (Armstrong translation).

33. See Armstrong, "Psyche, Ourselves, World-Soul, and Gaia in Plotinus," 116.

CHAPTER 4. THE LIGHT OF NATURE AND THE ALCHEMICAL IMAGINATION

1. See Eliade, *The Forge and the Crucible,* chapter 5, "Rites and Mysteries in Metallurgy." For the ancient roots of alchemy, see also Lindsay, *The Origins of Alchemy in Graeco-Roman Egypt.*

2. For a discussion of the primordial idea of minerals growing and ripening in the womb of the Earth, see Eliade, *The Forge and the Crucible,* chapter 4, "Terra Mater, Petra Genitrix." Eliade quotes the writer Cardan, "Metallic materials are to mountains no other than trees and have their roots, trunk, branches and leaves. . . . What is a mine if not a plant covered with earth?" (45).

3. Copernicus, *On the Revolutions of the Heavenly Spheres* 1.10 (Duncan translation, 50).

4. Telesio, *On the Nature of Things According to Their Own Proper Principles,* 308.

5. Bruno, *The Expulsion of the Triumphant Beast,* 72.

6. See Fideler, *Jesus Christ, Sun of God: Ancient Cosmology and Early Christian Symbolism.* For the Stoics the Sun was an overflowing fount of *pneuma* and *logos.* Poseidonius, for example, maintained that the world was permeated by a vital force or life-power (*zōtikē dynamis*) that flows from the Sun.

7. Quoted in Toulmin and Goodfield, *The Architecture of Matter,* 118.

8. Quoted in Burckhardt, *Alchemy: Science of the Cosmos, Science of the Soul,* 25.

9. Quotation from *The Sophic Hydrolith,* in Waite, editor, *The Hermetic Museum,* 1:116.

10. Jung, "The Spirit Mercurius," in *Alchemical Studies,* 209, quoting *Metallorum metamorphosis.*

11. Ibid., quoting *The Sophic Hydrolith*; see also Waite, *Hermetic Museum,* 1:78.

12. Ibid., 214, citing *Coelum Sephiroticum*.

13. *The Sophic Hydrolith* in Waite, *Hermetic Museum*, 1:78.

14. Jung, "The Spirit Mercurius," in *Alchemical Studies*, 214, citing Happelius, "Aphorismi Basiliani," in *Theatrum Chemicum*.

15. For Jung's account, see "The Concept of the Collective Unconscious," in *The Archetypes of the Collective Unconscious*, 50–53.

16. Jung, *Psychology and Alchemy*, 34.

17. For Jung, the unified god-image of Christ represented an image or model of the self, yet it also functioned as "the tutelary image or amulet against the archetypal powers that threatened to possess everyone" (*Psychology and Alchemy*, 36). In Jung's view, with the birth of Christianity came a changing of the gods, or a change in the dominants of the collective unconscious. The emergence of the Christ image reflected an individuation process in the collective psyche, but "while the dogmas of the Church offered analogies to the alchemical process, these analogies, in strict contrast to alchemy, had become detached from the world of nature with the historical figure of the Redeemer" (*Psychology and Alchemy*, 35). Nonetheless, "whereas in the Church the increasing differentiation of ritual and dogma alienated consciousness from its natural roots in the unconscious, alchemy and astrology were ceaselessly engaged in preserving the bridge to nature, i.e., to the unconscious psyche, from decay" (*Psychology and Alchemy*, 34).

18. Jung, "Paracelsus as a Spiritual Phenomenon," in *Alchemical Studies*, 185.

19. "If a man puts his hand to the opus, he repeats, as the alchemists say, God's work of creation" (Jung, "The Spirit Mercurius," *Alchemical Studies*, 239).

20. For the mythology of the Gnostic Revealer, see Fideler, *Jesus Christ, Sun of God: Ancient Cosmology and Early Christian Symbolism*, chapter 6.

21. Jung, "Paracelsus as a Spiritual Phenomenon," in *Alchemical Studies*, 161.

22. Quoted in Jones, *The Redemption of Matter*, 44.

23. Paracelsus in *Paracelsus: Selected Writings*, 144.

24. Jung, "Psychoanalysis and Neurosis," in *Freud and Psychoanalysis*, 250.

25. Jung, "Psychology and Religion," in *Psychology and Religion: East and West*, 75.

26. Jones, *The Redemption of Matter*, 41.

27. Paracelsus in *Paracelsus: Selected Writings*, 255.

28. Jung, "Paracelsus as a Spiritual Phenomenon," *Alchemical Studies*, 114, quoting Paracelsus, *Astronomia magna*.

29. Jung, "Paracelsus as a Spiritual Phenomenon," *Alchemical Studies*, 115.

30. Jones, *The Redemption of Matter,* 42.

31. See Prigogine and Stengers, *Order Out of Chaos.*

CHAPTER 5. THE LUSHNESS OF EARTH AND
THE SPIRIT OF THE DESERT

1. Plato, *Laws* 740A (Stephen Clark translation).

2. Plato, *Phaedrus* 279B–C.

3. James Hillman noted that "the soul's inherent multiplicity demands a theological fantasy of equal differentiation" (*Re-Visioning Psychology,* 167). My discussion of the monotheistic and polytheistic imaginations is indebted to Hillman's idea of "psychological polytheism" set forth in *Revisioning Psychology.* For Hillman's psychological vision of the contemporary meaning of the World Soul, see his *"Anima Mundi:* The Return of Soul to the World."

4. Athanassakis, translator, *The Orphic Hymns.*

5. The classic study of this unease is the work by E. R. Dodds, *Pagan and Christian in an Age of Anxiety.* Even the philosopher Plotinus, for whom the entire universe was a living theophany of divine beauty, "seemed ashamed of being in his body" according to Porphyry, Plotinus's biographer.

6. Tarnas, *The Passion of the Western Mind,* 100.

7. Ibid., 112.

8. Ambrose and Tertullian quoted by Ferris, in *Coming of Age in the Milky Way,* 42.

9. Lactanius, *The Divine Institutes* 2.6, in Roberts and Donaldson, *The Ante-Nicene Fathers,* VII. Lactanius was arguing here against the Stoic idea of a living, intelligent cosmos, of which humanity is a part.

10. Theodore Roszak, *Where the Wasteland Ends,* 123.

11. Lactanius, *The Divine Institutes* 2.6.

12. Given this outlook, it's no wonder that Lynn White, Jr., concluded in his famous essay on "The Historical Roots of Our Ecologic Crisis" that certain aspects of the Christian tradition were decisive in fostering our modern ecological crisis. Specifically, he argued that "our science and technology have grown out of Christian attitudes toward man's relation to nature which are almost universally held not only by Christians and neo-Christians but also by those who fondly regard themselves as post-Christians. Despite Copernicus, all the cosmos rotates around our little globe. Despite Darwin, we are *not,* in our hearts, part of the natural process. We are superior to nature, contemptuous of it, willing to use it for our slightest whim." He concluded

that "what we do about ecology depends on our ideas of the man-nature relationship. More science and more technology are not going to get us out of the present ecologic crisis until we find a new religion, or rethink our old one" (1206).

13. Quoted by Winthrop Wetherbee in Silvestris, *Cosmographia,* 7.

14. Writing in Silvestris, *Cosmographia,* 12.

15. Allers, "Microcosmus from Anaximandros to Paracelsus," 360n107.

16. Ibid.

17. Chenu, *Nature, Man, and Society in the Twelfth Century,* 69.

18. Ibid., 21.

19. Ibid., 22.

20. Ibid., 69.

21. Copleston, *A History of Philosophy,* 2.1:191.

22. Allers, "Microcosmus from Anaximandros to Paracelsus," 359.

23. See ibid., 386–87.

CHAPTER 6. THE LAST FLOWERING

1. For a discussion of "The World as Organism" in Renaissance thought, see Merchant, *The Death of Nature,* chapter 4.

2. Leonardo da Vinci, quoted in Betty Roszak, "The Two Worlds of Magic," vii.

3. As he wrote, "The cosmos is animate just like any animate thing, and more effectively so" (Ficino, *Three Books on Life* 3.2).

4. Merchant, *The Death of Nature,* 80.

5. Campanella, *The City of the Sun,* 112–13.

6. Cited in Merchant, *The Death of Nature,* 115.

7. della Porta, *Natural Magick,* 14.

8. Ficino, *The Book of Life* (Boer translation), vii.

9. Ficino, *Opera omina,* 944; in Kristeller, *The Philosophy of Marsilio Ficino,* 22–23.

10. Ficino, *Three Books on Life* 3.4 (Kaske and Clark, 259).

11. Skolimowski, *The Participatory Mind,* 131.

12. Tarnas, *The Passion of the Western Mind,* 213.

13. Kristeller, *The Philosophy of Marsilio Ficino,* 114.

14. As Rudolf Allers noted, "The recrudesence of microcosmism, in its truly metaphysical meaning, occurs in ages which usually are labelled 'Renaissance.'" He also concluded "that Renaissance is always Platonic in its philosophical aspect" and that "this was indubitably the case with the Great

Renaissance" ("Microcosmus from Anaximandros to Paracelsus," 334–35).

15. Quoted by Betty Roszak, "The Two Worlds of Magic," vii.

16. On this central Western cosmological idea, see Allers, "Microcosmus from Anaximandros to Paracelsus." See also the study by Conger, *Theories of Macrocosms and Microcosms in the History of Philosophy.*

17. See Aristotle, *De anima* 3.8.431.B21, and Allers, "Microcosmus from Anaximandros to Paracelsus," 330.

18. *Asclepius* 6, in Brian Copenhaver, translator, *Hermetica,* 69.

19. Ibid., 70.

20. Ibid.

21. Ibid., 69.

22. The exact quotation reads: "It was not for small things but for great that God created men, who, knowing the great, are not satisfied with small things. Indeed, it was for the limitless alone that He created men, who are the only beings on earth to have re-discovered their infinite nature and who are not fully satisfied by anything limited, however great that thing may be" (Ficino, *The Letters of Marsilio Ficino,* vol. 6, no. 6).

23. Marsilio Ficino, letter to Pellegrino degli Agli dated June 13, 1458; quoted in Field, *The Origins of the Platonic Academy of Florence,* 176.

24. Ficino, *Platonic Theology* 1.6; quoted in Robb, *Neoplatonism of the Italian Renaissance,* 86.

25. See discussion in Cassirer, *The Individual and the Cosmos in Renaissance Philosophy,* 110.

26. Plotinus, *Enneads* 4.4.40 (MacKenna translation).

27. As Plotinus explained, "The phenomenon of sympathy; the response between soul and soul is due to the mere fact that all spring from the self-same soul (the hypostasis Soul) from which springs the Soul of the All" (*Enneads* 4.3.8; MacKenna translation).

28. Plotinus, *Enneads* 4.9.3 (Armstrong translation). See also *Enneads* 4.3.8, 4.4.26, and 4.4.40.

29. Kristeller, *The Philosophy of Marsilio Ficino,* 120, quoting Ficino, *Opera omina,* 121.

30. Moore, *The Planets Within,* 45.

31. Ibid., translating Ficino, *Three Books on Life* 3.1.

32. Warden, "Orpheus and Ficino," 95.

33. Ibid.

34. Bruno, *Cause, Principle, and Unity,* 87.

35. Ibid., 85.

36. Ibid.

37. Ibid., 81.

38. Ibid.

39. Ibid.

40. Ibid., 82.

41. Ibid., 83.

42. Ibid., 89.

43. Ibid., 87.

44. Ibid., 88.

45. della Porta, *Natural Magick*, 2.

46. Debus, *The English Paracelsians*, 21.

47. Due to their knowledge of celestial phenomena, the three Magi, or wise men, from Persia were able to foresee the birth of the Christ child.

48. Paracelsus, *The Hermetic and Alchemical Writings of Paracelsus*, 1:1.

49. Ibid., 1:2.

50. R. Bostocke, quoted in Debus, *The English Paracelsians*, 24.

51. Paracelsus, *Astronomia Magna*, in *Paracelsus: Essential Readings*, 144.

52. Paracelsus, *Selected Writings*, 18.

53. See Poncé, "The Alchemical Light," 172.

54. Paracelsus, *Astronomia Magna*, in *Paracelsus: Essential Readings*, 110.

55. See Debus, *The English Paracelsians*, 21. In the *Astronomia Magna*, Paracelsus explained how "logic intervened to extinguish both the light of Nature and the light of wisdom and introduced an alien doctrine which relegated both kinds of wisdom" (*Paracelsus: Essential Readings*, 115).

56. Nicholas Goodrick-Clarke, writing in *Paracelsus: Essential Readings*, 25.

57. Paracelsus, *Astronomia Magna*, in *Paracelsus: Essential Readings*, 119.

58. Marsilio Ficino, quoted by Cassirer, *The Individual and the Cosmos in Renaissance Philosophy*, 133.

59. This quote is a summary, by Leo Strauss, of the Enlightenment philosopher John Locke's attitude toward the natural world. See Strauss, *Natural Right and History*, 250–51.

CHAPTER 7. THE MECHANIZATION OF THE WORLD

1. For a study of the important contributions that the magical, mechanistic, and organic traditions all made to the Scientific Revolution, see the study by Hugh Kearney, *Science and Change: 1500–1700*.

2. See Michael J. Crowe, *Theories of the World from Antiquity to the Copernican Revolution,* chapter 6. As Crowe points out, "in a sense the choice between the two systems rested on aesthetic criteria."

3. For the significance of the Sun in Renaissance Neoplatonism, see Marsilio Ficino's work *Concerning the Sun.* Copernicus was acquainted with similar ideas and was intimate with a student of Ficino's.

4. The full quotation is: "Philosophy is written in the great book which is ever before our eyes—I mean the universe—but we cannot understand it if we do not first learn the language and grasp the symbols in which it is written. The book is written in the mathematical language, and the symbols are triangles, circles, and other geometrical figures, without whose help it is impossible to comprehend a single word of it; without which one wanders in vain through a dark labyrinth" (Galileo, *Opere Complete di Galileo Galilei* 4.171, quoted in E. A. Burtt, *The Metaphysical Foundations of Modern Physical Science,* 75).

5. Galileo Galilei, *Opere* 7.213; in Galileo, *Two New Sciences,* 170.

6. Edmund Husserl identified this as a key turning point in Western thought that challenged humanity's relationship to the *Lebenswelt* or "lifeworld." See Husserl, *The Crisis of the European Sciences and Transcendental Phenomenology.* See also chapter 2, "Husserlian Perspectives on Galilean Physics," in Aron Gurwitsch, *Phenomenology and the Theory of Science.*

7. Descartes quoted by Stewart Shapiro, editor, in *The Oxford Handbook of Philosophy of Mathematics and Logic,* 38.

8. Kenny, *Oxford History of Western Philosophy,* 113.

9. How it was that the entirely immaterial human mind could maintain a relationship with an extended, machine-like body remained a stumbling block of the Cartesian system. In the Sixth Meditation and in *The Passions of the Soul,* Descartes explained that a tiny gland, the pineal gland in the brain, is the point of contact where the body and mind interact. This is the only point where the body can directly affect the mind, but Descartes was unable to explain the way in which the interaction took place since his other premises, in effect, ruled it out. As one of his correspondents, Princess Elizabeth wrote, "I could more readily allow that the soul has matter and extension than that an immaterial being has the capacity of moving a body and being affected by it."

10. Goethe, *Dichtung und Wahrheit,* quoted by Bly, *News of the Universe,* 31.

11. See Abram, "The Mechanical and the Organic: On the Impact of Metaphor in Science," 67–68.

12. Descartes, *Principles of Philosophy,* part 4, section 187.

13. Descartes, *The World,* chapter 7, in *The Philosophical Writings of Descartes,* 1:92.

14. *Corpus Hermeticum* 11.4, "Mind to Hermes," translated by Yates, *Giordano Bruno and the Hermetic Tradition,* 31.

15. Descartes, *Principles of Philosophy,* part 4, section 188.

16. Descartes, quoted by Debus, *Man and Nature in the Renaissance,* 107.

17. Thomas Hobbes, introduction to *Leviathan,* in *The English Works of Thomas Hobbes,* 3:ix.

18. Nicholas Malebranche, *Oeuvres de Malebranche* (Paris: Libraire Philosophique J. Vrin, 1962), vol. 2, p. 394, quoted in Easlea, *Witch Hunting, Magic, and the New Philosophy,* 144.

19. Descartes, *Discourse on Method,* part 2, in *The Philosophical Writings of Descartes,* 1:120.

20. Descartes, *Discourse on Method, Optics, Geometry, and Meteorology,* translated by P. J. Olscamp, 361.

21. Kenny, *Oxford History of Western Philosophy,* 127.

22. Descartes, *Discourse on Method,* part 6, in *The Philosophical Writings of Descartes,* 1:142–43.

23. White, *Medieval Technology and Social Change,* 122.

24. Ibid., 124.

25. Ibid., 125.

26. Reproduced in Gimpel, *The Medieval Machine,* 148.

27. Descartes, Sixth Meditation, in *The Meditations and Selections from the Principles,* translated by John Veitch, 98.

28. Jones, *The Redemption of Matter,* 58.

29. Descartes, "Lettre à Mersenne," April 15, 1630, *Oeuvres,* vol. 1, p. 145; quoted in Merchant, *The Death of Nature,* 205.

30. Theodore Roszak, *Where the Wasteland Ends,* 186.

31. Newton, *Opticks,* quoted in Jones, *The Redemption of Matter,* 59.

32. Newton, *Principia,* 544.

33. Ibid.

34. Tarnas, *The Passion of the Western Mind,* 269.

35. In Fauvel et al., *Let Newton be!,* 1. Pope's couplet was published in his *Epitaphs* of 1730.

36. Edmund Halley, "Ode to Newton," in Newton, *Principia,* xiii–xv.

37. Theodore Roszak, *Where the Wasteland Ends,* 221. For more on this theme,

see the essays in Fauvel et al., *Let Newton be!,* particularly Derek Gjertsen, "Newton's Success," and Maureen McNeil, "Newton as National Hero."

38. John Maynard Keynes, "Newton, the Man," in Royal Society, *Newton Tercentenary Celebrations,* 27–43.

39. I am here indebted to the analysis of Morris Berman, *The Reenchantment of the World,* chapter 4, and David Kubrin's article, "Newton's Inside Out!: Magic, Class Struggle, and the Rise of Mechanism in the West."

40. Berman, *The Reenchantment of the World,* 125–26.

41. See Kubrin, "Newton's Inside Out!," 113, 116.

42. Kubrin, "Newton's Inside Out!," 97.

43. Specifically, Newton postulated the existence of an aetherial medium, since he found the thought of unmediated "action-at-a-distance" to be incomprehensible. As he wrote in a letter to Bentley, "That gravity should be innate, inherent, and essential to matter, so that one body may act upon another at a distance thro' a vacuum, without the mediation of any thing else, by and through which their action and force may be conveyed from one another, is to me so great an absurdity, that I believe no man who has in philosophical matters a competent faculty of thinking, can ever fall into it" (Newton, *Isaac Newton's Papers and Letters on Natural Philosophy,* 302–3).

44. Letter from Newton to Richard Bently, January 17, 1692, in *Isaac Newton's Papers and Letters on Natural Philosophy,* 298.

45. "I have not been able to discover the cause of those properties of gravity from phenomena, and [so] I frame no hypotheses; and hypotheses, whether metaphysical or physical, whether of occult qualities or mechanical, have no place in experimental philosophy" (Newton, *Principia,* 547).

46. Newton, *Principia,* 447.

47. Jones, *The Redemption of Matter,* 59.

48. Newton, *Principia,* 544.

49. Voltaire, *The Ignorant Philosopher,* quoted in Dampier, *A History of Science and Its Relations with Philosophy and Religion,* 197. As Dampier points out, while Voltaire's analysis is problematic, "Newton's French disciples taught that the Newtonian system indicated reality as a great machine, in all essentials already known, so that man, body and soul, became part of an invincible and mechanical necessity." In this respect, Voltaire "expresses vividly the current French assumptions as to the philosophic and religious import of the Newtonian cosmology" (Dampier, 197).

CHAPTER 8. IN THE NAME OF UTILITY

1. My argument concerning Bacon's ethos of domination is indebted to Theodore Roszak, *Where the Wasteland Ends,* chapter 5; William Leiss, *The Domination of Nature,* chapter 3; Carolyn Merchant, *The Death of Nature,* chapter 7; and David Easlea, *Witch Hunting, Magic, and the New Philosophy: An Introduction to Debates of the Scientific Revolution, 1450–1750,* chapter 3.

2. Francis Bacon, quoted in Bury, *The Idea of Progress,* 50.

3. Ibid., 56.

4. Ibid., 53.

5. Bacon, in *Novum Organum,* book 1, aphorism 129, edited by Joseph Devey, available at http://oll.libertyfund.org/titles/1432.

6. Collins, *Meditations, Poems, Pages from a Sketchbook,* 31.

7. Friedrich Nietzsche, quoted in Krupp, *Skywatchers, Shamans, and Kings,* 209.

8. For a study of Bacon's indebtedness, see Rossi, *Francis Bacon: From Magic to Science,* chapter 1.

9. Easlea, *Witch Hunting, Magic, and the New Philosophy,* 127.

10. Bacon, quoted in Debus, *Man and Nature in the Renaissance,* 103.

11. Bacon, quoted in Easlea, *Witch Hunting, Magic, and the New Philosophy,* 128.

12. Bacon, quoted in Leiss, *The Domination of Nature,* 51.

13. Bacon, *Novum Organum,* quoted in Theodore Roszak, *Where the Wasteland Ends,* 147.

14. Ibid., 160.

15. Bacon, quoted in Theodore Roszak, *Where the Wasteland Ends,* 163.

16. Bacon, quoted in Leiss, *The Domination of Nature,* xxv.

17. Bacon, *The Dignity and Advancement of Learning,* in *The Works of Francis Bacon,* 4:298.

18. Bacon, Preface to *The Great Instauration,* in *The Works of Francis Bacon,* 4:20.

19. On Bacon's use of imagery from the witch trials, see Merchant, *The Death of Nature,* 168–69.

20. Bacon, *The Great Instauration,* in *The Works of Francis Bacon,* 4:29.

21. Bacon, *The Dignity and Advancement of Learning,* in *The Works of Francis Bacon,* 4:296.

22. Bacon, *Novum Organum,* in *The Works of Francis Bacon,* 4:42.

23. Bacon, *Thoughts and Conclusions,* in Farrington, *The Philosophy of Francis Bacon,* 93.

24. Ibid.

25. Bacon, *The Dignity and Advancement of Learning,* in *The Works of Francis Bacon,* 4:373.

26. Bacon, *The New Organon,* in *The Works of Francis Bacon,* 4:115.

27. Bacon, *The Masculine Birth of Time,* in Farrington, *The Philosophy of Francis Bacon,* 59; see also Bacon, *Thoughts and Conclusions,* in Farrington, *The Philosophy of Francis Bacon,* 92–93.

28. Bacon, *Thoughts and Conclusions,* in Farrington, *The Philosophy of Francis Bacon,* 92.

29. Locke, *Two Treatises of Government,* "Second Essay," section 42 (Laslett edition, 315).

30. See Strauss, *Natural Right and History,* 250–51.

31. Bentham, *An Introduction to the Principles of Morals and Legislation,* 1.

32. Jevons, *Theory of Political Economy,* 1.

33. Bentham, *An Introduction to the Principles of Morals and Legislation,* 98.

34. Jevons, *Theory of Political Economy,* 77.

35. Ibid., 77, 38.

36. Specifically, Newton believed that due to the effects of gravity operating on all its parts, the clockwork mechanism of the solar system might need to be adjusted periodically by God. Laplace's system of celestial mechanics did away with the necessity of such divine intervention, and in his own time he came to be seen as the archetype of "the atheist scientist."

CHAPTER 9. PSYCHE REGAINED

1. Blake, quoted by Raine, "Science and Imagination in William Blake," 29.

2. My discussion in this section and most of the quotations are indebted to Whyte's study.

3. See Plotinus, *Enneads* 1.4.10.

4. This is the major critique of modern philosophy presented by William Barrett in his book *Death of the Soul: From Descartes to the Computer.*

5. In Whyte, *The Unconscious before Freud,* 91.

6. Ibid.

7. Ibid., 96.

8. Ibid., 99.

9. Ibid., 114.

10. Ibid., 133.

11. Ibid., 148.

12. Ibid., 149.

13. Ibid., 176.

14. Wordsworth, *The Recluse,* lines 816–21, in *The Complete Poetical Works of William Wordsworth,* 388.

15. In Whyte, *The Unconscious before Freud,* 127. On Goethe's philosophy of nature, see the anthology edited by Naydler, *Goethe on Science.* See also Bortoft, *The Wholeness of Nature: Goethe's Way toward a Science of Conscious Participation in Nature.*

16. Blake, *Milton,* book 2, plate 32, line 18, in *The Complete Poetry and Prose of William Blake,* 132.

17. Blake, *Jerusalem,* 1.14–16, in *The Complete Poetry and Prose of William Blake,* 153.

18. Letter to Thomas Butts dated November 22, 1802, in *The Complete Poetry and Prose of William Blake,* 722.

19. Letter dated August 23, 1799, in Blake, *The Complete Poetry and Prose of William Blake,* 702.

20. Wordsworth, *The Prelude,* book 14, lines 159–62, in *The Complete Poetical Works of William Wordsworth,* 373.

21. Wordsworth, *The Excursion,* opening lines of book 9, in *The Complete Poetical Works of William Wordsworth,* 579.

22. Quoted in Theodore Roszak, *Where the Wasteland Ends,* 328.

23. In Barfield, *What Coleridge Thought,* 44.

24. Coleridge, *Aids to Reflection,* cited in Barfield, *What Coleridge Thought,* 44.

25. Coleridge, *On Poesy or Art,* in *Biographia Literaria,* 2:257–58. See also Bonifazi, *The Soul of the World,* 136.

26. Coleridge, *Biographia Literaria,* 2:65.

27. In Barfield, *What Coleridge Thought,* 80. In this point and in the rest of his natural philosophy, Coleridge was highly influenced by his reading of Schelling.

28. *On Poesy or Art,* in *Biographia Literaria,* 2:255. See also Barfield, *What Coleridge Thought,* 81.

29. *The Friend,* 1:155, in Barfield, *What Coleridge Thought,* 99.

30. Barfield, *What Coleridge Thought,* 100–101.

31. *The Friend,* 1:440, in Barfield, *What Coleridge Thought,* 100.

32. *The Friend,* 1:521, in Barfield, *What Coleridge Thought,* 103.

33. Schelling, quoted in Whyte, *The Unconscious before Freud,* 125.

34. Freud quoted in Whyte, *The Unconscious before Freud,* 169.

35. Freud, Lecture 31, "The Anatomy of the Mental Personality," in *New Introductory Lectures on Psycho-analysis.*

36. Whyte, *The Unconscious before Freud,* 179.

37. Jung, "Yoga and the West," in *Psychology and Religion: West and East,* 536–37.

38. Jung, *Memories, Dreams, Reflections,* 168.

39. Jung, "Psychology and Religion," in *Psychology and Religion: West and East,* 35.

40. Nietzsche, *The Gay Science,* 26.

41. Jung, "Basic Postulates of Analytical Psychology," in *The Structure and Dynamics of the Psyche,* 349–50.

42. Burdach quoted in Whyte, *The Unconscious before Freud,* 148.

43. In the United States, the population did not become predominantly urban until 1910.

44. Romanyshyn, "Egos, Angels, and the Colors of Nature," 176.

45. Ibid.

46. Ibid., 177

47. Freud, quoted in Theodore Roszak, "Where Psyche Meets Gaia," 11.

48. Roszak, "Where Psyche Meets Gaia," 10.

49. Coleridge, *Biographia Literaria,* 2:65.

CHAPTER 10. THE MIRROR OF NATURE

1. Rexroth, "The Lights in the Sky Are Stars," in Bly, *News of the Universe,* 136.

2. Burtt, *The Metaphysical Foundations of Modern Physical Science,* 17.

3. In Jones, *The Redemption of Matter,* 61.

4. Gerald Feinberg, quoted in Pagels, *The Cosmic Code,* 213.

5. Eiseley, *The Immense Journey,* 210.

6. My account here of the early development of atomic physics is indebted to Jones, *The Redemption of Matter,* chapter 5.

7. In Pine, *Science and the Human Prospect,* 224.

8. According to contemporary cosmologists, the universe as a whole may be "the ultimate free lunch," having spontaneously arisen out of the emptiness of the quantum vacuum, a theory first set forth by Edward Tryon in 1973. In this scenario the enormous energy in the universe is canceled out by the

opposing force of gravitational attraction. If correct, the universe has zero net energy and is a quantum fluctuation that has emerged from nothing. See Guth, *The Inflationary Universe,* chapter 1.

9. Popper, "Materialism Transcends Itself," 8, in Popper and Eccles, *The Self and Its Brain.*

10. d'Espagnat, "The Quantum Theory and Reality," 158.

11. Feynman, Leighton, and Sands, *The Feynman Lectures on Physics,* 3:1.

12. Ibid, 3:18–19.

13. Albert Einstein, quoted in Kafatos and Nadeau, *The Conscious Universe: Part and Whole in Modern Physical Theory,* 117.

14. For an account of the experimental verification of nonlocality, see Gribbin, *In Search of Schrödinger's Cat,* chapter 10.

15. See, for example, Gribbin, *In Search of Schrödinger's Cat,* 229.

16. Eddington, in Lang and Gingerich, *A Source Book in Astronomy and Astrophysics: 1900–1975,* 288.

17. de Duve, *Vital Dust,* 118.

18. Ibid., 121.

19. Ibid., 292–93.

20. Shapley, *Of Stars and Men,* 113.

21. Ibid., 107.

22. Kauffman, *At Home in the Universe,* 149.

CHAPTER 11. THE PATTERN WHICH CONNECTS

1. Young, *The Unfinished Universe,* 42.

2. Ibid., 121.

3. Ibid., 130.

4. Ibid., 145.

5. Ibid., 149.

6. Daniel Koshland, "A Response-Regulated Model in a Simple Sensory System," *Science* 196: 1055–63, quoted in Margulis and Sagan, *What Is Life?,* 179.

7. Quoted in Theodore Roszak, "Nature and Nature's God," 15.

8. Jeans, *The Mysterious Universe,* 158.

9. Samuel Butler, quoted in Margulis and Sagan, *What Is Life?,* 183.

10. Charles Darwin, *Life and Letters* (London: John Murray, 1888), 3:18, quoted in Margulis and Sagan, *What Is Life?,* 56.

11. See, for example, Kauffman, *At Home in the Universe: The Search for the Laws of Self-Organization and Complexity.*

12. See Bateson, *Mind and Nature*, chapter 4, for his six criteria of mental processes.

13. Bateson, quoted in Capra, *The Turning Point*, 290.

14. Cited by Hadot, *The Veil of Isis: An Essay on the History of the Idea of Nature*, 25.

15. See Maturana and Varela, *Autopoiesis and Cognition* and *The Tree of Knowledge*. An account of their Santiago theory, which identifies cognition (the process of knowing) with life, appears in Capra, *The Web of Life*. See also Margulis, "Big Trouble in Biology: Physiological Autopoiesis versus Mechanistic Neo-Darwinism," in Margulis and Sagan, *Slanted Truths*, chapter 20.

16. With his description of a holon's self-assertive and integrative faces, Koestler unwittingly revived the observation of the ancient philosopher Empedocles that the powers of Strife (differentiation) and Love (integration) are both present in the fabric of life. See Koestler, *Janus: A Summing Up*.

17. See Margulis and Sagan, *What Is Life?*, chapter 5, "Permanent Mergers." For a technical treatment, see Margulis, *Symbiosis in Cell Evolution*.

18. For a discussion of the oxygen holocaust, see chapter 6 in Margulis and Sagan, *Microcosmos: Four Billion Years of Microbial Evolution*.

19. Lovelock, *The Ages of Gaia*, 18. As he wrote, "Through Gaia theory I now see the system of the material Earth and the living organisms on it, evolving so that self-regulation is an emergent property. In such a system active feedback processes operate automatically and solar energy sustains comfortable conditions for life. The conditions are only constant in the short term and evolve in synchrony with the changing needs of the biota as it evolves. Life and its environment are so closely coupled that evolution concerns Gaia, not the organisms or the environment taken separately" (19–20).

20. M. Newman, "Evolution of the Solar Constant," in Ponnamperuma and Margulis, editors, *Limits to Life*. See also Joseph, *Gaia: The Growth of an Idea*, 121–25.

21. See Lovelock, *The Ages of Gaia*, chapter 3.

22. Margulis and Sagan, *What Is Life?*, 28.

23. Davies, *God and the New Physics*, 179.

24. Dyson, *Disturbing the Universe*, 251.

25. Harris, *Cosmos and Anthropos*, 58.

26. Swimme and Berry, *The Universe Story*, 54

27. Plato, *Timaeus* 30D3–31A1.

CHAPTER 12. THE TURNING POINT

1. Eugene Cernan, quoted in White, *The Overview Effect: Space Exploration and Human Evolution,* 206–7.

2. Schweickart, in Katz, Marsh, and Thompson, *Earth's Answer,* 12.

3. Mitchell, *The Way of the Explorer,* 58.

4. Ibid., 58–59.

5. Schweickart, in Katz, Marsh, and Thompson, *Earth's Answer,* 12–13.

6. Marcus Aurelius, *Meditations* 7.47–48, quoted in Hadot, *Philosophy as a Way of Life,* 244. Pierre Hadot made a special study of the spiritual exercises used by Greek philosophers and discusses "The View from Above" in a chapter of that title, in *Philosophy as a Way of Life,* 238–50.

7. Hadot, *Philosophy as a Way of Life,* 244.

8. Ibid., 273.

9. See Planetary Collective, *Overview,* at: www.overviewthemovie.com/#!/watch/.

10. See the astonishing film compiled by photographer Knate Myers, *View from the ISS at Night,* http://vimeo.com/45878034#.

11. Brand, "Photography Changes Our Relationship to Our Planet."

12. Fideler, "Alexandria, the Cosmopolis: Global Community, Then and Now." An excerpt from this talk is available at www.cosmopolisproject.org/what-is-a-cosmopolis/.

13. Thomas, *The Lives of a Cell,* 145.

14. Margulis and Sagan, *What Is Life?,* 28.

15. Echoing the need to rediscover our place in a contemporary cosmopolis, Nancy Abrams and Joel Primack note, "Right now humanity's overriding need is for a transculturally shared vision for how to solve global problems, and a cosmic society is the only serious candidate we know for an organizing principle that would allow such a shared vision to flourish" (Abrams and Primack, *The New Universe and the Human Future: How a Shared Cosmology Could Transform the World,* 143).

16. Benyus, *Biomimicry: Innovation Inspired by Nature,* 5.

17. Primack and Abrams, *The View from the Center of the Universe,* 253–54.

18. Article on "World Footprint," website of the Global Footprint Network (www.footprintnetwork.org/en/index.php/GFN/page/world_footprint/).

19. Interview with Hazel Henderson, in Danitz and Zelov, *Ecological Design.*

20. MacLeish, "A Reflection: Riders on Earth Together, Brothers in Eternal Cold."

CHAPTER 13. THE ALCHEMY OF ENGAGEMENT

1. Benyus, TED talk, "Biomimicry in Action."
2. Ibid.
3. As Benyus notes, "After 3.8 billion years of research and development, failures are fossils, and what surrounds us is the secret to survival" (*Biomimicry: Innovation Inspired by Nature*, 3).
4. Kealy Devoy, "Day 3: One Sun with Paul Hawken," April 14, 2012, http://blogs.nicholas.duke.edu/cleanenergy/day-3-one-sun-with-paul-hawken/.
5. Scott Cooney, "Paul Hawken on Solar, Population, GDP, and Solutions in Smallness," August 6, 2012, www.triplepundit.com/2012/08/paul-hawken-solar-population-gdp-solutions-smallness/.
6. Van der Ryn and Cowan, *Ecological Design*, 9.
7. Benyus, *Biomimicry: Innovation Inspired by Nature*, xi.
8. For a discussion of these two large-scale bioshelters, see Nancy Jack Todd, *A Safe and Sustainable World: The Promise of Ecological Design*, chapters 6 and 7.
9. John Todd, "Living Machines" lecture, Duquesne University.
10. Ibid.
11. John Todd, "Ecological Design," E. F. Schumacher Society lecture.
12. John Todd, "Living Machines" lecture, Duquesne University.
13. Nancy Jack Todd and John Todd, *From Eco-Cities to Living Machines*, xviii. My emphasis.
14. Ibid., xxi.
15. Hawken, "Natural Capitalism: Brother, Can You Spare a Paradigm?," 191.
16. Primack and Abrams, *The View from the Center of the Universe*, 240.
17. Ibid., 242.
18. Ibid., 288.
19. Nancy Jack Todd, *A Safe and Sustainable World*, 189.
20. See Skolimowski, *The Participatory Mind*, 61–73.
21. Benyus, "Biomimicry: What Would Nature Do Here?," 7.
22. John Todd, "Ecological Design," E. F. Schumacher Society lecture.
23. Interview with John Todd in Danitz and Zelov, *Ecological Design*.
24. Nancy and John Todd, *From Eco-Cities to Living Machines*, xix.
25. Hawken, "Natural Capitalism: Brother, Can You Spare a Paradigm?," 148.
26. For reliable statistics about the planetary environment, see World Resources Institute, *A Guide to World Resources 2000–2001: People and Ecosystems; The Fraying Web of Life* (available at: www.wri.org/publication/

world-resources-2000-2001-people-and-ecosystems-fraying-web-life); the Global Environment Outlook reports published by the United Nations Development Programme (most recently GEO5, available at: www.unep .org/geo/geo5.asp); the Living Planet Reports published by the World Wildlife Foundation (available at: http://wwf.panda.org/about_our_earth/ all_publications/living_planet_report); the State of the World Reports published and available for sale from Worldwatch Institute (www.world watch.org/bookstore/state-of-the-world) along with their publication Vital Signs (http://vitalsigns.worldwatch.org). A useful publication listing statistics from reliable sources is *Environmental Facts: Facts and Figures to Inspire Action toward Zero Waste*, available from Eco-Cycle at http://ecocycle.org/ files/pdfs/Eco-CycleEnvironmentalFacts.pdf. Information and articles regarding species extinction can be found at the Species Alliance website: http://speciesalliance.org.

27. World Resources Institute, *Materials Flows in the United States: A Physical Accounting of the U.S. Industrial Economy* (Washington, D.C.: World Resources Institute, 2008), chapter 1. Available at: http://pdf.wri.org/mate rial_flows_in_the_united_states.pdf.

28. United States Environmental Protection Agency, *Sustainable Materials Management: The Road Ahead* (2009), 4 (www.epa.gov/smm/pdf/vision2 .pdf).

29. Wilson, *The Future of Life,* 33.

30. United States Environmental Protection Agency, *Sustainable Materials Management,* 5.

31. World Resources Institute, *A Guide to World Resources 2000–2001,* 51.

32. Ibid., 104.

33. United Nations Development Programme, *Global Environment Outlook 5* (2012), 134.

34. World Resources Institute, *A Guide to World Resources 2000–2001,* 116.

35. United Nations Environment Programme report cited by BBC science correspondent Corinne Podger in "Quarter of Mammals 'Face Extinction,'" http://news.bbc.co.uk/2/hi/science/nature/2000325.stm. See also United Nations Environment Programme, *Global Environment Outlook 3* (2002); available online at www.unep.org/geo/geo3.asp.

36. Of the four hundred biologists questioned in the *Biodiversity in the Next Millennium* survey, "the majority (70 percent) think that during the next thirty years as many as one-fifth of all species alive will become extinct, and

one third think that as many as half of all species on Earth will die out in that time." American Museum of Natural History press release, April 20, 1998 (archived at www.mysterium.com/amnh.html).

37. World Wildlife Foundation, *Living Planet Report 2012: Biodiversity, Biocapacity, and Better Choices,* 40; see also "World Footprint," www.footprint network.org/en/index.php/gfn/page/world_footprint.

38. World Wildlife Foundation, *Living Planet Report 2012,* 43.

39. For a discussion of different concepts of sustainability, see Van der Ryn and Cowan, *Ecological Design,* chapter 1.

40. Rocky Mountain Institute, *Visitor's Guide,* 70.

41. To learn more about the Living Building Challenge, visit: http://living future.org/lbc/about.

42. Noble, "Regenerative Design," summarizing a presentation by Sim Van der Ryn, "Surpassability: The Future We Can Create Now," given at the Environmental Design Research Association annual conference in 2007 (EDRA 38).

43. Evliya Çelebi (1611–1682), quoted in an exhibit on "Piped Water and the Cult of Water," Museum of Sarajevo, Bosnia and Herzegovina.

44. Muhamed Nerkesija (ca. 1584–ca. 1635), quoted in an exhibit on "Piped Water and the Cult of Water," Museum of Sarajevo, Bosnia and Herzegovina.

45. See Delumeau, *History of Paradise: The Garden of Eden in Myth and Tradition,* 4.

46. Naydler, *Gardening as a Sacred Art,* 20.

47. Ibid., 36.

48. See Watkins, editor, *American Heritage Dictionary of Indo-European Roots,* for the roots of *divine* (deiw-) and *holy* (kailo-).

49. Naydler, *Gardening as a Sacred Art,* 87.

Bibliography

Abraham, Ralph. *Chaos, Gaia, Eros.* San Francisco: Harper San Francisco, 1995.

Abram, David. "The Mechanical and the Organic: On the Impact of Metaphor in Science." In *Scientists on Gaia,* edited by Stephen Schneider and Penelope Boston, 66–74. Cambridge, Mass.: MIT Press, 1991.

———. *Spell of the Sensuous: Perception and Language in a More than Human World.* New York: Vintage, 1997.

Abrams, Nancy Ellen, and Joel R. Primack. *The New Universe and the Human Future: How a Shared Cosmology Could Transform the World.* New Haven, Conn.: Yale University Press, 2011.

Allers, Rudolf. "Microcosmus from Anaximandros to Paracelsus." *Traditio* 2 (1944): 319–407.

Armstrong, A. H., editor. *Classical Mediterranean Spirituality: Egyptian, Greek, Roman.* New York: Crossroad, 1986.

Armstrong, A. H. "Psyche, Ourselves, World-Soul, and Gaia in Plotinus." *Sphinx* 5 (London: London Convivium for Archetypal Studies, n.d.), 114–21.

Athanassakis, Apostolos M., translator. *The Orphic Hymns.* Atlanta: Scholars Press, 1988.

Ausubel, Kenny, and J. P. Harpignies, editors. *Nature's Operating Instructions: The True Biotechnologies.* San Francisco: Sierra Club Books, 2004.

Bacon, Francis. *The Masculine Birth of Time.* In Farrington, *The Philosophy of Francis Bacon,* 59–72.

———. *Thoughts and Conclusions.* In Farrington, *The Philosophy of Francis Bacon,* 73–102.

———. *The Works of Francis Bacon.* Edited by James Spedding, Robert Ellis, and Douglas Heath. 14 vols. London: Longman, 1870.

Barfield, Owen. *What Coleridge Thought*. Middleton, Conn.: Wesleyan University Press, 1971.

Barrett, William. *Death of the Soul: From Descartes to the Computer*. Garden City, N.Y.: Anchor Books, 1987.

Bateson, Gregory. *Mind and Nature: A Necessary Unity*. New York: E. P. Dutton, 1979.

Bentham, Jeremy. *An Introduction to the Principles of Morals and Legislation*. Oxford, U.K.: Oxford University Press, 1907.

Benyus, Janine. "Biomimicry in Action." Filmed July 2009, Oxford, U.K. TED video, 20:15. Posted August 2009. www.youtube.com/watch?v=k_GFql2w5WU.

———. *Biomimicry: Innovation Inspired by Nature*. New York: Harper Perennial, 2002.

———. "Biomimicry: What Would Nature Do Here?" In Ausubel and Harpignies, editors, *Nature's Operating Instructions*, 3–16.

Bergson, Henri. *Creative Evolution*. New York: Cosimo, 2005. (Orig. pub. in English by Modern Library, 1911.)

Berman, Morris. *The Reenchantment of the World*. Ithaca, N.Y.: Cornell University Press, 1981.

Blake, William. *The Complete Poetry and Prose of William Blake*. Edited by David V. Erdman. New York: Anchor Books, 1988.

Bly, Robert, editor. *News of the Universe: Poems of Twofold Consciousness*. San Francisco: Sierra Club Books, 1980.

Bonifazi, Conrad. *The Soul of the World: An Account of the Inwardness of Things*. Lanham, Md.: University Press of America, 1978.

Bortoft, Henri. *The Wholeness of Nature: Goethe's Way toward a Science of Conscious Participation in Nature*. Hudson, N.Y.: Lindisfarne Press, 1997.

Brand, Stewart. "Photography Changes Our Relationship to Our Planet." Smithsonian Institution website: *click! Photography Changes Everything*. http://click.si.edu/Story.aspx?story=31

Bruno, Giordano. *Cause, Principle, and Unity*. Translated by Jack Lindsay. New York: International Publishers, 1964.

———. *The Expulsion of the Triumphant Beast*. Translated by Arthur Imerti. New Brunswick, N.J.: Rutgers University Press, 1964.

Burckhardt, Titus. *Alchemy: Science of the Cosmos, Science of the Soul*. Baltimore: Penguin, 1971.

Burtt, E. A. *The Metaphysical Foundations of Modern Physical Science.* Revised edition. New York: Doubleday, 1954.

Bury, J. B. *The Idea of Progress.* New York: Dover, 1955.

Campanella, Tommaso. *The City of the Sun.* Translated by Daniel Donno. Berkeley: University of California Press, 1981.

Campbell, Joseph. *Myths to Live By.* New York: Bantam, 1973.

———. *The Power of Myth.* New York: Doubleday, 1988.

Capra, Fritjof. *The Turning Point: Science, Society, and the Rising Culture.* New York: Simon & Schuster, 1982.

———. *The Web of Life: A New Scientific Study of Living Systems.* New York: Doubleday, 1996.

Cassirer, Ernst. *The Individual and the Cosmos in Renaissance Philosophy.* New York: Harper & Row, 1964.

Chenu, M.-D. *Nature, Man, and Society in the Twelfth Century.* Chicago: University of Chicago Press, 1983.

Clark, Stephen. "Ancient Philosophy." In *The Oxford History of Western Philosophy,* edited by Anthony Kenny, 1–56. New York: Oxford University Press, 1994.

Clement of Alexandria. *The Exhortation to the Greeks.* Loeb Classical Library. Cambridge, Mass.: Harvard University Press, 1919.

Coleridge, Samuel Taylor. *Biographia Literaria.* Edited by J. Shawcross. 2 vols. Oxford, U.K.: Oxford University Press, 1968.

———. *The Friend.* Edited by Barbara Rooke. 2 vols. Princeton, N.J.: Princeton University Press, 1969.

Colish, Marcia L. *The Stoic Tradition from Antiquity to the Middle Ages.* 2 vols. Leiden, Netherlands: E. J. Brill, 1985.

Collingwood, R. G. *The Idea of Nature.* Oxford, U.K.: Oxford University Press, 1945.

Collins, Cecil. *Meditations, Poems, Pages from a Sketchbook.* Ipswich, U.K.: Golgonooza Press, 1997.

Conger, George P. *Theories of Macrocosms and Microcosms in the History of Philosophy.* New York: Columbia University Press, 1922.

Copenhaver, Brian P. *Hermetica: The Greek Corpus Hermeticum and the Latin Asclepius in a New English Translation.* Cambridge, U.K.: Cambridge University Press, 1992.

Copernicus, Nicholas. *On the Revolutions of the Heavenly Spheres.* Translated by A. M. Duncan. New York: Barnes & Noble, 1976.

Copleston, Frederick. *A History of Philosophy.* 7 vols. New York: Image Books, 1965.

Corbin, Henry. *Temple and Contemplation.* London: KPI, 1986.

Crowe, Michael J. *Theories of the World from Antiquity to the Copernican Revolution.* New York: Dover, 1990.

Cushman, Robert. *Therapeia: Plato's Conception of Philosophy.* Chapel Hill: University of North Carolina Press, 1958.

Dampier, William Cecil. *A History of Science and its Relations with Philosophy and Religion.* Fourth edition. Cambridge, U.K.: Cambridge University Press, 1948.

Danitz, Brian, and Christopher Zelov, directors. *Ecological Design: Inventing the Future.* Hellertown, Pa.: Knossus Project, 1994.

Davidson, Norman. *Sky Phenomena: A Guide to Naked-Eye Observation of the Stars.* Hudson, N.Y.: Lindisfarne Press, 1993.

Davies, Paul. *God and the New Physics.* New York: Simon & Schuster, 1983.

Debus, Allen G. *The English Paracelsians.* New York: Franklin Watts, 1966.

———. *Man and Nature in the Renaissance.* New York: Cambridge University Press, 1978.

de Duve, Christian. *Vital Dust: Life as a Cosmic Imperative.* New York: Basic Books, 1995.

della Porta, Giambattista. *Natural Magick* (1558). Facsimile reprint of the 1658 translation. New York: Basic Books, 1957.

Delumeau, Jean. *History of Paradise: The Garden of Eden in Myth and Tradition.* New York: Continuum, 1995.

Descartes, René. *Discourse on Method, Optics, Geometry, and Meteorology.* Translated by Paul J. Olscamp. Indianapolis: Bobbs-Merrill, 1965.

———. *The Meditations and Selections from the Principles.* Translated by John Veitch. Chicago: Open Court, 1908.

———. *The Philosophical Writings of Descartes.* Translated by John Cottingham, Robert Stoothoff, and Dugald Murdoch. 3 vols. Cambridge, U.K.: Cambridge University Press, 1985.

———. *Principles of Philosophy.* Translated by Valentine Rodger Miller and Reese P. Miller. Dordrecht, Netherlands: Reidel, 1983.

d'Espagnat, Bernard. "The Quantum Theory and Reality." *Scientific American* (November 1979), 158–81.

Diogenes Laertius. *Lives of the Eminent Philosophers.* 2 vols. Loeb Classical Library. Cambridge, Mass.: Harvard University Press, 1925.

Dodds, E. R. *Pagan and Christian in an Age of Anxiety.* Cambridge, U.K.: Cambridge University Press, 1965.

Durham, Frank, and Robert Purrington. *Frame of the Universe: A History of Physical Cosmology.* New York: Columbia University Press, 1983.

Dyson, Freeman. *Disturbing the Universe.* New York: Harper & Row, 1979.

Easlea, Brian. *Witch Hunting, Magic, and the New Philosophy: An Introduction to Debates of the Scientific Revolution, 1450–1750.* Brighton, U.K.: Harvester Press, 1980.

Einstein, Albert. "The Cosmic Religious Feeling." In *Alexandria* 4 (Grand Rapids: Phanes Press, 1997), 11–14.

Eiseley, Loren. *The Immense Journey.* New York: Random House, 1946.

Eliade, Mircea. *The Forge and the Crucible: The Origins and Structures of Alchemy.* New York: Harper & Row, 1971.

Eliot, T. S. *The Rock: A Pageant Play.* New York: Harcourt, Brace and Co., 1934.

Emerson, Ralph Waldo. *The Works of Ralph Waldo Emerson.* 4 vols. New York: Charles C. Bigelow, n.d.

Fallico, Arturo, and Herman Shapiro, editors and translators. *Renaissance Philosophy.* 2 vols. New York: Random House, 1967–69.

Farrington, Benjamin. *The Philosophy of Francis Bacon.* Liverpool, U.K.: Liverpool University Press, 1964.

Fauvel, John, Raymond Flood, Michael Shortland, and Robin Wilson, editors. *Let Newton be!* Oxford, U.K.: Oxford University Press, 1988.

Ferris, Timothy. *Coming of Age in the Milky Way.* New York: William Morrow, 1988.

Feynman, Richard P., Robert B. Leighton, and Matthew Sands. *The Feynman Lectures on Physics.* 3 vols. Reading, Mass.: Addison-Wesley, 1963–65.

Ficino, Marsilio. *The Book of Life.* Translated by Charles Boer. Dallas: Spring Publications, 1980.

———. *Three Books on Life.* Translated by Carol Kaske and John Clark. Binghamton, N.Y.: Medieval and Renaissance Texts and Studies, 1989.

———. *Commentary on Plato's Symposium on Love.* Translated by Sears Jayne. Dallas: Spring, 1985.

———. *Concerning the Sun* (1493). In Fallico and Shapiro, editors and translators, *Renaissance Philosophy,* 1:118–141.

———. *The Letters of Marsilio Ficino.* Translated by members of the Language Department of the School of Economic Science, London. London: Shepheard-Walwyn, 1975–2010.

Fideler, David. "Alexandria, the Cosmopolis: Global Community, Then and Now." Keynote lecture, conference on Ancient Alexandria: Greco-Egyptian Birthplace of the Western Mind, Bibliotheca Alexandrina, Alexandria, Egypt, June 9–14, 2012. (Excerpt available online at: www.cosmopolisproject.org/what-is-a-cosmopolis.)

———. "Introduction." In *The Pythagorean Sourcebook and Library*, Kenneth Sylvan Guthrie, compiler and translator, 19–54. Grand Rapids, Mich.: Phanes Press, 1987.

———. *Jesus Christ, Sun of God: Ancient Cosmology and Early Christian Symbolism*. Wheaton, Ill.: Quest Books, 1993.

———. "Science's Missing Half: Epistemological Pluralism and the Search for an Inclusive Cosmology." *Alexandria* 5 (Grand Rapids, Mich.: Phanes Press, 2000), 41–73.

Field, Arthur. *The Origins of the Platonic Academy of Florence*. Princeton, N.J.: Princeton University Press, 1988.

Freud, Sigmund. *New Introductory Lectures on Psycho-analysis*. London: Hogarth Press, 1933.

Galileo Galilei. *Two New Sciences*. Translated by Stillman Drake. Madison: University of Wisconsin Press, 1974.

Gimpel, Jean. *The Medieval Machine: The Industrial Revolution of the Middle Ages*. New York: Penguin, 1977.

Goethe, Johann Wolfgang. *The Maxims and Reflections of Goethe*. Translated by Bailey Saunders. New York: Macmillan, 1906.

———. *Goethe on Science: An Anthology of Goethe's Scientific Writings*. Edited by Jeremy Naydler. Edinburgh: Floris Books, 1996.

Gribbin, John. *In Search of Schrödinger's Cat: Quantum Physics and Reality*. New York: Bantam, 1984.

Gurwitsch, Aron. *Phenomenology and the Theory of Science*. Evanston, Ill.: Northwestern University, 1974.

Guth, Alan. *The Inflationary Universe*. Reading, Mass.: Addison-Wesley, 1997.

Guthrie, Kenneth Sylvan, compiler and translator. *The Pythagorean Sourcebook and Library: An Anthology of Ancient Writings Which Relate to Pythagoras and Pythagorean Philosophy*. Edited and introduced by David Fideler. Grand Rapids, Mich.: Phanes Press, 1987.

Guthrie, W. K. C. *A History of Greek Philosophy*. 6 vols. Cambridge, U.K.: Cambridge University Press, 1962–1981.

Hadot, Pierre. *Philosophy as a Way of Life: Spiritual Exercises from Socrates to*

Foucault. Translated by Michael Chase. Malden, Mass.: Blackwell, 1995.

———. *The Veil of Isis: An Essay on the History of the Idea of Nature.* Translated by Michael Chase. Cambridge, Mass.: Harvard University Press, 2006.

Hahn, Roger. "Laplace and the Mechanistic Universe." In Lindberg and Numbers, editors, *God and Nature: Historical Essays on the Encounter between Christianity and Science,* 256–76.

Harris, Errol E. *Cosmos and Anthropos: A Philosophical Interpretation of the Anthropic Cosmological Principle.* Atlantic Highlands, N.J.: Humanities Press International, 1991.

Harrison, Edward. *Cosmology: The Science of the Universe.* Cambridge, U.K.: Cambridge University Press, 1981.

Hawken, Paul. "Natural Capitalism: Brother, Can You Spare a Paradigm?" In Ausubel and Harpignies, editors, *Nature's Operating Instructions,* 147–60.

Hillman, James. *Re-Visioning Psychology.* New York: Harper & Row, 1975.

———. *"Anima Mundi:* The Return of Soul to the World." *Spring* 1982 (Dallas: Spring Publications, 1982), 71–93.

———. "Concerning the Stone: Alchemical Images of the Goal." *Sphinx* 5 (London: London Convivium for Archetypal Studies, n.d.), 234–65.

Hillman, James and Michael Ventura. *We've Had a Hundred Years of Psychotherapy and the World Is Getting Worse.* San Francisco: Harper San Francisco, 1993.

Hobbes, Thomas. *The English Works of Thomas Hobbes.* Edited by William Molesworth. 11 vols. London: J. Bohn, 1839–1845. Reprint, Aalen, W. Germany: Scientia Aalen, 1962.

Horowitz, Irving. *The Renaissance Philosophy of Giordano Bruno.* New York: Ross, 1952.

Husserl, Edmund. *The Crisis of the European Sciences and Transcendental Phenomenology.* Evanston, Ill.: Northwestern University Press, 1970.

James, William. *A Pluralistic Universe.* New York: Longmans and Green, 1909. Reprint, Lincoln: University of Nebraska Press, 1996.

Jeans, James. *The Mysterious Universe.* New York: Macmillan, 1930.

Jevons, William Stanley. *The Theory of Political Economy* (1871). Fifth edition. New York: Kelly & Millman, 1957.

Jones, James W. *The Redemption of Matter.* Lanham, Md.: University Press of America, 1984.

Joseph, Lawrence E. *Gaia: The Growth of an Idea.* New York: St. Martin's Press, 1990.

Jung, C. G. *Alchemical Studies.* Collected Works, 13. Princeton, N.J.: Princeton University Press, 1967.

———. *The Archetypes of the Collective Unconscious.* Collected Works, 9.1. Princeton, N.J.: Princeton University Press, 1968.

———. *Freud and Psychoanalysis.* Collected Works, 4. Princeton, N.J.: Princeton University Press, 1961.

———. *Memories, Dreams, Reflections.* New York: Vintage Books, 1965.

———. *Psychology and Alchemy.* Collected Works, 12. Princeton, N.J.: Princeton University Press, 1968.

———. *Psychology and Religion: West and East.* Collected Works, 11. Princeton, N.J.: Princeton University Press, 1969.

———. *The Structure and Dynamics of the Psyche.* Collected Works, 8. Princeton, N.J.: Princeton University Press, 1975.

Kafatos, Menas, and Robert Nadeau. *The Conscious Universe: Part and Whole in Modern Physical Theory.* New York: Springer-Verlag, 1990.

Katz, Michael, William Marsh, and Gail Thompson, editors. *Earth's Answer: Explorations of Planetary Culture at the Lindisfarne Conferences.* New York: Harper & Row, 1977.

Kauffman, Stuart. *At Home in the Universe: The Search for the Laws of Self-Organization and Complexity.* New York: Oxford University Press, 1995.

Kearney, Hugh. *Science and Change: 1500–1700.* New York: World University Library, 1971.

Kellert, Stephen R., and Edward O. Wilson, editors. *The Biophilia Hypothesis.* Washington, D.C.: Island Press, 1993.

Kenny, Anthony, editor. *The Oxford History of Western Philosophy.* New York: Oxford University Press, 1994.

Kerr, Walter. *The Decline of Pleasure.* New York: Touchstone, 1962.

Koestler, Arthur. *Janus: A Summing Up.* New York: Vintage Books, 1978.

Kristeller, P. O. *The Philosophy of Marsilio Fincino.* New York: Columbia University Press, 1943.

Krupp, E. C. "Light in the Temples." In *Records in Stone,* edited by Clive Ruggles, 473–99. Cambridge, U.K.: Cambridge University Press, 1988.

———. *Skywatchers, Shamans, and Kings: Astronomy and the Archaeology of Power.* New York: Wiley, 1997.

Kubrin, David. "Newton's Inside Out!: Magic, Class Struggle, and the Rise of Mechanism in the West." In *The Analytic Spirit: Essays in the History of*

Science in Honor of Henry Guerlac, edited by Harry Woolf, 96–121. Ithaca, N.Y.: Cornell University Press, 1980.

Lactanius. *The Divine Institutes.* In Roberts and Donaldson, editors, *The Ante-Nicene Fathers,* vol. 7.

Lang, Kenneth, and Owen Gingerich, editors. *A Source Book in Astronomy and Astrophysics, 1900–1975.* Cambridge, Mass.: Harvard University Press, 1979.

Lankford, John, editor. *The History of Astronomy: An Encyclopedia.* New York: Garland, 1996.

Leiss, William. *The Domination of Nature.* New York: George Braziller, 1972.

Linberg, David C., and Ronald L. Numbers, editors. *God and Nature: Historical Essays on the Encounter between Christianity and Science.* Berkeley and Los Angeles: University of California Press, 1986.

Lindsay, Jack. *The Origins of Alchemy in Graeco-Roman Egypt.* London: Frederick Muller, 1970.

Locke, John. *Two Treatises of Government.* Edited by Peter Laslett. Cambridge, U.K.: Cambridge University Press, 1967.

Lockyer, Norman. *The Dawn of Astronomy.* London: Cassell, 1894.

Lovelock, James. *The Ages of Gaia.* New York: W. W. Norton, 1988.

MacLeish, Archibald. "A Reflection: Riders on Earth Together, Brothers in Eternal Cold." *New York Times,* December 25, 1968. http://graphics8.nytimes.com/packages/pdf/opinion/20081224earth1.pdf.

Marcus Aurelius. *Meditations.* Translated by Maxwell Staniforth. New York: Penguin, 1964.

Margulis, Lynn. *Symbiosis in Cell Evolution.* Second edition. New York: W. H. Freeman, 1993.

Margulis, Lynn, and Dorion Sagan. *Microcosmos: Four Billion Years of Microbial Evolution.* Berkeley: University of California Press, 1997.

———. *Slanted Truths: Essays on Gaia, Symbiosis, and Evolution.* New York: Springer-Verlag, 1997.

———. *What Is Life?* New York: Simon & Schuster, 1995.

Marshack, Alexander. "Lunar Notation on Upper Paleolithic Remains." *Science* 146 (November 1964): 743–45.

———. *The Roots of Civilization: The Cognitive Beginnings of Man's First Art, Symbol and Notation.* New York: McGraw-Hill, 1972.

Maturana, Humberto, and Francisco Varela. *Autopoiesis and Cognition.* Dordrecht, Netherlands: D. Reidel, 1980.

———. *The Tree of Knowledge.* Boston: Shambhala, 1987.

Meeker, Joseph W. *The Comedy of Survival*. New York: Charles Scribner's Sons, 1974.

Merchant, Carolyn. *The Death of Nature*. San Francisco: Harper & Row, 1980.

Mitchell, Edgar. *The Way of the Explorer*. New York: Putnam, 1996.

Moline, Jon. *Plato's Theory of Understanding*. Madison: University of Wisconsin Press, 1981.

Moore, Thomas. *The Planets Within: The Astrological Psychology of Marsilio Ficino*. Lewisburg, Pa.: Bucknell University Press, 1982. Reprint, Great Barrington, Mass.: Lindisfarne Press, 1990.

Nagel, Thomas. *The View from Nowhere*. New York: Oxford University Press, 1986.

Naydler, Jeremy. *Gardening as a Sacred Art*. Edinburgh: Floris Books, 2011.

Nelson, Bruce. "The Theology of the Invisible." In *Alexandria* 4 (Grand Rapids, Mich.: Phanes Press, 1997), 195–201.

Newton, Isaac. *Isaac Newton's Papers and Letters on Natural Philosophy and Related Documents*. Edited by I. Bernard Cohen. Cambridge, Mass.: Harvard University Press, 1958.

———. *Principia Mathematica Philosophiae Naturalis* (1687). Translated as *Mathematical Principles of Natural Philosophy and His System of the World* by Florian Cajori and Andrew Motte. Berkeley: University of California Press, 1934.

Nietzsche, Friedrich. *The Gay Science*. Mineola, N.Y.: Dover Philosophical Classics, 2006.

Noble, Christina. "Regenerative Design." Article originally published in *Forward: Architecture and Design Journal* (Fall 2007). http://contourarchitecture .com/wordpress/blog/regenerative-design.

North, John. *The Norton History of Astronomy and Cosmology*. New York: Norton, 1996.

———. *Stonehenge: Prehistoric Man and the Cosmos*. New York: Free Press, 1997.

Pagels, Heinz R. *The Cosmic Code*. New York: Simon and Schuster, 1982.

Paracelsus. *The Hermetic and Alchemical Writings of Paracelsus*. 2 vols. Berkeley, Calif.: Shambhala, 1976.

———. *Paracelsus: Essential Readings*. Selected and translated by Nicholas Goodrick-Clarke. Wellingborough, U.K.: Crucible, 1990.

———. *Paracelsus: Selected Writings*. Edited by Jolande Jacobi. Princeton, N.J.: Princeton University Press, 1979.

Pine, Ronald C. *Science and the Human Prospect*. Belmont, Calif.: Wadsworth, 1988.

Plato. *Works*. 12 vols. Loeb Classical Library. Cambridge, Mass.: Harvard University Press, 1914–1927.

———. *Plato: The Collected Dialogues, Including the Letters*. Edited by Edith Hamilton and Huntington Cairns. New York: Pantheon, 1961.

———. *Plato's Timaeus*. Translated by F. M. Cornford. Indianapolis: Bobbs-Merrill, 1959.

Plotinus. *The Enneads*. Translated by A. H. Armstrong. 7 vols. Loeb Classical Library. Cambridge, Mass.: Harvard University Press, 1966–1988.

———. *The Enneads*. Translated by Stephen MacKenna. Burdett, N.Y.: Larson Publications, 1992.

Poncé, Charles. "The Alchemical Light." In *The Alchemical Tradition in the Late Twentieth Century,* edited by Richard Grossinger, 172–82. Berkeley, Calif.: North Atlantic Books, 1983.

Ponnamperuma, C., and Lynn Margulis, editors. *Limits to Life*. Dordrecht, Netherlands: D. Reidel, 1980.

Popper, Karl R., and John C. Eccles. *The Self and Its Brain*. New York: Springer-Verlag, 1977.

Porphyry. *Porphyry's Launching-Points to the Realm of Mind: An Introduction to the Neoplatonic Philosophy of Plotinus*. Translated by Kenneth Sylvan Guthrie with an introduction by Michael Hornum. Grand Rapids, Mich.: Phanes Press, 1988.

Prigogine, Ilya, and Isabelle Stengers. *Order Out of Chaos*. New York: Bantam, 1984.

Primack, Joel R., and Nancy Ellen Abrams. *The View from the Center of the Universe*. New York: Riverhead Books, 2006.

Raine, Kathleen. "Science and Imagination in William Blake." In Kathleen Raine, *Golgonooza, City of Imagination: Last Studies in Blake,* 9–29. Ipswich, U.K.: Golgonooza Press, 1991.

Robb, Nesca A. *Neoplatonism of the Italian Renaissance*. London: Allen & Unwin, 1935.

Roberts, Alexander, and Donaldson, James, editors. *The Ante-Nicene Fathers: Translations of the Writings of the Fathers down to A.D. 325.* 10 vols. Edinburgh, 1868. Reprint, Grand Rapids, Mich.: William B. Eerdmans, 1981.

Robinson, John. *An Introduction to Early Greek Philosophy*. New York: Houghton-Mifflin, 1968.

Rocky Mountain Institute. *Visitor's Guide.* Sixth edition. Snowmass, Colo.: Rocky Mountain Institute, 2007. (Available at: www.rmi.org/Content/Files/Locations_LovinsHome_Visitors_Guide_2007.pdf.)

Romanyshyn, Robert. "Egos, Angels, and the Colors of Nature." In *Alexandria* 4 (Grand Rapids, Mich.: Phanes Press, 1987), 165–80.

Rosenblum, Bruce, and Fred Kuttner. *The Quantum Enigma: Physics Encounters Consciousness.* Second edition. New York: Oxford University Press, 2011.

Rossi, Paolo. *Francis Bacon: From Magic to Science.* Chicago: University of Chicago Press, 1968.

Roszak, Betty. "The Two Worlds of Magic." In *The Book of the New Alchemists,* edited by Nancy Jack Todd, vii–ix. New York: Dutton, 1976.

Roszak, Theodore. "Nature and Nature's God: Modern Cosmology and the Rebirth of Natural Philosophy." *Michigan Quarterly Review* (Winter 1995): 1–32.

———. *The Voice of the Earth: An Exploration of Ecopsychology.* New York: Simon & Schuster, 1992.

———. "Where Psyche Meets Gaia." In *Ecopsychology,* edited by Theodore Roszak, May Gomes, and Allen Kanner, 1–17. San Francisco: Sierra Club Books, 1995.

———. *Where the Wasteland Ends.* New York: Doubleday, 1972. Reprint, Berkeley, Calif.: Celestial Arts, 1989.

Rowe, Stephen C. *Rediscovering the West: An Inquiry into Nothingness and Relatedness.* Albany: State University of New York Press, 1994.

Royal Society. *Newton Tercentenary Celebrations.* Cambridge, U.K.: Cambridge University Press, 1947.

Seneca. *Epistles.* Translated by Richard M. Gummere. 3 vols. Loeb Classical Library. Cambridge, Mass.: Harvard University Press, 1917–1925.

———. *The Stoic Philosophy of Seneca: Essays and Letters.* Translated by Moses Hadas. New York: W. W. Norton, 1958.

Shapiro, Stewart, editor. *The Oxford Handbook of Philosophy of Mathematics and Logic.* New York: Oxford University Press, 2005.

Shapley, Harlow. *Flights from Chaos: A Survey of Material Systems from Atoms to Galaxies.* New York: McGraw-Hill, 1930.

———. *Of Stars and Men: Human Response to an Expanding Universe.* Boston: Beacon Press, 1958.

Silvestris, Bernard. *The Cosmographia of Bernardus Silvestris.* Translated by Winthrop Wetherbee. New York: Columbia University Press, 1973.

Skolimowski, Henryk. *The Participatory Mind.* New York: Penguin, 1994.

Strauss, Leo. *Natural Right and History.* Chicago: University of Chicago Press, 1953.

Swimme, Brian, and Thomas Berry. *The Universe Story: From the Primordial Flaring Forth to the Ecozoic Era.* San Francisco: Harper San Francisco, 1992.

Tarnas, Richard. *The Passion of the Western Mind.* New York: Harmony Books, 1991.

Telesio, Bernardino. *On the Nature of Things According to Their Own Proper Principles* (1565). In Fallico and Shapiro, editors and translators, *Renaissance Philosophy,* 1:301–38.

Thomas, Lewis. *The Lives of a Cell.* New York: Viking Press, 1974.

Todd, John. "Ecological Design: Reinventing the Future." Twenty-first Annual E. F. Schumacher Lectures, October 2001, E. F. Schumacher Center, Amherst, Massachusetts. http://centerforneweconomics.org/publications/lectures/Todd/John/Ecological-Design/.

———. "Living Machines: Ecological Water and Waste Management." Lecture filmed November 7, 2002, Duquesne University, Pittsburgh, Pennsylvania, 43:54. Posted February 2013. www.youtube.com/watch?v=wojrOpH5O7M.

Todd, Nancy Jack. *A Safe and Sustainable World: The Promise of Ecological Design.* Washington, D.C: Island Press, 2005.

Todd, Nancy Jack, and John Todd. *From Eco-Cities to Living Machines: Principles of Ecological Design.* Berkeley, Calif.: North Atlantic Books, 1993.

Toulmin, Stephen, and June Goodfield. *The Architecture of Matter.* New York: Harper & Row, 1962.

United Nations Development Programme. *Global Environment Outlook 5.* Nairobi, Kenya: United Nations Development Programme, 2012. (Available at: www.unep.org/geo/geo5.asp.)

United States Environmental Protection Agency. *Sustainable Materials Management: The Road Ahead.* Washington, D.C.: Environmental Protection Agency, 2009. (Available at: www.epa.gov/smm/pdf/vision2.pdf.)

Vallentin, Antonina. *Einstein: A Biography.* London: Weidenfeld and Nicloson, 1954.

Van der Ryn, Sim, and Stuart Cowan. *Ecological Design.* Washington, D.C.: Island Press, 1996.

von Simson, Otto. *The Gothic Cathedral: Origins of Gothic Architecture and the Medieval Concept of Order.* New York: Pantheon, 1956.

Waite, Arthur E., editor. *The Hermetic Museum.* 2 vols. London, 1839. Reprint, 2 vols. in 1, York Beach, Maine: Samuel Weiser, 1973.

Warden, John. "Orpheus and Ficino." In *Orpheus: The Metamorphoses of a Myth,* edited by John Warden, 85–110. Toronto: University of Toronto Press, 1982.

Watkins, Calvert, editor. *The American Heritage Dictionary of Indo-European Roots.* Boston: Houghton Mifflin, 1985.

White, Frank. *The Overview Effect: Space Exploration and Human Evolution.* Boston: Houghton Mifflin, 1986.

White, Lynn. "The Historical Roots of Our Ecologic Crisis." *Science* 155 (1967): 1203–7.

———. *Medieval Technology and Social Change.* Oxford: Clarendon, 1962.

Whyte, Lancelot Law. *The Unconscious before Freud.* New York: Basic Books, 1960.

Wilson, Edward O. *Biophilia.* Cambridge, Mass.: Harvard University Press, 1984.

———. *The Future of Life.* New York: Alfred A. Knopf, 2002.

Wordsworth, William. *The Complete Poetical Works of William Wordsworth.* New York: Thomas Crowell, n.d.

World Resources Institute. *A Guide to World Resources 2000–2001: People and Ecosystems; The Fraying Web of Life.* Washington, D.C.: World Resources Institute. (Available at: www.wri.org/publication/ world-resources-2000-2001-people-and-ecosystems-fraying-web-life.)

———. *Materials Flows in the United States: A Physical Accounting of the U.S. Industrial Economy.* Washington, D.C.: World Resources Institute, 2008. (Available at: http://pdf.wri.org/material_flows_in_the_united_states.pdf.)

World Wildlife Foundation. *Living Planet Report 2012: Biodiversity, Biocapacity, and Better Choices.* Gland, Switzerland: WWF International, 2012. (Available at: http://wwf.panda.org/about_our_earth/all_publications/ living_planet_report/2012_lpr.)

Yates, Francis A. *Giordano Bruno and the Hermetic Tradition.* Chicago: University of Chicago Press, 1964.

Young, Louise B. *The Unfinished Universe.* New York: Oxford University Press, 1993.

Index

About the Author

David Fideler has worked as a college professor, editor and publisher, educational consultant, and the director of a humanities center. He studied ancient Greek philosophy and Mediterranean religions at the University of Pennsylvania and holds a Ph.D. in philosophy and the history of science and cosmology.

Through his work, he has attempted to build bridges between the world of learning and contemporary life.

At the age of twenty-four, he founded Phanes Press, with the primary aim of publishing *The Pythagorean Sourcebook and Library*. Initially focusing on works in ancient philosophy, Phanes Press went on to publish interdisciplinary works in creativity, cultural issues, spirituality, ecology, and psychology. He has also edited five volumes of a humanities journal published in book form, *Alexandria: Cosmology, Philosophy, Myth, and Culture*, and is editor of the Cosmopolis Project website (www.cosmopolisproject.org).

A recognized authority on the Pythagorean school, Fideler contributed encyclopedia articles on Pythagoras and Pythagoreanism to *Classical and Medieval Literature Criticism* and *The New Dictionary of the History of Ideas*.

Born in the United States, he lives in Sarajevo with his wife and son.